THE NEW CONSTRUCTIVISM IN INTERNATIONAL RELATIONS THEORY

David M. McCourt

GW00645435

BRISTOL
UNIVERSITY
PRESS

First published in Great Britain in 2023 by

Bristol University Press
University of Bristol
1-9 Old Park Hill
Bristol
BS2 8BB
UK
t: +44 (0)117 374 6645
e: bup-info@bristol.ac.uk

Details of international sales and distribution partners are available at bristoluniversitypress.co.uk

British Library Cataloguing in Publication Data
A catalogue record for this book is available from the British Library

ISBN 978-1-5292-1782-7 hardcover
ISBN 978-1-5292-1783-4 paperback
ISBN 978-1-5292-1784-1 ePub
ISBN 978-1-5292-1785-8 ePdf

Cover design: Liam Roberts
Front cover image: Carlos de toro

Bristol University Press uses environmentally responsible print partners.

Printed in Great Britain by CPI Group (UK) Ltd, Croydon, CR0 4YY.

Contents

Acknowledgements

The New Constructivism synthesizes what I have learned over 15 years reading, recognizing, becoming, and – hopefully – contributing to Constructivism in IR theory. In all those endeavours, I am immensely grateful to many people, some of whom I will unfortunately forget in these acknowledgements. To them, my sincere apologies. The synthesis remains my own, warts and all.

First, to the following constructivists and fellow travellers my appreciation is immeasurable: Jon Acuff; Rebecca Adler-Nissen; Jacques Amoureux; Alex Barder; Jordan Branch; Benjamin de Carvalho; Mauro Caraccioli; Jon Carlson; Jeremie Cornut; Charlotte Epstein; Jamie Frueh, Stacie Goddard; Harry Gould; Inanna Hamati-Ataya; Jarrod Hayes; Eric Heinze; Andrew Hom; Jacques Hymans; Patrick Thaddeus Jackson; Oliver Kessler; Ron Krebs; Joseph MacKay; Halvard Leira; Dan Levine; Daniel Nexon; Vincent Pouliot; Mark Raymond; Andrew Ross; Laura Sjoberg; Ty Solomon; Brent J. Steele; Michael Struett; and Jelena Subotić. I am grateful for kind invitations to symposiums on Constructivism held in Weimer, Germany, in January 2014 – organized by Oliver Kessler – and the University of Southern California in early 2015 – organized by Jarrod Hayes, Mariano Bertucci, and Patrick James – which pushed along my thinking immensely.

All theory, we know, is perspectival, and the perspective adopted here was incubated at the European University Institute (EUI) in Florence between 2005 and 2009, under the eye of the incomparable Friedrich Kratochwil. The label 'founding father' of IR Constructivism is entirely too narrow to encapsulate the breadth of his learning. The same can be said of Nicholas Onuf and Alexander Wendt, to both of whom I owe thanks. In Florence, sincere thanks go to fellow Fritzians Xymena Kurowska, Hannes Peltonen, Christian Bueger, and Andrew Glencross.

The book's argument expands and reformulates a case first made in the pages of *International Studies Quarterly* in 2016. I am thankful to then-editor Daniel Nexon for organizing an online symposium on the article, and to the following for kindly agreeing to participate: Ted Hopf, Stacie Goddard, Alexander Montgomery, Oliver Kessler, Cecilia Lynch, Ty Solomon, and Swati Srivastava.

I have been fortunate to be employed in the Department of Sociology at the University of California, Davis, since 2014. My perspective on IR has been deeply shaped by becoming a sociologist, as is clear from the following. I have come to appreciate both the usefulness of a canon – whether Marx, Weber, DuBois and Durkheim, et al or Morgenthau, Carr, and Waltz – and the disciplinary harm canonization can do. While far from uncritical of sociology, the field offers a professional space similar in breadth to international studies within which to think and explore new ideas and approaches. I am thankful to my colleagues for their support of my activities in IR and Sociology, and especially to Eddy U for suggesting a book-length treatment of years of thinking about Constructivism.

At Bristol University Press, Stephen Wenham and Caroline Astley have been a pleasure to work with. I am grateful for Stephen's ongoing enthusiasm about the project. I hope this contributes in some small way to the Press' own success.

Finally, thanks to my family. My parents, Al and Julia, have bought me more Constructivist IR theory books than they would want to be reminded. My brilliant wife Stephanie Mudge has poked fun with me at the idiosyncrasies of both American and European IR. And thanks to my boys, Leighton and Julian, for giving me nightly writing slots while sat in the car park at their soccer practices.

Preface

In a recent paper submitted to a prominent international affairs journal, I claimed that my approach 'hewed to a constructivist way of thinking'. I made the point almost in passing, not giving it much thought. I should have known better.

The reviewers were quick to refute any association between what I was doing and 'Social Constructivism'. Constructivism, they emphasized, focuses on the role of interaction in creating mutual identities in world politics, 'or something along those lines'. My paper was on the topic of expert contestation in the making of US national security policy. It explored the intermingling of political struggles over the framing of America's national interest vis-à-vis a major power competitor with professional competition over the nature of foreign policy expertise. One reviewer pointed out, quite correctly, that Constructivism is not concerned with beliefs and ideas alone, factors important in the story I was telling. Since identity making in interaction was explicitly absent from the piece, both reviewers concluded that a claim about its constructivist pedigree should be removed.

To me at least, the paper was unambiguously constructivist. I was not adopting a realist perspective, one focused on the supposed verities of power politics, whether in a classical – prudential or *realpolitik* – or structural guise. Equally, the paper was not rationalist in its research design. It did not picture policy-making as an effort at utility maximization within a bargaining game – whether with a full- or partial-information game. Finally, the paper was not an exercise in critical or post-modernist theorizing. Despite the Gramscian overtones of its focus on America's policy-making elites, the paper was not trying to unmask hidden power structures in society with the aim of helping overturn them. Rather, the paper was an explanatory exercise – in a broad understanding of the word – aimed at accounting for the effects of professional contestation on discursive representations of the United States in world politics. It was about how the world was *constructed* and the social world(s) of those doing the constructing – the experts and policy-makers. It all seemed solidly constructivist fair to me.

Again, I should have known better. The politics of Constructivism as an approach in International Relations (IR) theory are often fraught, and frequently downright hostile. At least the reviewers in question were polite about it. And they were quick.

What is Constructivism in IR theory? Why did my claim need to be shot down? As the old saying goes, you will receive as many answers to the question of what Constructivism is as constructivists you ask – or, more appropriately, textbooks you read. Everyone seems to have a say on the nature of Constructivism, generating voluminous scholarship throughout its time as an approach in IR – roughly from the late 1980s until today.[1] Constructivism remains a matter of controversy, and this book will surely not settle matters.

Nonetheless, this book is about Constructivism as an approach in IR theory. The book defends the claim that recent developments in constructivist theorizing – recent meaning the last ten years or so, so recent in the slow pace of the academy – add up to a qualitatively new approach, which should be labelled as such: *the New Constructivism.* Central to the New Constructivism are new theoretical perspectives and vocabularies, like practice theory, relationalism, and actor-network theory, new empirical interests, like affect and emotions, and methodological innovations like network analysis and Multiple Correspondence Analysis (MCA). While many of the promoters of these approaches have downplayed or denied their links to Constructivism, in this book I seek to set the record straight – showing how they are principally developments *within* Constructivism, rather than outside it. Written to appeal to a wide readership, from advanced undergraduates and graduate students casting around for theoretical moorings to practising constructivists, the book presents a manifesto for this New Constructivism via a tour of the contemporary constructivist landscape.

The tour begins with classic constructivist work on culture, norms, and identity in world politics. I show that over time this classical or 'Old' Constructivism narrowed its field of conceptual vision, such that practice theory, relationalism, and the other components of the New Constructivism seemed to stand outside it, ripe for 'bringing in', to adopt a tired if seemingly-ever-useful political science cliché. In other words, Constructivism *became* a theoretical approach almost solely focused on the role of norms, identity, and culture in world politics. Crucially, norms, identity, and culture came to be viewed within this new approach as relatively fixed things, things that could even be 'tested' alongside other 'factors' in foreign policy-making, like material interests. The effect was to downplay precisely the *constructing* of world politics, the attempt to create, modify, or break norms, identities, and culture, in international affairs. Practice theory and relationalism in particular are aimed at breaking down social factors into the varied processes by which they are constructed, processes that shape but do not fully determine social outcomes.

My reviewer was not, therefore, entirely wrong in their characterization of Constructivism when they echoed a predominant, but I argue, outdated understanding of Constructivism. Constructivists absolutely *can* make insightful arguments about how social factors like culture and norms shape the identities of states as they interact in world politics. Against rationalist and realist accounts especially, such arguments remain extremely useful, as I will show later in the book. My reviewer did not, however, recognize that Constructivism has also moved on, or at least significantly expanded its field of vision, adding new and exciting dimensions not only concerned with the mutual constitution of state identities. After reading this book, they will recognize the New Constructivism. At least that is my hope.

Why bother? Why do new developments *have* to be viewed as internal to Constructivism? As well as witnessing the rise of the New Constructivism – as I will contend – the last ten years has also witnessed a turn away from paradigms in general. For leading IR theorist David Lake, for instance, the 'isms' are more of a hindrance to knowledge construction than a help.[2] By organizing our work into academic 'sects', and privileging intramural debate – of which this book is undeniably an example – over cross-paradigm testing of theory in search of policy relevance, 'we are not giving society what it deserves even in terms of basic theoretical and empirical knowledge about world politics, a domain that we as scholars claim as our own'.[3] This book therefore seems to fly in the face of two common senses: what Constructivism is, and that paradigm-centric debate is, or at least should be, a thing of the past.

Identifying the New Constructivism, however, is imperative for three related reasons, which I defend further in the following Introduction: empirical pay-off, intellectual consistency, and the formation of groups of scholars who share a perspective on international politics and how it should be studied, however broad those groups may be.

Empirical pay-off must be front and centre. On that, I am in full agreement with Lake. Constructivism, like all theories and frameworks, is ultimately an aid to interpretation, a device we use to help us tell better, more accurate, convincing, and insightful stories about world politics. Theories are thinking and communication aids. But different types of scholars find different types of stories convincing. As a constructivist, someone can tell me until they are blue in the face about the effects of differentials in power on national interest formation, which realism foregrounds. But I will still want to know how those factors influence how real individuals and groups interpret purported reality. How does someone *know* what is in the national interest? Contra rationalists, I will doggedly defend the notion that a thick description of the constitutive rules underpinning a particular bargaining scenario are as scientifically valid and important as a formalized and solved model of the game itself. Contrary to the narrowed vision of Constructivism that developed over time, in both cases a full analysis might require sensitivity to the practical, taken-for-granted knowledge in a foreign ministry, or the scholarly community of national security experts in a given capital – aspects key to the New Constructivism.

The arguments of Lake and others aside, therefore, whether they recognize the fact or not, constructivists – Old and New – *are* the social group interested in New Constructivist arguments.[4] We are the ones who will find New Constructivist arguments convincing in terms of empirical pay-off. In telling the story of Constructivism in IR, of how it narrowed and had to be re-born, I am not, therefore, defending paradigms for no reason. I am trying to get constructivists of every stripe on the same page, to get down to the real work of telling good stories about world politics.

Intellectual consistency, group identity, and empirical pay-off are thus all intimately related. Hence it matters that, with a few important recent exceptions, most assessments of Constructivism – of what it *is*, and what objects and method of analysis are constructivist – fail to remain true to the central tenets of Constructivism, failing to remain grounded in historically, geographically, and institutionally specific dynamics. As I explore in greater detail in the following chapter, the starting point for any definition of Constructivism should not be 'Constructivism is …' but 'Constructivism does …', and 'what do people do with and through "Constructivism?"' Thought of in this way, Constructivism does not refer to a narrow set of concepts, but as a space within IR – viewed itself in social and cultural terms – for bringing in from cognate fields like sociology, history, and psychology, insights into the processes by which international political reality is made. The New Constructivism is the result of a new generation of scholars *doing* that importation.

The task is pressing. Despite its prominence, Constructivism is in danger of losing its momentum as it remains stuck in detailing the effects of a narrow band of inputs to state action. As a space within IR understood as not only an intellectual enterprise, but a set of part nationally rooted/part internationalized *professions*, Constructivism needs to be continually refreshed to carry on. Yet hostility in discussions about the nature of Constructivism reflects precisely the weakness of Constructivism and constructivists within the various social worlds they inhabit – academies and policy-making circles, at both the state and international levels. Constructivism does not fare well at the top academic departments in IR and political science – not technical or scientific enough in the US, not critical enough in the United Kingdom, Europe, and beyond. Constructivists attacking one in another, in simple terms, is the academic working class attacking itself.

In place of such internecine strife, I hope to prove that the New Constructivism is a vibrant and powerful approach to world politics. I foreground eight key features underpinning its potential. The New Constructivism is (1) anti-foundationalist; (2) rigorously anti-essentialist; (3) methodologically omnivorous; (4) conceptually pluralist; (5) reflexive;

(6) necessarily historical; (7) politically agnostic; and (8) attuned to emotions and affect in human action. I unpack this list in more depth in the following Introduction. Suffice it here to say that while some of these features are prominent in alternative approaches, especially post-positivist perspectives and feminism, Constructivism is the only home to all of them.

Using an array of exemplary works, and my own ongoing work on United States and British national security policy, I highlight throughout the immediate applicability of Constructivism to the real world of international politics. To be sure, this is well-trodden ground, but purposefully so. Part of the aim of the book is for junior researchers who want to 'try on' the New Constructivism in their first forays into identifying and answering puzzles about world politics. Precisely where changing national interests seem most obvious, most unproblematic, is where the New Constructivism is most needed.

Introduction: What Is Constructivism?

Constructivism in International Relations theory is ...

I should pause right there. We are accustomed to defining things in academic discourse and everyday life using the definer-in-chief – 'is'. The exercise comes automatically, unreflexively. When we want to bring the nature of a phenomenon to the surface, we begin with a definition – however provisional – so we can all begin from the same place. The habit is rooted in the structure of language itself, after all. Ordinary language tells us the world is made up of things, discrete 'its' that do things.[1] Why should it be any different with IR Constructivism?

While 'defining one's terms' is drilled into us early in our education, in the case of Constructivism, the practice represents a problematic starting point. Even sophisticated constructivists can fall into the trap – for one, for example, 'Constructivism is about the social embeddedness of human consciousness and its role in international life.'[2] This definition is not incorrect so much as only one of many possible definitions of 'it'. (What is 'consciousness', after all?) The problem comes because Constructivism resists such *substantialization* or *essentialization*: casting Constructivism as a stable thing the nature of which words can straightforwardly capture. Indeed, Constructivism resists substantialization or essentialization in not one but two ways: Constructivism is neither a single thing in IR, be it a theory, approach, perspective, or whatever, nor is it a theory or approach that studies things in world politics. To ask what Constructivism *is*, therefore, is to pose a crucial question in the wrong way for the object at hand.

Let me try again, then. In this book, I will defend a view of Constructivism less as an essence than a particular kind of *space* within the professionalized study of international political life – be it political science departments in the United States, or departments of Politics, Government, or International Studies, as elsewhere in the world. The main characteristic of Constructivism

1

as a space is that it is where a certain *process* obtains: the process of looking at how international political life – its main actors, institutions, rules, language, norms, cultural meanings, identities, roles – are constituted, made, or, simply, *constructed*. Where every other theory or approach in IR can be understood as a thing that studies things – a theory that studies the effects of power in the case of realism, or an approach that models utility maximization in full- or partial-information games, as in rationalism – Constructivism is a process that, in turn, studies the processes of doing, and trying to grasp the doings of, international political life.

Constructivists tend to follow a specific process in their research also. They usually reach beyond IR's disciplinary boundaries to cognate fields for ways to foreground the construction of world politics, fields such as philosophy, social theory, sociology, social psychology, and cultural anthropology. Why do they do this? In part, they do it for epistemic authority. Whereas other popular perspectives, particularly rationalism, can draw on the authority of science and scientific method, constructivists can draw on the authority of thinkers such as Michel Foucault, Anthony Giddens, Judith Butler, Pierre Bourdieu, and others. But the question of *why* constructivists reach beyond IR's disciplinary confines is, again, not the right question. Foregrounding process, the nature of Constructivism is that space in IR where constructivists further the project of what, following sociologist C. Wright Mills, I term 'classic social analysis'.[3] By classic social analysis, Mills means a tradition that includes such thinkers from Herbert Spence and August Comte, to Emile Durkheim, Karl Mannheim, Karl Marx, and Max Weber. As John Gerard Ruggie has shown, Constructivism had its antecedents primarily in the work of Durkheim and Weber.[4] Tellingly, bringing Mills' list up to date would have to include Foucault et al, as well as previously marginalized figures like W.E.B. Du Bois, as I make clear in later chapters.[5] If we *have* to use the word 'is' to characterize constructivism, then IR is the-space-in-IR's-varied-institutional-bases-where-classic-social-analysis-is-practiced – to coin a nice, catchy term.

I am not the first to point out the usefulness of thinking of IR theorizing as classic social analysis,[6] nor is the association without its problems – again, the lack of women and non-White scholars in the aforementioned list is striking, centring the question of the relationship between constructivism and feminism, critical race theory, and post-colonialism, matters discussed in Chapter 6.[7] Nonetheless, with those caveats in hand, the case for viewing Constructivism as classic-social-analysis-in-IR is useful since it sets up the argument that Constructivism understood as a space within IR and political science for doing something different from the mainstream, is a *positive* condition – a Good Thing.[8] Constructivism represents IR's 'sociological imagination', to again draw from Mills. As heirs to classic social analysis, the type of knowledge aimed at by constructivists is different from – but as useful and important as, I would even say more so – the timeless, general, abstract, and context-free knowledge aimed at by the scientistic mainstream. As Friedrich Kratochwil in particular has shown, Constructivism is uniquely *problem-driven* and attuned to the practical and not merely theoretical nature of political knowledge.[9]

Plan of the chapter

In the remainder of this introduction, I lay out a framework for thinking about Constructivism in IR theory consistent with constructivist premises, and show why it matters by identifying the core features of the New Constructivism using the very tools the new perspective puts at our disposal.

Most stocktaking efforts address Constructivism as a set of disembodied ideas, usually the role in world politics of shared norms, national identities, and national and international culture.[10] While useful for comparing Constructivism to other approaches like realism, liberalism, and rational choice, both pedagogically and in terms of research design, such a way of describing Constructivism is, in fact, very *un-constructivist*. Again, it fixes Constructivism as 1) a singular theoretical approach, one 2) focused on certain types of things. Constructivism is not a singular theory, however, nor is it a perspective focused on settled things, but one that centres on the processes and relationships that underpin social and political life.[11] But *essentializing* constructivist IR theory has left scholars unable to see the connections between Constructivism and exciting new developments, such as the recent turn to 'practice'.[12] As I show, early constructivists emphasized the importance of practice and practical knowledge in international affairs. However, such insights were quickly overshadowed by more easily operationalizable concepts, such as norms, identity, and culture.

Foregrounding IR Constructivism's own social and historical origins reveals that Constructivism in IR theory is the process of incorporating insights on the social construction of international reality from cognate disciplines, especially sociology but philosophy, social theory, cultural anthropology, geography, and social psychology. It is a space from which scholars can remind their colleagues that outcomes in world politics are the products of historically, culturally, and geographically specific processes. My claim is not that constructivist explanations of outcomes in world politics *cannot* be based on shared norms, and so on, but that there is more to Constructivism than norms, culture, and identity – together, the emergence of New Constructivist ideas like practice theory, relationalism, and others detailed in the book, add up to a New Constructivism in IR theory.

3

Constructivism in International Relations: a constructivist stocktaking

Constructivism has come a long way since its emergence in IR theory over three decades ago. Brought into the field by early constructivists to 'socialize' the then-reigning rationalist approaches – neorealism and neoliberal institutionalism – Constructivism today is a broad church.[13] Yet, predominant treatments of Constructivism in handbooks and introductory texts tend to equate Constructivism with a narrow set of correctives to mainstream perspectives rooted mostly in work from the 1990s and early 2000s. From that viewpoint, Constructivism is an interpretivist approach focusing on the role of culture, norms, and identity, in state action. For some positivist scholars, Constructivism even offers hypotheses for the role of such social factors, which can be tested alongside rationalist and materialist alternatives. Accordingly, recent developments in the field – like practice theory, relationalism, and social network analysis – are often described as separate from Constructivism. Like many of us might wish we were, Constructivism is stuck in the 1990s.

The typical way of characterizing analytical approaches like Constructivism in IR, like in any other discipline, is to grasp the core ideas they put forward, in this case about the basic features of world politics and how we should study them. From this perspective, although Constructivism is acknowledged to be a broad approach rather than a theory, it has nevertheless been distilled to a set of core tenets.[14]

The most basic tenets of Constructivism are the primacy of social facts and meaning. As Martha Finnemore and Kathryn Sikkink put it, 'Constructivism ... asserts that human interaction is shaped primarily by ideational factors, not simply material ones; that the most important ideational factors are widely shared or "intersubjective" beliefs, which are not reducible to individuals; and that these shared beliefs construct the interests of purposive actors'.[15] A more recent contribution notes how: 'The central insight of Constructivism is that collectively held ideas shape the social, economic, and political world in which we live.'[16] As such, Constructivism's emergence in IR is thus usually dated to the late 1980s–early 1990s, to the work of Friedrich Kratochwil, Nicholas Onuf, and John Gerard Ruggie, who each stressed the intersubjective basis of social life, and to Alexander Wendt, who in 1992 translated the insight into terms even the most ardent objectivist could understand: 'anarchy is what states make of it'.[17] In other words, the lack of a supranational state for states only translated to the Hobbesian 'war of all against all' if states believed it to be so.

Constructivists' assertion of the primacy of social facts, meaning, and intersubjective reality, has had important implications for what both Constructivism's proponents *and those not aligned with the approach* think constructivists study. Arguably more important than the founding constructivist theories was a first wave of empirical contributions which showed a field in the grips of a neorealist/neoliberal institutionalist consensus (at least in the US)[18] that norms and identities underpinned state interest formation,[19] that the practice of world politics had its basis in fundamental institutions, like state sovereignty and diplomacy,[20] that non-state actors could be as important as states,[21] and that security was rooted in different national cultures and self-conceptions.[22] These works launched Constructivism as what Peter Katzenstein, Robert Keohane, and Stephen Krasner call a *general theoretical orientation*.[23] What Katzenstein et al refer to as *specific research programmes* followed on the role of collective and state identity,[24] political culture,[25] and specifically norms in world politics – an agenda that shows no signs of slowing down a quarter of a century later.[26]

Viewed as an approach that posits the importance of social facts, meanings, and ideas to world politics, the second tenet of Constructivism concerns what methodology is consequently most appropriate. Constructivism has been understood as a different approach to knowledge production than positivism – sometimes labelled neo-positivism[27] – which remains predominant in American political science.[28] Constructivism's methodological implications have been variously characterized, and there is far from a consensus.[29] But given the stress constructivists place on intersubjective meaning, Max Weber's notion of *verstehen* and its typical translation as 'interpretation' have formed the bedrock of attempts to develop a specifically constructivist methodology.[30] The notions of 'constitutive' theory, as opposed to purely 'causal' analysis,[31] and the search for 'understanding' over 'explanation',[32] are also commonplace.

Together, these core contributions have come to characterize Constructivism as an approach to the study of IR. Yet they fail to capture the nature of Constructivism because they fall into a specific type of the essentializing trap with which I began this chapter. They offer an ideational account of Constructivism, a set of ideas about the world – which, confusingly, are about the way Constructivism supposedly foregrounds things like ideas. However, research is only one of the processes by which perspectives – like Constructivism – are produced and reproduced in academic disciplines understood as themselves social spaces, specifically professions. Approaches also diffuse through the writing and use of textbooks, discussion at conferences, the teaching of graduate students, and the placing of those graduate students in academic positions. Approaches and theories like Constructivism thus enter academic fields at particular times and places, in the work of particular people, and are picked up and used by multiple actors for their own purposes. They are thus conditioned by forces beyond the control of any individual: they are, put simply, socially constructed.

As I make clear in the following chapter, the predominant characterization sketched here is not per se wrong – after all, from a constructivist perspective definitions are always provisional, always a *claim* on the nature of reality, not reality itself. But the characterization is partial or narrow, capturing only the most prominent arguments made by the most prominent – almost exclusively American-trained – scholars, and not all the claims that could be made in Constructivism's name. Nonetheless, the aforementioned sketch does show how, relatively quickly after its emergence in IR, Constructivism was essentialized, in two senses: first, as a coherent approach that could be compared to others and made legible to the field; and second, as an approach that studies things: be they norms, identities, culture, or whatever. This serves in practice to close off Constructivism to new objects of interest, like emotions, practice, and relationality, and new methods, like network analysis.[33]

Again, what happened to Constructivism? To answer that question, what is needed, simply put, is an accounting of Constructivism in IR that acknowledges how it has been shaped by the field, and therefore what it *may have been*, and *could be in the future*. What is needed is an adequately constructivist assessment of the nature of Constructivism.

The social life of International Relations Constructivism

Since human life offers no Archimedean perspective, and hence no clear starting point to the social life of Constructivism, we must begin in the middle – with the matter of where and when. The significance of Constructivism's emergence in the context of late 1980s US IR is thereby crucial. It draws attention to the nature of IR as a field and the specific social contexts in which it exists. Traditionally traced back to the first Chair at the University of Wales at Aberystwyth and especially to the post-WWII US, where it became bound up with American global hegemony, the 1980s and 1990s saw IR go global.[34] Yet strong national and regional characteristics remain. A straightforward distinction between IR as a sub-field of political science – as in the US – and as a stand-alone discipline – for much of the rest of the world – has important implications for what Constructivism *does* in different contexts.

Constructivism does something very different in the US than it does outside America. As already noted, Constructivism emerged in the US as a counterpoint to neorealism and neoliberal institutionalism, and their specific arguments regarding the role of regimes in international organization,[35] and more generally on the origins of state interests.[36] But over time the context of US political science has shifted significantly. Realism is no longer the predominant paradigm and liberal institutionalism its neat Other. The picture is far more complex.

No single theoretical approach predominates. Indeed, respondents to different waves of the 'Teaching and Research in International Politics' surveys often rank Constructivism their theory-of-choice.[37] But in general what might be termed a form of 'soft rationalism' is the dominating perspective: the notion that politics is ultimately rooted in calculating individuals in changing institutional contexts – what Helen Milner labelled over two decades ago the 'choice-in-constraints' model.[38] Individuals may be driven by ideas or psychological blinders, but from a soft rationalist perspective, they are ultimately still utility-maximizing creatures. That perspective lends itself to recent innovations in scientific method, particularly the use of experiments, where respondents are primed to respond to different prompts.[39]

In terms of what it *does*, consequently, Constructivism in US IR is now the main counterpoint to rationalism and its scientific offshoots.[40] Constructivism serves to remind rationalists that the initial actor type and background rules they model are not given by nature, but by practice.[41] Constructivism can provide insights as to why individuals diverge from strict instrumental rationality, in Max Weber's terms.

In non-US IR, by contrast, neither the 'Neo-Neos' – neorealism and neoliberal institutionalism – nor more recently rationalism have ever been predominant. In Europe especially, more sociological approaches akin to Constructivism – like the English School and the Copenhagen School, to name just two – were already there and remain strong.[42] There was then no significant 'Other' for constructivists to argue against, as the Neo-Neos provided in America. As such, Constructivism's insights look familiar beyond the US, and problematically tied to older US-centric concerns and styles of theorizing (especially in its Wendtian variety.) Whereas US-based constructivists drew on philosophical and social theoretic work from Europe to make arguments aimed at realists, neoliberal institutionalists and rationalists – from Foucault and Jürgen Habermas, to Anthony Giddens and Pierre Bourdieu[43] – in European IR these thinkers have been drawn upon more organically, and not as part of something that can only be brought into IR as 'Constructivism'.

The creation of the academic journal *International Political Sociology* (*IPS*) in 2007 is significant in this regard. *IPS* is dominated by work that can be considered constructivist from the aforementioned standard view. But much of it does not label itself constructivist. This is because it is largely European or at least non-US in origin. This should come as no surprise. Beyond the US, Constructivism is – or more accurately *does* – IPS. As first-generation constructivist Christian Reus-Smit has noted, 'Constructivists are political sociologists, no more no less.'[44] Such a total equivalence undoubtedly goes too far, but the point remains.

Foregrounding the geographic context in which IR has developed also highlights the important fact that the discipline of IR sits within particular nationally and regionally rooted *professions*. These professions decide who counts as a member and who prospers, something achieved through credentialing, publishing, the distribution of jobs, and thus the maintenance of a prestige hierarchy. As much a set of ideas, then, Constructivism is a *stake* and form of capital within professional struggles. From this perspective, the pertinent issue is the professional standing Constructivism has attained within IR's diverse professional contexts, especially the level of prestige accorded to constructivist scholarship and scholars.[45]

Constructivism's professional standing is difficult to measure. In the US, surface assessments suggest a healthy standing. Alexander Wendt is often cited as among the most influential IR scholars,[46] and Kathryn Sikkink is Professor in the Kennedy School at Harvard – the litmus test for much in American higher education. But closer inspection suggests a more sobering tale. In Jelena Subotić's accounting, only some 31 of 499 tenure-track political science professors in the top 50 programmes in the United States list IR as their first or second specialization. In the top 25, the numbers are 23 of 292.[47] Moreover, notwithstanding the fact that Wendt has openly recanted on his constructivist beliefs,[48] the ability of the first generation of constructivists to position their students in the highest echelons of the political science profession has been limited. Beyond the US, by contrast, Constructivism's standing is very strong. If we define Constructivism broadly, it can be seen to be in many ways predominant, with scholars such as Karin Fierke, Stefano Guzzini, Ole Waever, Lene Hansen, and Michael Williams at the top of the prestige hierarchy. Indeed, the two trends are not unrelated, as many of the first-generation and second constructivists secured job and publication opportunities overseas, including Friedrich Kratochwil (EUI, Italy), Christian Reus-Smit (University of Queensland), Jutta Weldes (Bristol), Richard Price (University of British Columbia), Ted Hopf (National University of Singapore), and Janice Bially Mattern (also at the National University of Singapore).

Michael Struett, Jarrod Hayes, and others have been forthright in chronicling the processes underpinning constructivists' struggles. In the case of peer review, for example, Struett describes the experience of constructivists submitting work to journals in the discipline the reviewers for which 'either do not understand constructivist epistemological, ontological, and methodological approaches, or [who] refuse to accept them as legitimate'.[49] Hayes centres difficulties in getting recognition for the scientific statues of the constructivist enterprise: on one conference panel, he recalls, a fellow participant dismissed his question by suggesting what Hayes does 'isn't science'.[50] Most constructivists have similar experiences. For Kratochwil, it was when a colleague informed him 'if it doesn't bleed or explode it isn't IR'.[51] For me, it was when – while doing graduate work in Europe – a well-known American IR scholar told me that if I was interested in a career in America, I'd 'have to learn the language of science'. The implication, of course, was that Constructivism is not science. (I strongly believe I *did* learn the language of science – it just isn't the naïve neo-positivism common in the US social sciences, nor is it a single language.)

These reflections are anecdotal. But they serve to highlight how an understanding of Constructivism as a set of theoretical ideas and empirical arguments misrecognizes what Constructivism is and does in IR, when the latter is grasped as a set of overlapping professional contexts. A more appropriate survey has been generated by the collective work of scholars such as Jarrod Hayes, Mariano Bertucci, Ayşe Zarakol, and Jelena Subotić. They have shown, among other things, that looked at objectively:

> Constructivism is an approach to the study of international relations that (a) makes security issues in the North Atlantic region its salient substantive and empirical focus of analysis, (b) is heavily oriented toward theory development, (c) aims to mainly produce constitutive knowledge, (d) is far from having an active concern with policy debates and recommendations, (e) largely disregards empirical analyses, and (f) relies almost exclusively on qualitative methods of analysis.[52]

As a final point, then, thus far I have focused on dynamics internal to IR to explain Constructivism's trajectory. Finally, however, as Alexander Barder and Daniel Levine note, the historical context of Constructivism's emergence was and remains crucial.[53] They show that at its birth Constructivism held a radical promise: to fully historicize and contextualize the categories of thought IR scholars used to make sense of the world – including the primacy of the nation-state, *raison d'état*, and sovereignty. For Ruggie, neorealism and neoliberal institutionalism – then Constructivism's chief 'Others' – are 'capable of explaining virtually nothing that is constitutive of the very possibility of IR: not territorial states, not systems of states, not any concrete international order, nor the whole host of institutional forms that states use, ranging from concepts of contracts and treaties to multilateral organizing principles'.[54] But over time, so-called *Via Media* Constructivism shook off its radical pretensions, adopting a more presentist and avowedly scientist style.[55]

The reason, for Barder and Levine, was that much *Via Media* Constructivism imbibed the post-Cold War optimism in world politics, and thus came to focus on the transformative and progressive potential of norms, human rights, taboos, culture, identity, and argument and persuasion in world politics. Constructivism, in other words – at least the *Via Media* variety popular in the US – became quite idealist. Fast-forward a decade and this context has vanished. The terrorist attacks of September 11, the invasion of Iraq, and the rise of the Islamic State and the wars in Syria and Ukraine, cast doubt on the happy liberal norms the constructivist approach emerged trumpeting.

Too much can be made of the historical context of Constructivism's emergence, however, particularly the end of the Cold War. For Onuf, 'The end of the Cold War had nothing to do with Constructivism's arrival on the scene.'[56] Constructivism, in his recollection – and we should value his viewpoint since he coined the term 'Constructivism'[57] – followed trends in the broader social sciences, notably the cultural turn: 'Drawing inspiration from continental social theory', Onuf recalls, 'humanists [beyond IR] declared that the philosophical assumptions underlying modern science are untenable'.[58] Yet, what is more likely – if difficult to prove – is that the end of the Cold War did stimulate acknowledgement of and research into the underappreciated role of transnational actors and shifting ideas, like *perestroika*. In other words, IR Constructivism may not have its roots in the Cold War's demise, but it gave Constructivism a significant injection soon after its inception.

The New Constructivism: overview of the main argument

The foregoing constructivist account of what happened to IR Constructivism sets up the main argument of the book. Recent developments in IR theory add up to a qualitatively new form of constructivist theorizing, despite the seemingly curious fact that the progenitors of those new developments – notably but not exclusively the practice and relational turns – have presented them as paradigm-neutral, outside the bounds of Constructivism. I say 'seemingly curious' because it should in fact come as no surprise that scholars have sought to distance their insights from Constructivism as they seek the academic distinction and professional rewards of 'the new'. Examining the process by which Constructivism narrowed over time to a doubly essentialized object – a thing that studies things – is not therefore of passing interest. Rather, it is essential because it perfectly illustrates many of the substantive features of the New Constructivism. In old constructivist terminology, Constructivism's trajectory in IR was a function of the predominant norms, identity, and culture of American political science, typically understood as a scientific enterprise privileging neo-positivism and the generation of abstract, general, and preferably quantifiable knowledge. Constructivism became normalized as a source of hypotheses to be tested against other theories, like realism. However, there is more to the story of Constructivism in IR than norms and culture – just as *there is more to constructivist IR than norms, identity, and culture.*

The reigning neo-positivism and scientism in US political science can be cast as a set of *practices*, or taken-for-granted ways of doing things, that shape possible strategies for conducting and presenting research. Those strategies exist alongside, or *in relation to*, other theories, approaches, and perspectives – whether prioritized over, downgraded alongside, or other associations besides. The narrowing of Constructivism was thereby a result of its success in slotting into American political science, understood as a relational social practice. Constructivists developed generative research agendas – on state socialization,[59] argumentation and persuasion,[60] and the diffusion of norms.[61] These agendas identified broad puzzles recognizable to political scientists of all stripes – and not just constructivists – of how to explain political action not aligned to objective interests.[62]

Constructivism's narrowing followed a general social pattern sociologist Andrew Abbott terms *fractionation*.[63] Fractionation is a process that sorts individuals into *fractal distinctions* according to given criteria. The quantitative-qualitative or rationalist-interpretive distinctions in social science – central to the story of IR Constructivism's trajectory – are, once again, strong examples. Put a group of social scientists into a room with a topic on which to design a research study – or indeed, with nothing to discuss – and this division will emerge. Quantitative, rationalist, and more scientistic scholars will find like-minded souls with whom to confer, as will more qualitative/interpretive scholars. But place these two groups in separate rooms and the process will repeat: the scientists will fracture between the more and less formal, the interpretivist scholars over issues like quantification and generalizability, and the fact/value distinction.[64] Usefully, Abbott uses social constructionism to illustrate the process: 'To a sociological theorist, OLS and LISREL amount to the same thing [that is, "quantitative approaches"], just as ethnomethodology and symbolic interactionism are indistinguishable to a sociological empiricist [that is, "constructivist"].'[65] For insiders, such distinctions are highly meaningful and drive fractal distinction.

The fractionation of Constructivism was a practical and relational process – deeply cultural and normative, but more besides. How did it happen? One way was via early characterizations of Constructivism as an approach in IR by prominent commentators like Jeffrey Checkel. Checkel and others, seeking a niche within American political science, argued that 'constructivists do not reject science or causal explanation; their quarrel is with mainstream theories is ontological, not epistemological'.[66] Other commentators emphasized Constructivism's modernism: for Katzenstein, Keohane, and Krasner, conventional constructivists, 'influenced by new trends in the humanities, put forward sociological perspectives that emphasized shared norms and values but which were in epistemological terms sharply differentiated from postmodernism'.[67] As Checkel noted, the early constructivists 'rescued the exploration of identity from the postmodernists'.[68] These were *relational* moves, attuned to the practice of American political science in differentiating Constructivism from other approaches and theories. These statements were thus true for some constructivists seeking to stay in the room with the scientists, but not those who would prefer to talk to critical and postmodernists, who share the constructivist concern with discourse, identity, and the normative grammar of social life.[69]

The fractionation of Constructivism was not, however, simply a result of privileged ways of defining Constructivism. It was also tied to objective power relations in IR as a social and professional field and practice, as noted earlier.[70] Constructivists are often accused of ignoring power, a theme I will return to – and refute – especially in Chapter 3. Here it is important to note how Constructivism has lacked a figurehead with the power and inclination to prevent, or at least manage, its fractionation.[71] While scholars like Kenneth Waltz and Robert Keohane ensured structural realism and neoliberal institutionalism reproduced themselves ideationally and generationally, prominent constructivists have remained agnostic about Constructivism. Alexander Wendt soon disavowed Constructivism.[72] Another contender for leadership of Constructivism, Peter Katzenstein, spans political science sub-fields and like Kratochwil and Onuf has not attempted to take on the constructivist mantle. With the exception of strong schools at Minnesota – under Raymond Duvall and Michael Barnett – and Cornell under Katzenstein, the result has fostered Constructivism's fraction. It is therefore telling that other figures heavily associated with Constructivism, like Emanuel Adler, are at the forefront of the practice turn.[73]

A predominant disciplinary understanding of Constructivism has been left behind of a coherent approach that analyzes the role of intersubjective meanings in world politics, represented by norms, culture, and identity, with Wendt's work its core theoretical foundation. One of its effects of essentializing Constructivism in this way – turning 'it' into a thing that studies things – is to place in shade the work of a number of critical IR scholars who might be considered constructivist but who announced their intention to speak 'the language of exile', refusing to 'be seduced … into abstractly theoretical discussions or self-enclosing simulations of idealized realities'.[74] Although they were doing the same thing as the constructivists – they drew specifically on Foucault to make arguments about the social construction of US foreign policy – post-structuralists like David Campbell and Roxanne-Lynn Doty are not typically understood as constructivists.[75]

The following chapter explores in greater depth the effects of the narrowing of Constructivism. As a final, telling, point, however, it should be noted how that recent constructivist-like turns emerged 20–25 years after the emergence of Constructivism: on a generational timescale. As Abbott notes, this is unsurprising: 'Twenty years is about the time it takes a group of academics to storm the ramparts, take the citadel, and settle down to the fruits of victory.'[76] Whether the constructivists took the citadel is questionable, but the pattern he identifies is familiar: first there is insightful theoretical works and empirical applications; then come treatises that consolidate the new approach;[77] and then new empirical work that obeys the law of diminishing returns. In social science generally, this process is iterations old. Constructionism emerged first at the turn of the 20th century, then in the 1930s, 1960s and 1980s, each time with a roughly 25-year interval in between.[78] The New Constructivism marks IR Constructivism's second phase.

The core features of the New Constructivism

Thus far, I have spoken in general terms about the New Constructivism as typified by practice theory and relationalism. I delve in greater detail into the substantive theoretical and methodological contributions of the New Constructivism, and what remains important from the old, in the remainder of the book. However, at this point, we can identify the core features of the New Constructivism. The New Constructivism is:

- rigorously anti-essentialist
- anti-foundationalist
- methodologically promiscuous
- conceptually pluralist
- reflexive
- necessarily historical
- politically agnostic
- attuned to emotions and affect

The New Constructivism does not have a single core feature. But if it did, it would be, first, anti-essentialism. Again, what was wrong with the Old Constructivism was the way it narrowed to focus almost exclusively on norms, identity, and culture understood as things. What was lost was the constructing process, *including naming and using concepts like norms, identity, and culture.* Nicholas Onuf puts the point best. Constructivists, new and old, stress the production in social life of what he rather whimsically terms 'moderate-sized dry goods:' words, concepts, labels, and frames with which we navigate the world.[79] The point is dead serious. For Onuf:

> The way we make useful, moderate-sized social objects with material properties, the way we infuse them with value, the way we do it together through a myriad of cognitive and linguistic operations: this is exactly what seems to entrance constructivists. And only constructivists. Everyone else starts with goods already in place.[80]

The point, in other words, is not that Constructivism *is* about norms, identity, and culture, and their role in international politics, nor about 'ideas', 'meaning', 'consciousness'. Rather, Constructivism centres how we make those things – *including as objects within disciplines like IR* – and how we infuse them with meaning and communicative ability, and then live our lives through, as, and within, those moderate-sized dry goods.

The New Constructivism's rigorous or consistent anti-essentialism extends to the philosophically thorny problem of foundations. The early empirical constructivists dodged that particular epistemological bullet, and for good reason. To remain on ontological grounds means the firmer territory of 'factors' in observable outcomes in world politics. But as Onuf has made clear, being a constructivist means at least having an *opinion* on the issue of foundations – of the grounds on which claims to knowledge can be made when social life is viewed as always grasped from specific institutional, temporal, and geographical, vantage points.[81] In other words, second, the New Constructivism is incompatible with unproblematic assertions of foundations to knowledge rooted in supposedly unchanging verities of scientific method, objectivism, or empiricism.

Constructivism's rejection of essences and foundations has too often, however, been misunderstood to imply a rejection of social science and its corollaries like measurement and objectivity. In its place is put interpretation and the study of discourse, aimed at uncovering subjective and intersubjective meaning, typically presented in prose form. Following Mills, I – third – defend a view of constructivism as methodologically promiscuous, by which I mean attuned to the most appropriate methods for the puzzle at hand. While traditional discourse analyses might be the most appropriate, constructivists should look far and wide for the best way to frame and prove their arguments. More concretely, as I explore in Chapter 5, this means not leaving new developments in computational methods to non-constructivists. Network analysis, topic modelling, and correspondence analysis, among others, each follow a logic that foregrounds relational social practices as the basis of political action. Constructivists should embrace them.

Fourth, the New Constructivism is conceptually pluralist, by which I mean it is a broad church able to house diverse conceptual categories. To be sure, as we will see, empirical work that analyzes language games is distinct from analyses based on, say, embodiment and emotions, or assemblages and social fields. The concepts or theoretical languages they employ are not of a piece, and might not sit together at all well when trying to make a coherent theoretically distinct account of some phenomenon in world politics. But the conceptual pluralism of the New Constructivism – that scholars can and should draw on an array of conceptual categories in their work, as the problem requires – should be seen as a strength, not a weakness.

One of the signal differences between the Old Constructivism and the New, as I detail in Chapter 4, fifth, is that the New Constructivism is thoroughly and self-consciously reflexive. Early constructivists pushed back against their rationalist colleagues' insistence on the supposedly objective laws of international affairs by demonstrating how the constitutive rules of world politics were not natural but *made* in and through human practice, at particular times and in particular places. As realism and liberalism gave way to rational choice approaches, constructivists countered again that the rules of the game of IR are not really external to the game, and can only be modelled as such by doing violence to reality. Yet, early constructivists largely failed to take the next step: to show how scholars and scientists – IR scholars included – were *themselves* involved in the constructing process.[82] The New Constructivism, I show, includes both the tools and the imperative to take that extra step, both at the level of specific outcomes constructivists seek to explain and understand, and at the general level of what Bentley Allan calls global 'cosmologies'.[83]

Sixth, the New Constructivism's reflexivity sits neatly alongside, and is informed by, another of its signal features – its essentially historical nature. The New Constructivism is not, then, simply the-space-in-IR's-varied-institutional-bases-where-classic-social-analysis-is-practiced, it is the space where *historical social analysis* is practiced. One of the most important aspects of all the classic social theorists, from Du Bois to Foucault, Marx to Norbert Elias, is the attempt to understand modernity in all of its complexity as emerging over time. Indeed, time itself is a social construct central to social and political projects – modern and otherwise – as Andrew Hom among others has expertly dissected.[84] Much Constructivism – Old and New – adopts a historical perspective. In Chapter 6, I argue that the New Constructivism's historicity is unique: neither the history-as-dataset view common in particular among rationalists, nor the historicist view of history as linear process.

Seventh, an important feature of the New Constructivism is its political agnosticism. Defending a view of Constructivism as unmoored from the desire for progressive social change enters an ongoing and lively debate. Several scholars, notably Jason Ralph, have highlighted the ways in which constructivist research can inform political debate by evaluating, and not merely charting, normative change in world politics.[85] Drawing on pragmatism, Ralph shows that norms work when they are useful, providing a role for the constructivist analyst in determining such meaning-in-use. For others, however, in particular Samuel Barkin and Laura Sjoberg, Constructivism does not have a politics – a theoretically informed view on what counts as good versus bad social change – and should not seek an alliance with critical theory in order to adopt one.[86] I track closely to the latter position. While Constructivism can provide the space for the sort of work Ralph suggests, it can also explain processes and change many of us would view with distaste. There is, in short, nothing inherent in its core theoretical properties preventing Constructivism's misuse.

Eighth, and finally, the New Constructivism is marked by several departures from the conceptual focus on norms, identity, and culture, in early constructivist research. Nowhere is this more evident than in the central place it affords to affect and emotions in the New Constructivism. The way social facts like norms, rules, and senses of self, relate to action is not completely – or often adequately – conceptualized by the common constructivist focus on understanding, sense-making, and knowing viewed

15

in an intellectualized form. Equally important, are affects, emotions, and feelings from shame and guilt, to horror and excitement.[87] Classic social analyst Emile Durkheim's concept of 'collective effervescence', for example, is meant to capture how social moods effect individuals viscerally, as the 'vital energies become hyper-excited, the passions more intense, the sensations more powerful'.[88]

Why bother?

Some readers may accept the foregoing and still be unconvinced of the need to undertake the task at hand. Why do IR scholars *need* to recognize a qualitatively new Constructivism on the theory scene? And consequently why should anyone bother to read this book? Two clear and related reasons stand out: first, because it will help them make better analyses of world politics – be better constructivists; second, it will help them recognize their own field, since, once again, if anyone in IR can understand what happened to *constructivism*, it is the constructivists.

I am always surprised that people do not think of Constructivism in the way presented here. In part, they do not because it is not polite – it violates the myth that disciplines are purely ideational phenomena. They also do not because it is defeatist – what good does it do to note Constructivism's disciplinary travails? They also do not like to dwell on the social construction of IR Constructivism because it smacks of navel-gazing, when what we really should be doing is getting on with the job of understanding and explaining world politics. All of these points are true: but they are also social constructs – what is more of a social fact than rules of politeness, or the social ends of an institutionalized arena like a profession or discipline? These rules are thus backed by a certain kind of power – the power to shape how we think and act.

The corollary of the use of that sort of discursive power in the world of politics is to say something to the effect that understanding the discourse of the 'War on Terror' is all well and good, but it does not help us deal with the problem at hand, of say, whether to authorize a drone strike on a suspected militant. Again, this is true enough, but it misrecognizes the constructivist's role. In short, Gentle Reader – in Du Bois' felicitous phrase[89] – if you are looking for 'shovel ready' knowledge, you're in the wrong place – and likely in the wrong business. *But that is precisely the point.* Of all the perspectives in IR, and the social sciences more broadly, Constructivism is the one that tells us why we think of knowledge in that way at all, why people want what they want from theory – without, that is, engaging in a critique of modernity, scientism, and so on *in toto*. It is a fine line to tread and it is not surprising many prefer to cross it entirely – give up on science, explanation, causation, as hopelessly lost to the powers that be. As a constructivist, giving up is not an option because science, explanation, causation, and so on are, *social constructs*.

Likely criticisms: on paradigmatic thinking and 'sociolatry'

Some readers will likely chafe at this reading of recent developments in IR theory, particularly the practice and relational turns. Two criticisms in particular should be aired at the outset, powerful critiques associated with the work of Patrick Jackson and Daniel Nexon, and Patricia Owens, respectively. For Jackson and Nexon, the attempt to reclaim recent developments for Constructivism unnecessarily limits the possibilities of relationalism for IR. For Owens, the space of Constructivism represents the spectre of 'sociolatry' – or a dangerous obsession with social theorizing.[90]

Moving beyond the 'isms'?[91]

Patrick Jackson and Daniel Nexon object to my attempt to claim recent developments in constructivist-style theorizing for the New Constructivism.[92] In particular, they see the attempt as one that unnecessarily limits the possibilities of new approaches by subsuming them under the 'isms' – realism, liberalism, et al – that actually do not function as coherent research programmes as work in the philosophy of science notes. For Jackson and Nexon, Constructivism – like realism and liberalism – does not qualify as either a Lakatosian research programme or Kuhnian paradigm, since both research programmes and paradigms are formed of 'theories that share the same set of content as sources of incommensurability'.[93] Although useful as self-identifiers, the isms are philosophically meaningless since they can be used to generate competing and comparable theoretical accounts of world politics. The most plausible sources of incommensurability, Jackson and Nexon show, involve much larger debates about how to pursue social scientific knowledge.[94] Relationalism is just such a larger perspective.

What Jackson and Nexon ignore, however, is that commensuration is a social process, practical and relational in nature,[95] not an issue of philosophy. Again, for Abbott to a theorist 'OLS and LISREL' are both 'quantitative approaches', while for a quantitative scholar, 'ethnomethodology and symbolic interactionism are indistinguishable'.[96] Cooperative and non-cooperative game theory are thus both rationalist approaches to post-positivists; Foucauldian genealogy and Bourdieusian field theory are both critical theories to mainstream scholars. This does not mean that anything goes when defining approaches. Rather – and as practice-relationalism would stress – approaches are defined for practical purposes according to accepted usage within the IR community.

The work of Kuhn, Lakatos et al has no privileged purchase on how to describe, *commensurate*, the practice of a different science – not science viewed as some general phenomenon. Constructivism must be understood practically and relationally, and not essentially. It may well be the case that in 25 years' time the term Constructivism will no longer be active in IR. But for now Constructivism is a recognized marker. Constructivism is IR's sociological imagination: a space for expanding the mainstream's lenses in more socially and historically sensitive directions. Again, this is a point of similarity to an earlier era. In his 1997 assessment of Constructivism, Adler noted how 'at the core of the debate about Constructivism is … the nature of social science itself and, therefore, the discipline of International Relations'.[97] Since Adler wrote these words, rationalism has overtaken neorealism and neoliberal institutionalism as the predominant approach, while constructivism has narrowed. But IR still needs the space of Constructivism to 'teach their fellows in something like the way that geologists, seismologists, ecologists, and paleontologists, and other historically-oriented physical scientists keep their universalizing brethren in touch with reality'.[98]

Method, not madness

A second, equally powerful, critique comes from the work of Patricia Owens, for whom the entire exercise of this book might represent a dangerous example of IR's 'sociolatry', or obsession with social theorizing.[99] As Owens correctly diagnoses, IR scholars – like many self-defined social scientists – adopt the category of 'the social' unquestioningly, and utilize the work of social theory's primary thinkers, from Marx and Weber to Foucault, without reflecting on their origins.[100] For Owens, IR follows these thinkers in taking 'as axiomatic the reality of underlying social forces, social facts, social systems, social structures, social norms, social processes, socialisation, international society, global civil society, and so on'.[101]

IR's sociolatry is problematic, Owens argues, because it removes the social from the historical context of its emergence – which lies with changes in thinking about society that arose at the same time as the technologies of control associated with the modern nation-state, which then spread out via imperialism over the long 19th century. As she explains, 'The most important setting for the rise of social theory is the new meanings and set of distinctions between "government" and "economy" that accompanied the rise of modern capitalist states/empires in the eighteenth century.'[102] The 'social' and 'socialisation' were not neutral terms, but part of 'efforts to understand and justify the rise of commercial and its bourgeois "civil society"'.[103] The social, Owens shows, was at its heart a depoliticizing discourse, as: 'By the nineteenth century, much more concerted and largely state-led efforts to demobilise recently mobilised and unruly populations (including in the colonies) were accompanied by new sociological discourses and practices – socialisation, social norms, traditional society, social policy, social insurance – explicitly seeking non-political explanations and remedies for violent revolts.'[104]

Owens' critique is nothing short of masterful. As she correctly asks, 'What was the historical context for the emergence of distinctly social thought and why does it matter for the story told in IR about methodological advance?'[105] Her answer:

> International theory cannot begin to answer these questions if it remains in the realm of the philosophy of social science; if it ignores the historicity of its theoretical categories; if accepts the tautology that sociology is the study of what 'social actors do'; and if it presumes that social theories are the only or true heirs of the secular relational constitution of the human world.[106]

Owens' investigations strike at the heart of Constructivism. To the extent that my view of Constructivism is the-space-in-IR's-varied-institutional-bases-where-classic-social-analysis-is-practiced, Owens' critique is potentially devastating. As she shows:

> The very notion of 'socialisation', so influential in contemporary international theory, was a product of a political and ideological crisis in liberal capitalist governance. Surveying the historical rise of sociological thought we find that the hegemony of social theory was achieved against various forms of what was understood (sometimes erroneously) as 'political'.

What is to be done? Abandon the endeavour entirely? Or press on?

Adopting the latter tack, the best response to Owens' critique of IR's sociolatry is to accept it, learn from it, and guard against the depoliticizing and dehistoricizing tendencies she rightly finds at the origins of social theorizing. In much the same way I suggest that constructivists should be able to give a constructivist account of its own origins and trajectory in IR, constructivists should be aware of social thinking's history beyond the field – with all its associations with state violence, internally and externally. Put another way, Owens' analysis *is precisely the sort of reflexive, historical analysis New Constructivists should seek to emulate.*[107] The ahistorical, knee-jerk adoption of social concepts, Owens rightly criticizes, should, as I hope to demonstrate in this book, be avoided.

Doing so shows that while social theorizing is far from immune from being co-opted for state violence – as recent use of social scientific work by the United States military demonstrates – its incorporation into IR via Constructivism also represents an important process within more the rationalistic and scientistic social sciences, especially in the United States.[108] A healthy field of IR needs the space of Constructivism. It is an institutional and intellectual space in which the scope and purpose of IR as a – historically reflexive – social science is kept open. The space of Constructivism is fragile. Constructivist research is pulled between the competing demands of science and the search for strongly generalizable theoretical conclusions, on the one hand, and the critical and more contextually specific impulse of the humanities, on the other.

Plan of the book

Having overviewed the volume, the rest of the book proceeds as follows. In the next chapter, I revisit the classic texts of Constructivism from the 1990s and early 2000s, setting them in their proper contexts within the field. I show that many of their central insights stand the test of time and still have much to offer current and prospective constructivists. Drawing on ongoing research into US foreign policy-making towards great power challengers like Russia and China, I show that sensitivity to international norms and US political culture, especially America's role as a hegemon, are still crucial to understanding the formation of US strategy. However, I also argue that Constructivism's toolkit is not limited to the concepts of culture, norms, or identity. To set the stage for the remainder of the book, and again in line with constructivist premises, I delve into the issue of how and why a narrow understanding of Constructivism took hold. Tracing Constructivism's development, I show that the approach fractured over the course of time, narrowing down to a set of hypotheses about the causal role of identity, culture, and norms in international political outcomes. In so doing, a number of dichotomies opened up – material versus ideational explanations, structure versus agency, explanation versus understanding, subjective versus objective accounts of social action – dichotomies that have produced the space for new approaches that can overcome them, setting the stage for the New Constructivism.

Chapter 2 analyzes the main approaches of the New Constructivism: practice theory, relationalism, network analysis, and actor-network theory. I first offer an overview of each perspective, and then describe how together they overcome the dichotomies described related to Constructivism discussed in the previous chapter, together forming a broad 'practice-relational' theoretical basis for the New Constructivism in IR. While practice theory is often thought limited to the work of French sociologist Pierre Bourdieu – as brought into the field by Vincent Pouliot and Rebecca Adler-Nissen, among others – following Christian Bueger and Frank Gadinger, I explore the full array of pragmatic and critical practice theories available to IR scholars.[109]

Similarly, I describe a broad account of relational and processual sociology, including the recent work of sociologist Andrew Abbott, network analysis and actor-network theory.[110] I describe how, by deploying distinct concepts, a practice-relational approach moves beyond problematic binaries like material versus ideational explanations, structure versus agency, and subjective versus objective accounts of social action. From a practice-relational perspective, political agents are always situated in social contexts imbued with power and knowledge. Bourdieu's concept of 'habitus', to take only one example, offers a way to explore empirically the co-constitution of agency and structure as it becomes embodied in the individual, coming to shape their political positions and dispositions. I show how a practice-relational view proves that approaches that downplay meaning are as misplaced as those that rely solely on objective power differentials to explain political life. Once again, many of these insights are not new – either to the Old Constructivism or the philosophical traditions like pragmatism early constructivists drew on.[111] Yet, they are revolutionary when compared with reigning rationalist views, both in contemporary IR theory and common-sense accounts of world politics.

Naming something new often suggests that all that has gone before can be discarded. Not so in the case of the New Constructivism. The following three chapters explore the core aspects of the New Constructivism in IR theory, cognizant at all times of the deep interconnections between Old and New. I begin in Chapter 3 with the continuing centrality of rules, law, and language to the New Constructivism, each of which were downplayed as constructivism developed in IR, a phenomenon noted by Charlotte Epstein, Mark Raymond, and others.[112] Rules, law, and language are long-standing constructivist concerns,[113] but they were pushed to one side as norms, culture, and identity emerged as the central concepts of the Old Constructivism. The effect was, in many caricatures of Constructivism, to see the approach as one fundamentally about the power of ideas in world politics – a concern held over from the late-1980s/early-1990s debate in political science more broadly about the role of ideas in policy-making.[114] By comparison to 'harder' approaches based on interests and more tangible manifestations of power – like military might – it is unsurprising that Constructivism became viewed as a 'soft' approach, useful for explaining outlying developments in world politics. The practice-relational sensitivity underpinning the New Constructivism, however, rejects such a characterization, placing power relations – effected through rules, law, and language – central to its accounts of world politics. In the case of law, for example, scholars such as Tanja Alberts and Nikolas Rajkovic – in addition to recent work of Kratochwil – have chronicled the immense power of legal rules to shape state interests, amounting to a form of liberal rule through law.[115]

Chapter 4 discusses the importance of reflexivity to the New Constructivism. It shows how a key distinction between the Old Constructivism and the

New is that the New Constructivism is self-consciously reflexive, fully cognizant of the way in which social actors – including the IR theorists – are not merely produced by social construction but engaged in the process of social construction. Many of the problematic intellectual binaries left over from the Old Constructivism are overcome by careful analysis of the role of specific agents like experts and elites in international political outcomes. I label these 'world-makers' as a nod to Nicholas Onuf's path-breaking 1989 volume *World of Our Making*. Theoretically, the impetus to focus on world-makers comes from a rejection – central to a practice-relational sensibility – of accounts of political action focused on norms, cultures, and identities understood in monolithic terms. Most clearly on display perhaps in the work of sociologist Bruno Latour, a rejection of a unified view of culture marks Christian Reus-Smit's recent work on culture in world politics.[116] One of the fundamental insights of this line of thinking is that it is not enough to account for political outcomes by citing the influence of norms, culture, and identities as ready-made artefacts, since their origins, trajectories, and differential effects must be accounted for – once again, foregrounding power in the process. Careful tracing of the impact of agents of different kinds, in other words, solves the agency-structure dilemma, which I illustrate with reference both to the explosion of work on experts and professionals in IR.[117]

What methodological commitments does the New Constructivism entail? The aim of Chapter 5 is to debunk two popular myths about Constructivism's methodological implications: first, that Constructivism is an interpretive approach focused on the reconstruction of subjective meanings; and second, that analysis of texts – speeches, strategy documents, newspaper articles, and memoirs, and so on – is therefore the only way of 'doing' Constructivism.[118] Counter to this common wisdom, I make the case that, instead, Constructivism should be seen as the inheritor of what sociologist C. Wright Mills called 'Classic Social Analysis': a perspective connecting the work of Karl Marx, Max Weber, and Emile Durkheim, and we should add Simone de Beauvoir, W.E.B. Du Bois, and others.[119] Situating the New Constructivism within classic social analysis has two key methodological implications. First, constructivists are much freer in terms of the methods they can use to substantiate their claims than is captured by the focus on interpreting texts. I illustrate using MCA, an approach that could be misconstrued as 'quantitative' and beyond the constructivist pale. Second, the New Constructivism remains within the pursuit of objective knowledge, despite the emphasis placed on intersubjectivity. From this perspective, Constructivism – both Old and New – sits uneasily alongside the main IR-specific theories, such as realism and liberalism, as it has broader concerns than the actions of states in international politics: not only are the social construction of national interests at issue, but the origins of state itself, for instance.

Chapter 6 addresses the question of constructivist ethics, which has emerged as a significant theme in the New Constructivism. Scholars like Martin Weber, Silviya Lechner, and Mervyn Frost have argued that relationalism and practice theory, respectively, are not only able to offer thicker accounts of the social construction of world politics than the Old Constructivism, but can also centre the ethical content of norms and culture in ways downplayed by earlier constructivist theorizing.[120] These scholars suggest that the practice-relational turn has so far downplayed normative/ethical matters due to its overreliance on Bourdieusian sociology. By drawing on new resources, such as German philosopher Axel Honneth, Weber et al argue that practice-relationalism can operate in a much-needed normative register. I assess these arguments, suggesting that the New Constructivism retains a core tension from the Old Constructivism when it comes to the issue of ethics and normativity. In many ways, a problem with Old Constructivism was not the lack of norms, but an over-abundance, which led many realists and rationalists to critique it as a somewhat 'soft' approach based on norms and taboos, rather than the 'hard' matter of power and interests.[121] I trace this tension to Constructivism's position in IR as a via media between more critical and scientific perspectives. For some, New Constructivism remains part of the modernist project of a social science of IR, and should therefore remain true to Max Weber's plea for a 'fact-value' distinction in theorizing. Such a position is closer to my own, which I advance but do not proselytize.

Chapter 7 further explores the New Constructivism's pluralist ethical commitments via an engagement with history, historical modes of knowing, and the question what *is* history in IR? Rather than diagnose specific solutions to be applied, like theoretical knowledge is supposed to do in common understandings, I argue that constructivist theory offers a phronetic understanding of knowledge as fostering 'prudence' and prudential political action. While powerful, such a position does not solve the problem of the relation between theory and practice in IR, but gives name to a type of knowledge the New Constructivism promises – knowledge sensitive to practice, context, history, and the world of artifice, a form worth defending from both problem-solving and critical theorizing.

In reprising the volume, in the conclusion I distil what is distinctive about the New Constructivism, and emphasize why it is imperative to pronounce the New Constructivism's existence at the present time. I argue that Constructivism – Old and New – is best understood as a space for a certain kind of work in IR, work that takes the field's scientific inclinations seriously while resolutely refusing to limit the nature of science to models imported from the natural sciences. Drawing on newer developments in sociology and cognate fields, the New Constructivism departs from the Old by foregrounding the relational and processual nature of social forms, their situatedness in temporally and spatially specific practical contexts. As a bridgehead to the broader historically and culturally sensitive social sciences, I emphasize the importance of keeping that space open vis-à-vis more scientistic approaches, on the one hand, and explicitly normative critical approaches, on the other.

Acknowledgements

This Introduction expands on an argument first made in David M. McCourt, The Future of Constructivism: A Constructivist Assessment. Republished with permission of the University of Michigan Press, from Mariano Bertucci, Jarrod Hayes, and Patrick James, eds. 2018, *Constructivism Reconsidered: Past, Present and Future*, pp 33–46, permission conveyed through Copyright Clearance Center, Inc.

1

The Old Constructivism

The premise of this book would seem to suggest that the Old Constructivism should be discarded. Not so. In this chapter, I show that the Old Constructivism still has many virtues. Many of its core contributions are as relevant as when first made over two decades ago, and as necessary to grapple with for newcomers to the field. Those fresh to Constructivism – in IR and political science in general – should revisit the foundational texts of Constructivism discussed here for themselves. While doing so, however, they should bear in mind two related points.

First, newcomers should recall what the authors of the early constructivist texts were arguing *against*, and why their arguments seemed exciting and refreshing to so many at the time, even dangerous to some of their critics.[1] Second, they should keep in mind the dynamics of IR as a field, dynamics that prioritize scholarship that looks beyond its borders for new insights over revisiting insights from within the field. Together, these caveats reinforce the conclusion that to acknowledge the evolution from the Old Constructivism to a new version of the same does not entail throwing the baby out with the proverbial bathwater. The virtues of the Old Constructivism remain.

Scholars at the forefront of mainstream American IR in the late 1980s and early 1990s had converged on a remarkably narrow set of core issues by the standards of today's variegated international studies profession. The so-called Neo-Neo debate revolved around the sources of state's interests within an international system understood to be anarchical – without a power above the sovereign state able to prevent or at least regulate inter-state conflict.[2] In the words of neorealist contributor to the debate Joseph Grieco, neoliberal institutionalism and neorealism each accepted the anarchical structure of the international system, but differed on whether under some circumstances – notably on trade – the search for relative gains with other states could trump the desire for absolute gains over rivals.[3]

Constructivism burst onto the US IR scene in the late 1980s and early 1990s in the midst of the Neo-Neo debate, drawing the field's attention to an exotic array of objects quite unlike the bombs, tanks, and gross national products, with which IR scholars were used to adjudicating the nature of international politics. In the place of national interests, power, and security dilemmas, constructivists highlighted the role of intersubjective meaning – how policy-makers interpreted, frame, and understood situations in world politics.[4] Constructivists considered the role of norms in the interpretive process, considerations of what is right, proper, and expected of leaders and decision-makers.[5] In so doing, they connected with international lawyers on the effects of legal rules and discourse.[6] Flying in the face of the Neo-Neo synthesis, they said that anarchy was not a given – that the structure of the international system could be changed through agency of individual decision-makers. Agents and structures were co-constituted, in a new phrase offered to the field.[7] Early empirical applications showed, crucially, that these concepts were not fancy buzzwords from – 'presumably Parisian' – social theory;[8] constructivists demonstrated how concrete outcomes *really were* affected by norms,[9] collective and state identity,[10] transnational networks,[11] and political culture,[12] in ways then-leading theories could not incorporate.

Disciplines have their collective pathologies, however. Historical research, for example, follows the dialectical arc of traditionalism, revisionism, and post-revisionist synthesis, alongside the search for the newest archive. In the case of IR, the search for generalizable contributions beyond the case at hand – so 'everyone' can be interested in anti-land mine activism in central Africa, for example – leads to the claim that X 'matters' in IR, usually meaning as an input into state action. Consider the sheer number of books and articles produced per year in IR with some variant on the title '(The role of) X in international relations/politics'.[13] The effect, however, is to exhaust interest in specific theoretical developments – a dynamic I explore later will soon come to limit the scope for new work in the practice turn specifically.[14]

Much of what is surprising about the Old Constructivism is precisely how much mileage scholars, in fact, got from the claim that norms, identity, culture, and so on, matter. One might think the claim would have exhausted itself rather sooner. The reason they have is that norms and so on *really do matter*, but most accounts of IR – official and scholarly – are written in the language of realism, of national interests and strategic calculations, not cultural discourses and international norms. The conceptual and methodological innovations of the New Constructivism prove the point that norms and so on matter, rather than render the Old Constructivism obsolete.

These two caveats must be kept in mind or else, to paraphrase Dickens' *A Christmas Carol*, nothing that follows will seem wondrous. Yet, I also explore in greater depth in this chapter the narrowing of Constructivism over the course of the 1990s and 2000s, which diluted the power of the Old Constructivism, giving rise to the New. I show that early constructivists were in many ways bound by the historical and institutional terms of their intervention – their purview limited by the very disciplinary blinders they had successfully challenged: the agent-structure debate; constitution versus causation; explanation versus understanding. Some newer constructivists criticize the Old Constructivists for not attacking these with more vigour,[15] but as I tried to show in the previous chapter, IR itself is a social space with its own institutional norms and practices, not just an intellectual arena. Incremental change of the sort on display in the emergence of Old Constructivism is what the IR field produces, not swift paradigmatic turnover.

The virtues of the Old Constructivism[16]

The virtues of the Old Constructivism are multiple. Here I focus on two broad sets of insights early constructivists placed at the forefront of IR scholarship: first, the normative foundations of IR, and the pervasive influence of culture on state action, at various levels; and second, the role of identity in the making of foreign policy, and the related methodological imperative to foreground meaning, sense-making, and interpretation in IR research. These broad categories do not exhaust the Old Constructivism, rather offering a convenient means by which to summarize a large body of research.

Culture and norms in international politics

As already noted, Constructivism emerged in IR in a context of a broader turn in the social sciences inspired by the 'cultural turn' in social theory. The key insight emerging from the encounter was that some of the field's then-predominant notions – security, the state, and national interests – had to be rethought as less neutral or universal, and more filled with cultural and hence normative content.[17] In many ways, as I explore throughout this book, constructivists remained engaged in the encounter with culturalist theorizing beyond IR, and puzzling what new developments there imply for research on – and indeed the nature of – world politics.

Culture, Peter Katzenstein explained in an authoritative early statement, is 'a broad label that denotes collective models of nation-state authority or identity, carried by custom or law'.[18] Culture as a concept is difficult to pin down, of which more later. Consequently, some early proponents avoided firm definitions of culture at all.[19] Most constructivists agreed, however, that culture inheres in some combination of collective beliefs, practices, identities, rules, and shared meanings. Drawing on anthropologist Clifford Geertz's then-influential descriptions, culture is the 'webs of meaning' within which humans live, which they 'themselves have spun'.[20] Culture forms the background knowledge of a community – how one typically thinks and acts: 'a web of intersubjective meanings, expressed through, and embedded within, language, images, bodies, practices, and artefacts'.[21]

Crucially, in culture the early constructivists found a vehicle for including in their analyses the inherently normative nature of international affairs – a way to analyze world politics not merely in terms of social physics of clashing billiard balls, but as an arena of life thick with rules, morals, beliefs, and prejudices. Culture thus has both descriptive and prescriptive content – a matter of 'is' and 'ought' – referring, to quote Katzenstein again, to 'both a set of evaluative standards (such as norms and values) and a set of cognitive standards (such as rules and models) that define what social actors exist in a system, how they operate, and how they relate to one another'.[22]

Perhaps the most oft-cited analysis of culture in IR – that of Alexander Wendt – picked up precisely here, with the issue of the type of social actors that exist in the global system, and how they relate to one another.[23] Wendt took head-on the structural realist theorizing of Kenneth Waltz, showing that it is far from lacking in culture.[24] The structural realist approach describes a 'Hobbesian' world of entrenched enmity. Noting how for many states this does not characterize their relations, Wendt described two alternative 'cultures of anarchy' states can inhabit: a 'Lockean' world of cautious rivalry and a 'Kantian' world of peaceful co-existence.[25] Wendt's approach helps explain differences in, for example, US grand strategy toward the West and Latin America – where Washington has forged long-lasting 'security communities' – and with parts of the world where more conflictual relations continue.[26]

While massively influential, Wendt's account maintained the parsimony of structural realism, and as such offered a relatively 'thin' vision of the effects of culture on world politics. A more generative constructivist literature offered a deeper understanding of international political culture, stressing how the sort of 'social facts' – societal constraints on individual behaviour – sociologist Emile Durkheim described in domestic society holds for international society too.[27] For norms researchers, international politics is far from the anomic world described by realists. It is filled with expectations about legitimate behaviour, expectations that put often strict bounds on what states can do and want to do.[28] Nina Tannenwald, for example, demonstrated the powerful effects of a taboo against first use of nuclear weapons.[29] Taboos, Tannenwald explained, are a certain type of cultural norm that have both *regulative* effects – the injunction in international law against first use – and *constitutive* effects – placing nuclear weapons in the 'do not use' category and creating a 'non-first user' category states can aspire to join and uphold.[30] Culture is thus normative in a dual sense, with the nuclear first-use taboo constitutive of *what it means to be a civilized country.*

Culture and norms made their first inroads into IR theory as features of the international system ignored by the then-reigning structural liberal and structural liberal theories. Other early constructivists brought culture down to the national and sub-national levels. For Colin Dueck, for example, structural realist, structural liberal, and structural-cultural accounts of US foreign policy all give insufficient weight to its uniquely *American* nature.[31] The centrality of US culture is evident in a commitment to a specific form of anti-authoritarian and market-oriented liberalism, and internationalism vacillating between moral-crusading and reluctant leadership. Similarly, Katzenstein and Andrew Oros have both demonstrated the culturally unique understanding of security in Japan, which is far more expansive than the American focus on the police and military, underpinning Japan's hesitation toward the use of force.[32]

Others still showed how culture shapes political action at the sub-state level, in domestic governing organizations. Lynn Eden, to illustrate, demonstrated the profound effects of organizational culture in American planning for the use of nuclear weapons.[33] Addressing the puzzle of why US military organizations in the post-war period developed very accurate predictions of nuclear blast radius, but consistently underestimated the radius for fire damage – which had such impact at Hiroshima. The answer, Eden emphasizes, influenced weapon procurement decisions, leading both the US and the Soviet Union to build tens of thousands of, effectively unusable, bombs. Eden answers with reference to the social construction of knowledge in US war planning organizations, specifically the 'knowledge-laden organizational routines' and 'organizational frames' that shaped the way planners understood nuclear weapons. They came to fold nuclear weapons into a 'blast damage frame' that had emerged during the 1930s and subsequently WWII – a frame that utterly failed to fit the world of nuclear weapons. Eden's analysis remains a powerful example of organizational culture and the frames through which culture influences action.[34]

A related, more recent, literature has continued in a similar vein by addressing the routines and habits underpinning foreign policy thinking.[35] Patrick Porter, for example, locates the sources of continuity in US grand strategy since the end of the Cold War in the habits and routines of the American foreign policy 'Establishment' – the many think tanks, research centres, and academic departments, mainly in Washington DC, that provide knowledge to the US government when it comes to foreign policy.[36] Porter describes how the Establishment narrows strategic debate to some version of US primacy along more or less liberal internationalist lines, limiting voices for other grand strategies such as restraint, pullback, or offshore balancing. Crucially, members of the Establishment are often unaware of how US foreign policy reproduces itself as an unintended consequence of their common modes of thinking and talking about global problems and American options.

These key contributions do not come close to exhausting the insights of the Old Constructivism. Yet, to many newcomers, it may appear strange that the cultural and normative aspects of international politics were so revolutionary. Others, including Foreign Policy Analysts, had sought for at least two decades to draw attention to the policy-making process, and the need to open up the 'Black Box' of the state structural theories insisted on keeping closed. Across the pond, the unfortunately named 'English School' of IR theory – unfortunate because few of its major figures or institutional bases were, in fact, English – had foregrounded the cultural aspects of international *society* as opposed to the culturally neutral concept of system popular in the US. Nonetheless, the early constructivists captured the imagination – and reading eyes – of the commanding heights of the IR world in the US. In so doing, the early constructivists proved that culture and norms can *matter* in world politics, shaping state action in ways realist and liberal theories would fail to predict.

By 2000 at the latest, however, the cultural and normative cat was out of the constructivist bag, scurrying around the house of American political science. There, the insights of Constructivism were shaped by the norms and culture of the US discipline. A distinction between rationalist and non-rationalist understandings of culture is a useful example of what happened.[37] Rationalists were quite happy to accept culture and norms mattered, in the form of cultural and normative expectations. But they viewed social expectations deriving from culture as inputs to be weighed like other costs in cost-benefit analyses. For non-rationalists, by contrast, culture is 'thicker' than rationalists allow, *constituting* the way social situations are made up – what moves are even thinkable for rational players to make in a given scenario.[38]

State identity and narrative knowing

Closely aligned to culture and norms in early constructivism, and suffering a similar fate, is the concept of state *identity*. Identity-based constructivist accounts of IR posit the will-to-self-knowledge and self-expression as a foundational feature of world politics, alongside the will-to-power central to realism. Foreign policy is as much about affirming a state's sense of who it *is* in world politics, as it is about material interests. Identity is deeply entwined with culture and norms. The identities states perform are manifestations of cultures at each of the aforementioned levels – the international, national, and sub-national. For example, whereas securing the US national interest in Northeast Asia might suggest a pre-emptive strike on North Korea, such action would violate America's sense of self. In the American collective imagination, the US is not the *type* of actor that violates norms of national sovereignty and the peaceful resolution of international disputes unless it must.

Like culture, identity too is a contested concept. Competing definitions abound.[39] Invoking identity opens up tricky philosophical questions about what identities are and where they come from. How *exactly* do considerations of 'American-ness' influence grand strategy? The implication that identities are unique also raises concerns about the generalizability. Scholars take different stances on these questions and develop different approaches to identity in IR. While any classificatory scheme does some violence, four broad inter-related approaches to identity can be identified: (1) identity as a story of a community's place in IR; (2) identity as a state's 'Self'; (3) critical approaches on the exclusionary practices of foreign policy; and (4) the constitutive role of sovereignty as expressing the moral purpose of the state in world politics.

National identity stories. The most straightforward approach explores the national identity stories that form the basis of foreign policy. In an early illustration, Eric Ringmar addressed the question of why Sweden became involved in the Thirty Years' War (1618–48).[40] Sweden's embroilment in the Europe-wide conflict was made possible by the construction during the late 16th and early 17th century of a Swedish national identity as a unified country – separate from Norway and Denmark with whom its history had been intertwined for 300 years. As a proud and separate country, founded by the ancient Goths, and a member of the Protestant countries of Europe, King Gustav Adolf (1594–1632) believed his purpose to be to take Sweden into the Thirty Years' War.

Again, foregrounding the identity-based motives for foreign policy was a crucial move for early constructivists because it responded to a puzzle left over from realist accounts of state action, namely where national interests come from. Realists downplay the question of how supposedly material conditions like national interests are interpreted as interests in the first place. Similarly rationalists downplay the origins of the preferences that structure bargaining games between states, as between individuals in domestic society. But as Wendt has argued, 'identities are the basis of interests', like Sweden's unified, protestant, identity.[41] In Martha Finnemore's formulation, before someone or some state can know what they *want*, they have to know who or what they *are*.[42] National identity stories provide this crucial aspect of state action missing from realist and rationalist accounts.

The *story* part of the national identity stories should not be neglected. For Ringmar, 'Our definitions of interest and identities are intimately related to the way in which we make sense of our world … it is on the basis of the meanings we construct that interests and identities are defined.' Meanings are constructed as and through narratives.[43] Narratives, Friedrich Kratochwil shows, construct meaning by emplotting events in the structure of a story, providing logical and chronological coherence by showing why something is the way it is by retelling its story of becoming.[44] As Ron Krebs has shown, national security narratives set out 'the broad contours for policy. Whether explicitly articulated or left implicit, it is the reason some beliefs seem naïve and that others seem realistic'.[45]

While generative, national identity stories made relatively little *conceptual* use of the concept of identity, however. Again, identities are stories about a national community, betrayed in public rhetoric. In certain renderings, identity-based explanations of foreign policy are largely indistinguishable from those based on 'ideas' or 'belief systems'.[46] Other approaches, consequently, foregrounded identity, in diverse ways.

Identity and the national 'Self'. For Brent Steele, identity is not simply a national story but a natural drive of the state to counter threats to its 'ontological security'.[47] This view expanded the concept of security from the physical world – territory, borders, and population – to the core beliefs about who or what a state is and the motivations that derive from threats to them. Jarrod Hayes, for example, showed how America's identity as a democratic country had crucial implications when it came to whether Cold War disputes with China and India would become security issues.[48] Democratic India was viewed by elites and the public in America as less threatening to the American Self than non-Democratic China – an insight which usefully socializes the long-standing thesis in IR that democracies are more cooperative with fellow democracies than alternative regime types.

The move to social psychology brought with it an increased sensitivity to emotions and affect in threat perception – a sensitivity more fully brought to fruition in the New Constructivism, as detailed later in the book.[49] Nonetheless, scholars like Jacques Hymans were aware of the identity-based meanings and emotions – in Hymans' case nuclear status – carries for different states.[50] National identity conceptions, he showed, have two dimensions: a *solidarity* dimension that corresponds to ideas about what a community stands for; and a *status* dimension made up of beliefs about where a state ranks in world politics.[51] The decision to cancel South Africa's nuclear programme after the end of apartheid, then, can be explained by the feeling of its leaders that South Africa's status and national purpose were not enhanced by nuclear capability. India and Pakistan, by contrast, had strong status concerns and solidarity reasons for wanting nuclear weapons, beyond the threat posed by the other. Hymans' work exemplified a rich literature focused on recognition and status-seeking, one that moves beyond constructivism's confines.[52]

Identity, difference, and foreign policy. The move to social psychology brought with it theoretical specificity absent from some national identity stories. Yet it also relied on cognitive and psychological processes in ways that can downplay the social and cultural factors initially attractive to constructivists. Both ontological security and national identity approaches can fail to grapple with the question of where state identities come from.[53] The problem of the origins of identities has been common to philosophical discourse since Hegel's discussion of the master-slave dialectic. There Hegel affirmed that identity – what something is – and difference – what something is not – are mutually constitutive. A master could not be a master without the slave, and vice versa. A third identity-based literature has thereby stressed the inherently *relational* nature of identities and the mutual constitution of 'Self' and 'Other'.[54]

'Broadly conceived as the mutual, cognitive, sociological, or emotional ties through which states understand themselves, especially in relation to others', Janice Bially Mattern noted, 'identity is an *embodiment* of shared categories of Self-Other understanding'.[55] Identities are formed through an 'on-going process of interaction and social learning'.[56] More recently, consequently, Iver Neumann and Ayşe Zarakol thus each foregrounded the social origins of foreign policies in the case of the 'problematic'.[57] Both countries have struggled to situate themselves against the West – neither fully within nor fully outside. What goes for marginal and stigmatized identities goes for seemingly unproblematic identities too. All identities are constructed against Others. These Others may be concrete other states, diffuse notions of what difference in international political culture, and past understandings of the state in question.

Identity affirmation, therefore, both at the individual and state level, is achieved through the playing distinct *social roles*.[58] Roles exist at the intersection of the unique and the general, mediating between identity and social structure. Contra thin visions of international culture as populated by roles such as enemy and rival, international society is filled with richer sets of roles, from great power, hegemon, to regional powers (which English School theorists have long acknowledged.)[59] Russian foreign policy since before the reign of Peter the Great (1672–1725), for example, has been shaped by repeated – frequently frustrated – attempts to play the role of *great power* in international affairs, a role defined by the Western Powers.[60] Russian foreign policy has vacillated between an intense desire for acceptance into the Western club and fierce rejection of all that it stands for, as evidenced today in Vladimir Putin's attempts to play a distinctly non-Western great power role. Russia's identity and the urge to affirm its preferred self in international politics is foregrounded from a role-based approach, but so too are the social and cultural constraints within which the process has taken place, mediated through the shifting expectations of the great power role.

A connected literature adopted a more critical tack, foregrounding the *political* as opposed to merely social constitution of identity. For David Campbell, foreign policy is the activity constitutive of identity.[61] Rather than the foreign – the other – foreign policy 'makes foreign' certain events and actors.[62] US foreign policy has been based on a series of shifting foreign threats constitutive of American identity: Britain, communism/the Soviet Union, drugs, and more recently terrorism. As Richard Ashley argues, 'foreign policy is "a specific form sort of *boundary producing political performance*".'[63]

Sovereignty, identity, and the State's moral purpose. A final early constructivist literature connected the socially constructed nature of state identity with its fundamentally moral character, returning us to the beginning of our discussion of how culture constitutes identities in IR. For Reus-Smit, national stories represented identities at the surface level of international society.[64] At a deeper level, fundamental institutions of international society – from multilateralism[65] and great power management,[66] to the many regimes that structure functional spheres of international cooperation – 'comprise the basic rules of practice that structure regime cooperation'.[67] Underpinning them all are the 'deep constitutive metavalues that comprise the normative foundations of international society'.[68] Again, as Katzenstein had noted, 'Cultural-institutional contexts do not merely constrain actors by changing the incentives that shape behavior. They do not simply regulate behavior. They also constitute the very actors whose conduct they seek to emulate.'[69] Centrally, the notion of sovereign statehood is the foundational metapractice of modern world politics, constituting the moral purpose of the state, and actors as knowledgeable social agents, at the same time as regulating their behaviour.[70]

The narrowing of Constructivism

By the early years of the new millennium, Constructivism found itself in a curious position. On the one hand, Constructivism was well on the way to being the third in IR's typical theoretical triptych alongside realism and liberalism, nudging Marxism or 'radicalism' from third spot. Constructivists had been allowed inside the tent. On the other, while highly productive, the constructivist approach had begun to split into a number of camps, with diverging understandings of the constructivist enterprise.

Scholars have described the emerging constructivist camps in different ways. For Ted Hopf, Constructivism split into two fractals: *conventional* and *critical* Constructivist varieties.[71] John Gerard Ruggie, by contrast, saw Constructivism splitting along three lines: first a *naturalistic* or scientistic Constructivism; second, a *neo-classical* variant akin to the classical social theorists such as Max Weber and Emile Durkheim, and a *postmodern* Constructivism indebted to various inspirations, notably Jacques Derrida.[72] Perhaps most straightforwardly, Maja Zehfuss associated 'three Constructivisms' with their principal exponents – Wendt, Kratochwil, and Onuf respectively.[73]

In each cases, the science/non-science divide was central to the process of fractalization. When describing Constructivism on the occasion of the journal *International Organization*'s half-centennial, for example, Katzenstein, Keohane, and Krasner emphasized Constructivism's modernism: 'constructivists … put forward sociological perspectives that emphasized shared norms and values but which were in epistemological terms sharply differentiated from postmodernism'.[74] For prominent constructivists, Constructivism's value was precisely that it represented a *via media* between positivism and interpretivism,[75] or – more radically – that the field should recognize Constructivism as positivist, once positivism's boundaries were expanded to include interpretivist work.[76]

Constructivism's fractal distinction and thus its narrowing cannot, however, be explained with reference to disagreements over epistemology or methodology alone. The reason is that Constructivism runs orthogonally to both. While Social Constructivism raises the issue of knowledge – of the actor and the observer – it has no specific philosophy of knowledge. Most constructivists, like their colleagues, gather empirical data to support arguments derived from theoretical analysis. The data is often simply of a different sort. As Patrick Jackson has persuasively demonstrated, Constructivism is not a methodological category either.[77] As a straightforward claim that the world is not given but made in practice, social construction can be studied using a wide range of methodologies, including large-n hypothesis testing.

The splitting of Constructivism should not be seen, therefore, as the inevitable result of philosophical differences over epistemology. Rather, it followed a social process of fractal distinction. Constructivism's narrowing was an effect of the predominant norms and incentive structures of the US academy, which broadly speaking favour the development of generalizable and abstract knowledge, rewarding ontological discovery and penalizing seemingly unnecessary philosophical speculation about the meaning of science and the nature of legitimate knowledge.

The value of Constructivism to US IR was frequently advertised thereby as an expanded ontology for the field. For Checkel, 'constructivists do not reject science or causal explanation; their quarrel is with mainstream theories is ontological, not epistemological'.[78] The effect of keeping matters on the terrain of ontology was to cement an understanding of constructivist theory as covering a distinct social ontology tied increasingly to a limited set of empirical objects: norms, culture, and identity. Later constructivist work explored issues like state socialization,[79] argumentation and persuasion,[80] and the diffusion of norms in international politics.[81] Such discussion could bring constructivists together with non-constructivists around shared problematics and methods. Yet, with some important exceptions,[82] the narrowing of Constructivism had the effect of inhibiting the development of new theoretical vocabularies in favour of meticulous empirical demonstration of the role of socially constructed drivers of state action versus more traditional material interest-based understandings. Constructivism's narrowing thus froze in place a particular account of constructivist theory increasingly closed to theoretical refinement.

Over time, the narrowed version of Constructivism that came to predominate in the US became less persuasive to non-American audiences. Constructivism's culturally and socially sensitive claims were far from novel internationally given the prevalence of the English School, Marxism, feminism, and critical theory, among other approaches.[83] Thus, while Constructivism emerged as an influential approach beyond the US in part because IR itself underwent intense internationalization over the 1990s and 2000s, the meaningfulness of the category Constructivism beyond America nonetheless very much rested on its continued strength *within* the American academy. There, a narrowed understanding increasingly held sway, an understanding that came to weaken the approach as time passed.

The Old Constructivism's problematic dichotomies

The narrowing of Constructivism – its double-essentialization as a singular approach that studies culture, norms, and identity as things rather than processes – led to a set of problematic dichotomies the New Constructivism is advertised as able to overcome.

First, a typical way of characterizing constructivism is as an ideational approach: 'The central insight of constructivism is that collectively held ideas shape the social, economic, and political world in which we live.'[84] Again, this shorthand is problematic. It not only makes it difficult to distinguish Constructivism from the ideas literature,[85] it brings associations of relativism and a rejection of science.[86] Constructivism is not idealist. As Finnemore and Sikkink noted, '[Constructivism] asserts that human interaction is shaped primarily by ideational factors, not simply material ones'.[87] While the exact relationship between ideational and material factors is vague, material factors are unmistakably included.[88]

Constructivism has been seen as idealist because of its focus on language and the difficulty of explaining political outcomes using language. The most common method, discourse analysis, is typically conflated with the need to interpret words as the vehicle for subjectively held ideas.[89] However, invoking meanings encoded in language is not sufficient to explain action since different courses of action can flow from the same word.[90] Downplayed thereby is the *practicality* and *relationality* of language. Words are not simply ideas; they are things individuals pick up and use in their everyday interactions, as scholars drawing on the theory of speech acts and the notion of securitization have shown.[91] This was central for early constructivists. 'Constructivism begins with deeds. Deeds done, acts taken, words spoken.'[92]

A second problematic binary linked to Old or narrowed Constructivism is agency versus structure.[93] Agent-structure co-constitution has become an impediment to theorizing because Constructivism is by turns conflated with agency and structure exclusively. For many, Constructivism is an approach that highlights the power of the agent to change their social environment, as in the example of transnational activists changing what states consider acceptable in terms of harm to their populations and others'.[94] But as Patrick Jackson complains, 'The argument here seems to be that any discussion of individuals and their preferences is somehow intrinsically linked to agency.'[95] Actors still exist in structural contexts. An alternative approach is to view Constructivism as based solely on structural factors, like norms and modes of legitimacy. Here agency goes missing.[96] Practice theory and relationalism both reject agency versus structure, focusing instead on stabilizations of ongoing processes.

Third, Constructivism became associated with a dichotomy between causal-versus-constitutive theorizing, with constructivism the domain of constitutive theory.[97] This gives priority to so-called *efficient* causation, which seeks to subsume observed events under general laws and serves to demote constitutive theory to non-causal status.[98] As Emirbayer notes, however, 'the notion of causes as immaterial entities such as "forces", "factors", "structures", which impel substances down the causal path',[99] is tied to substantialism. This was entrenched with the first empirical constructivist works, which drew on the notion of constitution to explore where state interests came from. For example, Klotz explored the role of norms of racial equality in constituting international responses to apartheid in South Africa.[100] Although Wendt attempted to dissolve the dichotomy, arguing that the social and natural sciences viewed causation similarly, causation is still often considered a positivist notion only.[101]

Practice theorists and relationalists explicitly reclaim causation and explanation.[102] Vincent Pouliot and Patrick Jackson draw on Max Weber's notion of *adequate causality* rather than efficient causation: 'we know that some configuration of factors is causally adequate if we cannot plausibly conceive of that configuration *not* producing the outcome in question'.[103] In line with the Weberian analysis based on ideal-types, since causes cannot be thought of in substantialist terms, the task is not to search for constant antecedents of observed events, but 'contingent practice that have historically made a given social fact possible'.[104] This highlights the role of concepts in social science. From this perspective, causes are not to be 'isolated "out there" but [considered as] heuristic focal points used by the researcher to make sense of social life'.[105] They 'are mental constructs devised to make sense of our interpretations and which belong to the realm of scientific knowledge'.[106]

Finally, Constructivism has been wrongly considered a purely 'qualitative' approach, as opposed to a 'quantitative' one. There is no good conceptual reason constructivists have shied away from the array of sophisticated data analysis and presentation techniques available to social scientists that blur the quantitative/qualitative distinction.[107] The practice and relational turns broaden Constructivism's methodological lenses, as I will detail in Chapter 5, techniques like social network analysis and MCA have particular potential.[108] They offer ways to objectify social processes and to explore their properties without falling into essentialization. Both remain under-utilized in IR.[109]

Conclusion

In the late 1990s, it seemed Constructivism was everywhere. Ten years later, the claim that international politics is socially constructed had become less exciting. By then, the issue was *how*, under what circumstances? As Amitav Acharya asked, 'whose norms matter?'[110] For Charlotte Epstein, 'Who speaks?' when we say identity matters.[111] Yet, as I will argue in the following chapter, scholars moved away from Constructivism for reasons beyond the diminishing novelty of the claim itself. The narrowing of constructivist theory had real analytical costs for Constructivism, leading scholars to de-essentialize constructivist notions like culture and identity in fresh and exciting ways.

Yet, by reaching beyond IR to social theory, social psychology, cultural anthropology, and cognate fields, those scholars involved de-essentializing culture, norms, and identity are doing the very same thing as the early constructivists. As I discuss further in the next chapter, *they are doing Constructivism*. For Abbott, the way in which IR Constructivism narrowed should be entirely unsurprising. It accords with a cyclical pattern associated with Construct*ionism* in the broader social sciences: 'first come insightful theoretical treatises and quirky but creative empirical work ... then systematic consolidation treatises ... and new empirical work that is solid but lacks the excitement of the initial treaties'.[112] The result of this process, Abbott notes, is that the basic claim that:

> social reality is given by practice rather than given ex ante has made at least four separate appearances in this century's social science: first in the pragmatism of Dewey and Mead, then in the relational Marxist epistemology of Mannheim, then in the strong constructionism of existentialism and phenomenology, and finally in recent theoretical work from France.[113]

In Abbott's view, the cyclical re-emergence of Constructivism in different guises means that '[t]here are different wrinkles to these appearances, and of course there is a new terminology in each case ... [but] there is no real progress, no fundamentally new concept. We simply keep recalling a good idea'.[114]

Acknowledgements

This chapter draws on material from a chapter in Thierry Balzacq and Ron Krebs, 2021, *Oxford Handbook of Grand Strategy*, by permission of Oxford University Press (https://global.oup.com/academic/product/the-oxford-handbook-of-grand-strategy-9780198840299?cc=us&lang=en&#)

The New Constructivism

The previous chapter left off on a rather dispiriting note, with sociologist Andrew Abbott's cynical-sounding conclusion that, when Constructivism reappears in the social sciences – as it does for him, on a roughly generational cycle – there are 'different wrinkles … and of course there is a new terminology … [but] there is no real progress, no fundamentally new concept. We simply keep recalling a good idea'.[1] In this chapter, I show that such a characterization of Construc*tionism* beyond IR both fits with the experience of the New Construc*tivism* in IR theory to some degree only, falling a little wide of the mark. It all depends on what we mean by *progress* and *fundamentally* new ideas.

Abbott is correct to the extent that the New Constructivism ultimately makes the same point as the Old: that international politics – like all human life – is a collective accomplishment. The social world, including the main categories and concepts we use to understand it – truth, science, knowledge, cosmologies – are constructed in and through practice. There is nothing natural about them. If *progress* and *fundamentally new ideas* are taken to mean something more than this, then no, the New Constructivism is not fundamentally distinct from the Old, and little progress has been made. But if progress is unmoored from the grip of prevailing understandings of the word 'science', understandings rooted in 'solving' problems we all agree on once and for all, the New Constructivism represents precisely the type of progress IR scholars should aim for. The New Constructivism offers an array of new concepts, perspectives, and methodologies designed to help us overcome the problematic dichotomies associated with the Old Constructivism outlined in Chapter 1, and to help us think about *exactly how* the socially constructed world shapes our collective and individual doings.

The New Constructivism, and those concepts, perspectives, and methods, has emerged from two recent 'turns' in IR theory: the turn to practices and relations.[2] Practice theory draws attention to everyday logics in world politics, and asserts that actors are driven less by abstract forces such as the national interest, preferences, or social norms, than by practical imperatives, habits, and embodied dispositions. Relationalism meanwhile rejects the idea that entities – whether states, international organizations, norms, or identities – are the basic units of world politics, replacing them with ongoing processes. Driven by the same anti-essentialism and anti-foundationalism, I here consider the turns to practice theory and relationalism a twin development, two sides of the same coin. Together, *practice-relationalism* represent the New Constructivism in IR. Taken as a piece, the aim of practice-relationalism is to ensure IR scholarship – particularly vis-à-vis the mainstream of US-centric IR – sensitive to the social and cultural contexts in which international politics takes place.

The New Constructivism should not, I emphasize, be considered limited to a concern with practice(s) and relations, as I will make clear. Practice theory and relationalism are expansive approaches. Both come in a number of flavours, and much work remains to be done in plumbing them for insights in the study of world politics. Nonetheless, the practice and relational turns – taken as a single movement in the field – are the instantiation of the re-emergence of Constructivism in IR.

The aim of this chapter, consequently, is four-fold. I first revisit the argument that the practice-relational turn should be considered a singular thing, the appearance of which represents a new round of constructivist theorizing in IR. Second, the bulk of the chapter overviews the major approaches and conceptual vocabularies of the New Constructivism. Admittedly, this is shifting terrain. However, I focus on field theory, network analysis, and actor-network theory (ANT), which have already proven their worth. Third, I offer an illustration of the empirical pay-off. Fourth, I close the circle between the Old Constructivism and the New by re-reading early constructivist tracts that, in retrospect, included a serious engagement with the notion of practices and relations. In short, the practice and relational turns should not have been necessary had the practice-sensitive and relational nature of early constructivism not been shorn from it as Constructivism narrowed over the 1990s and early 2000s.

Practice-relationalism: the New Constructivism

Practice theory is less a single theory than a broad set of approaches imported into IR from philosophy and social theory that display certain family resemblances.[3] What the label covers is a vision of social life composed of 'embodied, materially interwoven practices centrally organized around shared practical understandings'.[4] Practice theory opposes IR's two main ways of accounting for social action: the logic of consequences and the logic of appropriateness.[5] Knowledge is neither purely goal-oriented nor norm-driven, for practice theorists, but has an irreducibly engaged, practical component. Knowing what to do and how to do it are fundamentally conjoined as aspects of practical activity.

Foregrounded thereby in practice theory is the non-conscious aspect of much of what individuals do, which has typically been ignored in IR theory: often people behave in certain ways neither because they want to nor because they feel they should – as rationalist and norm-centred approaches suggest – but because it is 'what one does'. A consequent emphasis in practice theory is on the 'everyday' – the habits and commonsensical routines people develop to bring order to the complexity of social interaction[6] – and the affective and emotional underpinnings of social action.[7]

Diplomacy represents a useful example. IR scholars often pay less attention to the role of diplomacy in translating stated priorities into policies and agreements as might be warranted given its centrality to international politics.[8] From a practice perspective, however, diplomacy is a well-bounded social sphere with strong norms and conventions, clear physical locations and modes of entry – qualifications, social attributes, dispositions, and so on – and is where much of what IR scholars' study is actually carried out. Viewing diplomacy in practice theoretic terms thus has distinct advantages over alternatives. By embedding himself within the Norwegian diplomatic corps, for example, Iver Neumann shows that even something as simple as writing a speech is shaped by the practical process by which it is constructed.[9] Far from the unitary pronouncement of an objective national interest or state preference – as in realism and rationalism – or nation-state identity – as per narrowed Constructivism, Neumann demonstrates that speech writing is the result of countless day-to-day compromises characteristic of the practice of diplomacy. I discuss Neumann's insights in greater depth in Chapter 4.

Relationalism is a similarly broad approach brought in primarily from American sociology.[10] Relationalism's main premise is a rejection of the substantialism of most IR theory. Substantialism 'maintains that the ontological primitives of analysis are "things" or entities … [which] exist before interaction'.[11] In IR, neorealism and neoliberal institutionalism have been criticized for taking the international system, states, and state interests as immutable. Substantialism also affects non-state-centric theories like rational choice, however, where the cost-benefit maximizing human agent is assumed to exist prior to interaction.[12] Surprisingly, perhaps, the charge of substantialism extends to norms-based approaches – including narrowed constructivism – , which also tends to depict individuals as 'self-propelling, self-subsistent entities', only driven by norms.[13]

Relationalism is opposed to substantialism because it offers an undertheorized conception of agency. Treating social processes as essences leads to the view that action is undertaken not by individuals but by forces – like interests, preferences, or institutions – that propel essences into action. As sociologist Mustafa Emirbayer maintains, 'Social actors themselves, in gamelike transactions within ever-changing contexts, do all of the acting in social life, not some imaginary entities within or without them, as in the substantialist worldviews of self- or interaction.'[14] A relational perspective is therefore difficult to maintain and operationalize – as sociologist Norbert Elias notes, 'People to whom it seems self-evident that their own self (or their ego, or whatever else it may be called) exists, as it were, "inside" them … have difficulty assigning significance to those facts which indicate that individuals live from the first in interdependence with others.'[15] Relationalists nonetheless begin from the position that the social world as is made up of relations: 'Our task as analysts is to grasp the process through which such relations are aggregated and used to stabilize and reify some other relations as making up an entity or thing.'[16]

Taken together, practice-relationalism can be considered a twin approach because the aim in each is to recover a more appropriate understanding of the *social* in social explanation by foregrounding process over fixity, and its primary target is narrowed Constructivism. A more adequate form of social explanation requires sensitivity to both practice and relationality. By themselves, neither is sufficient, and neither need be considered ontologically primitive. Engagement in a practice is fundamentally relational. One cannot engage in a social practice like diplomacy alone, which implies also that relational positionality within a practice is important. Relational position, meanwhile, has causal efficacy only when individuals are engaged in coordinated practical activity. As Onuf made clear, 'What people take to be possible and what society makes permissible depend on one's vantage point, one's relation to practice, and not practice itself.'[17] Closer inspection of three influential practice and relational approaches – field theory, network analysis, and ANT – makes these interconnections clearer, and highlights some of the most powerful tools practice theory and relationalism offer IR, especially vis-à-vis the Old, narrowed, Constructivism.

Proponents of a turn to practice theory and relationalism in IR have not advertised their interventions as two parts of the same whole, however.[18] Some readers affiliated with the turns may well reject my reading of them.[19] Nonetheless, there are strong reasons to consider them a twin movement. While in important respects distinct, the turns to practice and relations display considerable overlap such that justifies the label of a practice-relational approach.[20]

First, both the practice and relational turns are explicitly advertised as capable of overcoming problematic dichotomies in IR theory,[21] like material versus ideational forms of explanation, agency versus structure, and explanation versus understanding. However, as the previous chapter showed, those dichotomies are very much to Constructivism's narrowing in IR theory.

Second, the proponents of the practice are both *doing* Constructivism as defined previously as trying to keep open the-space-in-IR's-varied-institutional-bases-where-classic-social-analysis-is-practiced. The turn to practice is explicitly an attempt to do what an earlier intervention on regimes did for the field in the early 1980s:[22] to identify a shared research object around which different approaches could coalesce. For Emanuel Adler – tellingly, also one of practice theory's main proponents – keeping the debate on ontological terrain helps stake out a 'middle ground' position similar to his earlier take on constructivism.[23] Rather than 'interparadigmatic competition, subsumption, synthesis, or even complementarity', like regimes, 'the concept of practice promises cross-fertilization – the engine of social scientific refinement'.[24] As a consequence, the practice turn is not advertised as a development within Constructivism because this would close off practice theory to realists, rationalists, and others.

Once again, relationalists like Patrick Jackson and Daniel Nexon reject the constructivist label less to erect a cross-paradigmatic umbrella than due to philosophical objections to the *isms* themselves.[25] For them, Constructivism does not qualify as either a Lakatosian research programme or Kuhnian paradigm, since both are formed of 'theories that share the same set of content as sources of incommensurability'.[26] For Kuhn, paradigms referred to theories that delineate a science's scope by highlighting shared puzzles about some sphere of the world.[27] Although useful as self-identifiers, many relationalists view the isms as philosophically meaningless therefore because, for example, realism and constructivism can each be used to generate competing and comparable accounts of world politics that agree on basic puzzles. The most plausible sources of incommensurability, and hence the most useful way to organize the field of IR, involve larger debates about how to pursue social scientific knowledge.

However, these justifications for viewing the turns to practice theory and relationalism as neutral of the isms run counter to the central insights of both approaches. A practice theoretic perspective would view IR itself as a practice: a distinct arena of social competition with its own practical logics. Whether meaningful or not, philosophically, the isms, like Constructivism, are highly meaningful in IR *practically*. They are recognizable markers that allow scholars to present themselves and their work in the field. A relational viewpoint would add that practice theoretic and relational arguments have to be made against or in relation to some other approach. Knocking down one ism therefore will constitute another, whether labelled an '-ism' or not. As a consequence, the timing and rationale of the practice and relational turns should not be understood as neutral of the isms since their own insights tell us that such neutrality is difficult to achieve in the social sciences. Relationalists advocate the isms' replacement – including Constructivism – with broader categories with which to differentiate the field: substantialism and relationalism. Practice theorists argue for engaged pluralism around international practices. Even if to reject it, the stakes of the practice-relational turn are tied to the isms, particularly Constructivism.

A more appropriate way of viewing the relationship between Constructivism and the turns to practice and relations is consequently to foreground what isms do in IR *in practice*. Constructivism's narrowing elided a broader vision of constructivism as a space in US IR for developing new theoretical arguments based on the social constructed nature of reality, not limited to any given concepts. Constructivism was intended as a space for theorizing world politics in a way that simultaneously engages with the mainstream by striving for generalizable, cumulative, scientific knowledge, yet which also grapples with the problems of practice, of intersubjective meanings and interpretation. Such a vision was clear at Constructivism's birth,[28] even to non-constructivists: 'The end of the Cold War ... opened up space for cultural and sociological perspectives, often referred to as "constructivist".'[29] Rather than proclaim practice theory and relationalism as developments entirely new, separate from Constructivism, they should be situated as internal, partially new features of the IR landscape: the New Constructivism in International Relations Theory.

Practice theory, relationalism and practice-relationalism

As a disciplinary movement internal to Constructivism in IR theory, the practice-relational turn offers an array of powerful theoretical tools for IR scholars as they design their empirical research projects. In this section, I outline three such sets of tools and approaches: field theory; network analysis; and ANT. These approaches by no means exhaust what practice-relationalism has to offer, far from it. But together with the contributions explored in the remainder of the chapters, they illustrate the power of the New Constructivism.

Field theory. Field theory 'is a more or less coherent approach in the social sciences whose essence is the explanation of regularities in individual action by recourse to position vis-à-vis others'.[30] Field theory rests on two metaphors: magnetic fields and battlefields – which evoke practically engaged individuals taking part in contests where their goals, strategies, and chances of success are conditioned by their position and attributes within the field. Although other versions of field theory exist – including one indigenous to US sociology[31] – Bourdieu's version has been drawn upon most extensively in IR as it offers a range of concepts designed to harness the power of this image.[32]

Fields for Bourdieu are analytically separable spheres of competition over a given stake, or field-specific form of *capital*. The examples of money in the economic field or prestige in the cultural field are typically given. As Pouliot notes, a commitment to the struggle over these stakes – what

Bourdieu terms *illusio* – is what forms the economic and cultural fields as separate social spheres.[33] Cultural prestige has little power in the economic field, while possession of wealth in itself cannot easily be translated into, for example, recognition of artistic capability in the cultural field.[34] Position within the field, which is based on possession of differential amounts of field-specific capital, strongly shapes the possible social strategies individuals can adopt in the struggle. Bourdieu's notion of *habitus*, finally, captures the embodied dispositional way individuals are shaped by their position within social fields – how they adapt to the field's composition, including its *doxa*, or taken-for-granted knowledge.

Field theory is both intensely practice-oriented and thoroughly relational. As John Levi Martin shows, the field terminology's strength is precisely its ability to grasp how '[t]he process whereby the actor takes in information about the world ... is not merely *relative* to this person's position in the field, it actually provides the actor information about his or her own position', and thus the actions that are open to them.[35] This has clear advantages over a narrowed constructivist account of social action based on structural norms or collective identities, which actors are somehow socialized into.

Field theory overturns this substantialist vision by overcoming what for Bourdieu is its root source: a *representational bias* typical of much contemporary theorizing in IR, social sciences, and modern culture more broadly.[36] The representational bias leads scholars to see the world they study as a spectacle, and themselves as occupying a position detached from the world.[37] Field theory overturns the representational bias by foregrounding the practically engaged and relational aspects of social action. It also includes a commitment to reflexivity, which places the scholar and their potential impact on events and the way events are categorized within purview of the analysis.[38]

Network analysis. The relational sensibility at the heart of field theory, and its emphasis on positionality, has points of overlap with network analysis.[39] Like field theory, network analysis represents an improvement on modes of explanation that ignore the social origins of interests and preferences, but also – crucially – those that view the social as an undifferentiated sphere that mechanistically communicates motivations to social actors. As sociologist Ann Mische notes, network analysis emerged out of a dissatisfaction with culturalist theorizing and a desire to explore in more concrete terms how culture matters by foregrounding its use and effects in social processes.[40]

The use of network analysis IR to improve upon the culturalist excesses of narrowed Constructivism thus makes good sense. Beginning from the 'premise that social life is created primarily and most importantly by relations and the patterns formed by these relations',[41] network analysis models social action in terms of *nodes* connected by different forms of *ties*.[42] Nodes are typically individuals or groups, but could be any form of network unit. Ties meanwhile can be any connection or transaction between two or more nodes, including friendship or authority relations, and the transfer of money, prestige, or recognition. The main focus in network analysis is on the shape of the network as determined by the strength, volume, and nature of the social ties that constitute it, and the number and position of network nodes.

From these basic building blocks network analysts have developed a powerful set of conceptual tools. To illustrate, Charli Carpenter uses network analysis to provide a better explanation for why some issues are picked up in global advocacy networks while others are passed over than the common-sense notion that interests and preferences predominate, or the will of powerful norm entrepreneurs.[43] Rather, the relational position within the network of certain advocacy groups is pivotal: '[T]he power to set − or vet − the network agenda should also be understood as a function of structural position within the wider networks of meaning, rather than primarily organizational capacity per se.'[44]

ANT. A final approach gaining ground is ANT. Sometimes referred to as 'material semiotics', the 'sociology of translation', 'actant rhizome ontology', or 'philosophical anthropology',[45] these diverse terms grasp part of the complex sensibility ANT brings to IR.[46] Indeed, of all the approaches under discussion, ANT is the one that most strongly resists efforts to tie down exactly what *it* is.

The term ANT was coined by Bruno Latour to give name to the form of sociological analysis he pioneered with others such as Steve Woolgar and Michael Callon in their empirical studies of scientific practice.[47] Rejecting the stylized vision of science characteristic of early sociology of science that viewed scientific knowledge as separate from society, Latour and Callon explored the multi-faceted relations that occur in laboratory life in practice − both between scientists and between scientists and material things within the laboratory, from laboratory supplies to equipment to research notebooks. Rather than view scientific practice as driven by the cultural norms of the laboratory, then − as might a narrowed constructivist approach − ANT begins with agents and artefacts, tracing inductively how complex relations and transactions produce seemingly objective scientific knowledge.

Taken beyond the laboratory setting, ANT represents a profound two-pronged attack on most social theory. First, it rejects not only the notion of substantialism but also the whole idea of 'the social' itself.[48] For Latour, the term has been a hindrance because it too often substitutes the vague label 'social' for a close analysis of the process of *associations* over time. Second, ANT also declines to limit the tracing of associations to relations between humans. The incorporation of non-human agents is one of ANT's most important features, as Tony Porter explains: 'Actor-network theory focuses on the importance of micro-level interactions between humans and "non-humans" such as other life forms, technical artifacts, or physical objects.'[49] The examples of computing equipment in High Frequency Trading in global finance and private military companies as new forms of actors in modern military markets demonstrate the serious limitations inherent in reducing the notion of agency to humans alone.[50]

Overcoming Constructivism's dualisms

Field theory, network analysis, and ANT should not be thought to exhaust practice theory and relationalism – any more than the study of norms, identity, and culture exhaust constructivism. They do, however, exemplify the powerful resources on offer in the attempt to shift IR theorizing from an approach focused on essences to one focused on processes. The move from essences/substances to processes overcomes the stale conceptual dichotomies that entered IR with Constructivism. Practice theory displays clear advantages over the linguistic/discursive excess of Old Constructivism. Relationalism offers advantages over the more rigidly structuralist perspective adopted by narrowed Constructivism. Each, finally, offers advantages when it comes to foregrounding the causal rather than merely constitutive nature of their explanations.

Practice theory dissolves the ideational-material dichotomy. From the ideational end it foregrounds how language and discourse functions in practice like material things, rather than as the vehicle for the subjective ideas that motivate 'socialized' individuals, as became associated with narrowed Constructivism.[51] When language and discourse are understood as subjectively held ideas, recourse to interests and revealed preferences remains preferable for many scholars since individuals' consciousness is an impenetrable domain. However, as philosophers of language have demonstrated following Ludwig Wittgenstein and John Austin, invoking meanings encoded in language is not sufficient to explain action since different behaviours can flow from the same word or linguistic rule. The reason is that words are not simply ideas that correspond neatly with an external world; they are things individuals pick up and use in their everyday interactions. Words or linguistic rules do not merely *regulate* behaviour, they also help *constitute* by making possible certain *strategies*. As Onuf stressed, 'To say that people and societies construct each other is not to imply that this is done wholly out of mind.'[52] Practice theory thus begins from the position that words are as much – material – 'things' as, say, nuclear warheads, and not from an unsustainable ideational-material binary.

From the material end, practice theory – together with relational work – offers a much-needed correction to misunderstandings over what exactly is materialist about much so-called materialist theorizing in IR. Practice theory allows greater attention to be paid to the objects and artefacts that can play a crucial mediating role in social interaction, drawing attention to how non-human actants – like technology and the physical environment – can act back, co-creating political configurations or *assemblages*.[53] The aim is to push beyond the anthropocentrism of much IR theory, which, whether focused on norms and identities, or preferences and interests, posits as the chief problem how humans understand the world. Downplayed in this in-built ideationalism, as Pouliot notes, is what social actors think *from* and not *about*: from the various materials of practice.[54]

The dissolution of the ideational-material dichotomy has points of overlap with a second problematic binary overcome by relationalism: agency-structure. Much of the materialism in materialist theories revolve around claims about the reality of structural factors that condition state behaviour, such as the distribution of economic and material power in the international system and the structural pay-offs in bargaining scenarios. Efforts to foreground ideas are then attempts to show how individuals can act on structural imperatives differently. The agency-structure debate has traversed much of the same terrain, with the notions of structuration or agent-structure co-constitution offering a neat solution to a thorny philosophical problem.

Relational approaches consciously put the philosophical dispute to one side. They reject the language of agency-structure in favour of different conceptual vocabularies for addressing how individuals and societies mutually construct one another, vocabularies that do not entail the possibility of meaningful individual or group action outside social relations. The shared focus is on practical involvement and positionality within fields, networks, actor-networks, or other frameworks. Here agency is then not an inherent feature of individuals but an effect of the differential-distribution of power, knowledge, and recognition in social topographies. In different ways, terms like 'node' and 'habitus' are each designed to grasp the connections between *position* – where one is located in social relations – and *disposition* – or what actors consequently want to do and feel the necessity to do. An actor-network sensibility goes even further, overturning the notion of both agency and seemingly fixed social locations associated with field theory and similar approaches. In ANT, action is always impelled by more than one actant,[55] and is a property of the actor-network, not individuals.

Third, and relatedly, practice theory and relationalism each offer resources for a renewed engagement with the causal-versus-constitutive dichotomy when it comes to explanation. The replacement of the problematic language of agency versus structure with process-focused concepts highlights the dangers of essentializing causes or viewing them as things to be 'isolated "out there" … rather than [considered as] heuristic focal points used by the researcher to make sense of social life'.[56] As Jackson notes, causes should instead be considered 'mental constructs devised to make sense of our interpretations and which belong to the realm of scientific knowledge'.[57]

Rejecting the mechanistic understanding of causation prominent in political science, practice theory, and relationalism thus offers different ways to reclaim causation and explanation without resorting to constitutive explanation. Both Pouliot and Jackson draw on Max Weber's notion of *adequate causality* rather than efficient causation: 'we know that some configuration of factors is causally adequate if we cannot plausibly conceive of that configuration *not* producing the outcome in question'.[58] In line with Weberian analysis based on ideal-types, since causes cannot be thought of in substantialist terms, the task is not to search for constant antecedents of observed events, but 'contingent practices that have historically made a given social fact possible'.[59]

Russian foreign policy and the West: an illustration

The value added by adopting practical and relational perspectives can be illustrated in the case of relations between the West and Russia after 1945 and after the Cold War.[60] Beginning with the earlier period, the puzzle lies in a continuing dissatisfaction with structural realist explanations of the Cold War's onset. As Ted Hopf makes clear,

> Distribution of power cannot explain the alliance patterns that emerged after World War II otherwise the United States would have been balanced against, not the Soviet Union. Instead, the issue must be how France, Britain, Germany, and the United States came to understand Soviet military capabilities and geographical proximity as threatening.[61]

Practical and relational approaches begin not from the West and the Soviet Union as entities with pre-given interests, identities, and preferences, but from the everyday activities and understandings of participants on both sides, and the relationships that emerged, conflictual rather than cooperative.

Jackson's approach is to reconceptualize Western civilization as a set of practices rather than as a given state of the world. He demonstrates how so-called *rhetorical commonplaces* – like the West as modern, civilized, democratic, and free – tie Western states to the project of Western civilization.[62] From this perspective, the Cold War did not follow from an objective Soviet threat. Conflict was rather a contingent result of political choices influenced by these commonplaces, like the formation of NATO with a rehabilitated West Germany as a member, which angered leaders in Moscow. Soviet actions in Eastern Europe weakened arguments of the West German Left in favour of a policy of neutrality because of the negative associations of the term socialist. By contrast, the Right could appeal to rhetoric of common heritage with the Allies to argue for moves towards the nascent Western security architecture.[63] What seems with hindsight the natural order of West Germany's integration into Western Europe was in fact tied to the relational dynamics of political discourse in Bonn in the late 1940s and early 1950s.

Neumann and Ole Jacob Sending offer another practical and relational perspective that helps explain the ending of the wartime alliance. They address Russia's great power identity over time and its relationship to Soviet foreign policy, breaking down the idea of a stable Soviet identity to explore the practical underpinnings of policy-making, and the relations created with the Western states. They draw on Foucault's notion of liberal governmentality: a historically specific mode of governing based on 'an imperative whereby letting go of the state's direct control of society [is] becoming a necessity ... for reasons of conforming to a new ... standard of governance'.[64] Looking back over the history of Russia's relations with the European great powers, they show that Russia's exclusion from the great power club, like after 1945, cannot be explained by the fact that it has never *been* a great power, nor that Russia has not been *accepted* as a great power. Rather, Russia's exclusion is due to its resistance to liberal governmentality to domestically engage, where it has not engaged in a process of governing less.[65]

Hopf meanwhile offers an explanation for why Moscow did not adopt liberal governing practices in Eastern Europe.[66] Rejecting the notion that the Soviet Union was essentially illiberal and uniformly threatening to the West, Hopf shows that the degree of liberalism in Soviet relations with its satellites varied widely during the Cold War depending on how secure the Soviet regime felt domestically. When a 'discourse of danger' predominated, as in the immediate post-war years, leaders were more hostile abroad; when leaders felt secure, as during most of Khrushchev's tenure, a discourse of Soviet uniqueness lead to a ratcheting down of aggressive rhetoric and a thaw in relations with satellites. The reason, Hopf stresses, is 'security is not entirely material, but also a toleration of difference and fallibility such that deviations and making errors are not signs of fatal flaws in the project'.[67] This relationship between domestic practices and foreign policy was missed in the West, which viewed the USSR as a monolith.

Patrick Morgan finally offers a practice perspective on how such understandings produced conflict.[68] Focusing on the role of deterrence, he shows that as a long-standing practice, deterrence emerged from after 1945 more messianic practice in nature, 'operating constantly within a profound and extended conflict with enormous stakes, a conflict considered so serious that the opponent was assumed to be poised to attack should an occasion ever arise, not only in a technical sense but because the opponent was *inherently* evil and aggressive'.[69] Total war against Germany, in other words, gave way to planning for total war against the USSR, this time nuclear. More than just an idea, however, deterrence was underpinned by the emergence of a vast domestic architecture, from the technology to effect nuclear deterrence to a body of theory and analysts to rationally analyze deterrence.

Conclusion

This chapter has sought to make the case for seeing the practice and relational turns as developments internal to Constructivism, and hence as core components of – if not exhausting – the New Constructivism. The case is worth making because equating Constructivism with one, narrow, version of it has the potential to undermine dialogue and debate between constructivists and non-constructivists. The frozen image of what I term in Old Constructivism as a culturalist and ideational approach – one focused on the normative structure of IR and deploying a descriptive and constitutive approach – lowers the bar for arguing with and against it.

The popularity of Open Economy Politics (OEP) in IPE provides a good illustration.[70] Unlike neoliberal institutionalism, which was 'enhanced by its affinity with the reigning king of the social sciences in the United States – economics',[71] OEP directly imports economics' vision of political actors as 'price takers with clearly ordered preferences [who] rank policies and outcomes based on how they effect their expected future outcomes'.[72] IR needs a strong constructivist perspective – adequately practical, relational, historical, and reflexive – because now-influential approaches underpinned by rationalism and neo-positivism lack sensitivity to the social fabric of international politics as much if not even more so than the neorealist-neoliberal institutionalist synthesis did in the late 1980s and early 1990s, when Constructivism made its initial appearance. New Constructivist approaches can and should offer robust counter-positions to OEP and similar perspectives, expanding the scope of inquiry and opposing what Fiona Adamson calls 'methodological nationalism'.[73]

A second and related reason for situating the practice and relational turns within the New Constructivism is that the potential for powerful constructivist/practice-relational counter-positions to appear depends on the vibrancy of the space of Constructivism in US IR – explored more in the book's Conclusion. Retracing Constructivism's narrowing suggests that a similar trajectory awaits practice-relationalism: first come novel theoretical treatises and quirky empirical work, then texts that consolidate the new approach's position, then works that are solid but unspectacular, followed by a re-emergence in a different guise. As a social space and not a singular theory, as Abbott explains, constructionism/ Constructivism is 'doomed to be a perpetual succession of flare ups', as the initial ontological insight that the world is socially constructed loses its novelty, and the norms of US political science towards more generalizable modes of analysis drive fractal distinction, which later facilitates another opening.[74] Constructivism in US IR narrowed for reasons to do with the dynamics of paradigmatic turnover in the social sciences, at least in America, and not because constructivist theorizing had run its course.

Constructivism as a project was not finished, as the emergence of practice theory and relationalism demonstrate.

My hope is that to be forewarned is to be forearmed: both constructivists and non-constructivists should recognize the space of Constructivism's cyclical tendencies. Non-constructivists must resist the temptation to argue against the straw man of narrowed Constructivism, and seek out more sophisticated arguments from the New Constructivism with which to engage. New Constructivists must continue to develop the new approaches discussed here and others, in full knowledge of the disciplinary dynamics that work to weaken claims to theoretical innovativeness. In the following four chapters, I expand outwards from the practice and relational turns to explore important contributions and new and enduring perspectives of the New Constructivism.

3

Rules, Law, and Language in the New Constructivism

Introduction

In this chapter, I re-centre language, rules, and law in the New Constructivism. Rules, law, and language lay at the core of the early theoretical Constructivist treatises, especially Nicholas Onuf's *World of Our Making* and Friedrich Kratochwil's *Rules, Norms, and Decisions*.[1] Each placed rule- and norm-governed reasoning as fundamental to political life, in the international no less than the domestic sphere. But as Constructivism gained ground in the discipline, especially in the empirical Old Constructivism that cemented its place in American political science, language, rules, and law, were sidelined.[2] Norms, identity, and culture became the conceptual touchstones of this new line of thought within an academic debate dominated by realist themes: the balance of power, national interests, and the search for security among independent sovereign states. More surprisingly, the New Constructivism also downplays language, law, and rules, in favour of practice, relationality, and the reality and post-humanism of the new materialism.[3] Old Constructivism and the practice-relational turn thus reflects and furthers two divisions that have rented Constructivism from language, rules, and law: first, between international law and legal theory and international politics and security such that the two barely speak;[4] and second between Constructivism and post-structuralism, where discourse seemed to render the project of social science itself in question. My aim in this chapter, consequently, is to show that these divisions were contingent, social processes, *constructions* we might say; retracing their separation can go some way towards knitting language, rules, and law, and Constructivism back together.

In short, although sensitive to practice(s), the inherent relationality – rather than fixity – of social life, and the body, emotions, and affect, the New Constructivism as a perspective or sensibility in IR should still revolve around language and discourse. Language and discourse are not all there is to social life to be sure; I do not here assert a return to a thoughtless nominalism. However, language remains the unavoidable medium between us and our world – providing understandings about how to 'go on' in social situations, and, crucially, political and legal reasoning and decision-making situations – with emotions and affect a key part of how such reasoning occurs – and hence the indispensable vehicle for its interpretation. Discourse is here understood as both material – thing-like – and ideational, or about expectations, hence the interest in language and rules, written and orally transmitted, and hence law. Norms, culture, and identities are aspects of discourses, discourses about what is normative and expected, for people of specified identities. As the commonly cited example goes: yes, the person standing on a beach looking on at an oncoming tsunami will die when it hits land, but no amount of asserting the wave's material reality can disprove the possibility that the person may, truly, believe themselves about to meet their maker or otherwise blessed by the tsunami's approach.

As the study of language and discourse and their effects on political framings, understandings, narratives, and therefore decision-making situations, Constructivism butts up firmly against the generalizing tendency of science and its prioritization of the general, abstract, and ahistorical. If, as critics worry, constructivist explanations and interpretations of world politics are always, and will always only be, analyses of changing discourse, how does knowledge accumulate and science progress? 'Bringing in' norms, identity, culture, and more recently practices to the study of state action and national interest formation primarily, should be seen as a way of answering that question within the discipline, of *performing progress*.[5] Once again, both the emergence of Constructivism and practice-relationalism have performed progress by highlighting new objects to analyze, remaining on the relatively agreeable grounds of ontology rather than its shakier philosophical groundings. But what Pouliot and Adler in particular hope might represent a 'gluon' for the field is, on closer inspection, a fudge of the real response constructivists should offer, which is that knowledge accumulation in the natural sciences is not the best guide to how knowledge works in the human sciences.

Again, as Andrew Abbott noted, some people make a name for themselves by coining a new term, with the process soon to start over. The real – Constructivist – response to the question of knowledge accumulation and progress in IR, despite the continuing centrality of language, rules, and law, should be 'yes, we are all studying discourse all the time, but there is still a large complex world to study, and plenty of stories to tell'. In Charlotte Epstein's words, the proper response is 'to advocate a return to language as necessary to deepening the understanding of the constructed-ness of IR's world, not simply to continue accumulating empirical evidence that it is so'.[6] Identifying new and unrecognized ways in which the world is socially constructed *represents progress in IR*. Can one imagine a scientific paper rejected from *Nature* or *Science* because 'all' it does is reassert that one's genes can contribute to one's propensity to develop some diseases. Of course not. Words still cause wars, but for some reason the point is old hat. In other words, despite the efforts of IR constructivists – and post-structuralists, historical sociologists, Skinnerian political theorists, and others – we are still learning *how* international politics is constructed – what erasures, connections, interruptions are built into the modern episteme. We have barely scratched the surface.

The chapter proceeds via an engagement with key recent constructivist works that retain the linguistic, legal, and rule-based character of Constructivism, especially Charlotte Epstein's prescient early call for Constructivism to re-engage with language and its role in international political life as a way to prolong 'Minerva's flight', and her recent exemplary work in the origins of the state.[7] Epstein too shows how early Constructivists, like Onuf and especially Alexander Wendt pushed post-structuralism to the side, in part to try to find solid ground, a centre – a universal, something beneath or behind discourse, performance, or the many other concepts we have come across to assess the socially constructedness of world politics, norms, identities, practice. For Wendt, as for many, the universal is the sovereign state – the rump material existing 'at the bottom' of language and discourse. For Epstein, to remain true to its premises, and make good on its promise, Constructivists must face the discursive nature of international politics 'all the way down'.[8]

In engaging Epstein, however, I widen the aperture to law and rules, two further concepts downplayed by the Old Constructivism, and still sidelined by practice theory and relationalism. On rules, I highlight what Mark Raymond calls 'secondary' or 'procedural' rules, rules that concern when and how rules should be applied in world politics. I also explore Lechner and Frost's trenchant critique of the practice turn as not only ignoring rules but actively hostile to them. While I dissent from their argument in crucial ways, their centring of rules represents a forceful argument to foreground rules. On law, I explore recent analyses by Tanja Aalberts and Nikolas Rajkovic, among others, who have tried to shift the focus on the nature and role of law in world politics away from the rule of law, to rule *through* law.

Expanding the discussion to rules and law, finally, demonstrates the pay-off of broadening the New Constructivism – which is to tell new stories about *rule* and the exercise of power. At its best, Constructivism reminds us that the world of is one of 'artifice' – constituted, constructed, and crafted, not given. As I show via revisiting Onuf's *World of Our Making*, only by recognizing the social constructedness of world politics can we ask the question of how rule works, who is doing the ruling, when, for what purpose, and with what consequences – intended and otherwise?

Language

From the outset, IR Constructivism confronted the key role of language as the medium of social construction, a fact often obscured – as already noted – in retrospective accounts that emphasize instead the role of ideas, like *perestroika*, and how the reigning materialist IR theories were unable to explain the tumultuous events surrounding the end of the Cold War. Pedagogically, the notion that the Cold War's demise necessitated Constructivism is useful. It provides a recognizable external stimulus to changes in the field, roughly coinciding with the time Constructivism appeared on the scene.[9] While pedagogically understandable, in actuality Constructivism emerged in IR *before* the end of the Cold War, drawing on themes beyond the discipline's borders, including feminism and the cultural turn in the broader social sciences. Friedrich Kratochwil and John Gerard Ruggie took the then-popular debate over the nature and staying power of international regimes to task over a mismatch between its object of inquiry – regimes as intersubjective features of world politics – and an objectivist mode of analysis fundamentally at odds with the intersubjectivity of regimes as bundles of norms and expectations, conveyed in and through language.[10]

As Kratochwil explained, 'our conventional understanding of social action and of the norms governing them is defective because of a fundamental misunderstanding of the function of language in social interaction, and because of a positivist epistemology that treats norms as "causes".'[11] Kratochwil instead explored the value of a mode of inquiry based on ordinary language analysis pioneered by Ludwig Wittgenstein and taken forward by J.L. Austin and John Searle. As is well known, a Wittgensteinian approach debunked the mirror theory of language of words 'matching' the world. There is, for example, nothing in the world to match a term such as 'although',[12] nor more importantly, language-reliant practices such as promising, demanding, deploying profanity, apologizing, and asserting.[13] The recognition that 'speech acts' – where saying and doing are one and same – are a crucial feature of interaction ignored by the mirror theory of language, laid the basis for insightful analyses of world politics, including the end of the Cold War,[14] and the incorporation into the realm of national security an array of objects of foreign policy concern.[15]

Language is thus a powerful weapon of critique, of denaturalizing the world as it appears, rather than merely reflecting it –

> serv[ing] as a powerful criticism of traditional taxonomies and 'truth' theories and derives our understandings not from the traditional notion of a meeting of a concept with a preexisting reality 'out there' – that is, not from reference or essentialist properties – *but from the use of concepts* and our ability to 'go on' with our individual and collective projects.[16]

Etymologically derived from *krinein*, 'to separate, divide or order', analysis of language and its uses is thus '"critical" in the sense of trying to establish "criteria" for the "right" or problematic use of concepts and their embeddedness in the semantic field informing the practices of actors'.[17]

Part of the *Via Media* project of the early empirical Constructivism, the theoretical work of Alexander Wendt, and Constructivism's disciplinary interpreters, however, was to push some of the more problematic implications of engaging with exotic, 'presumably Parisian' social theory.[18] Again, the reason are less to do with intellectual substance than style, and the rationalist and scientific norms and practices of US political science. As Jeff Checkel noted in an early review, once Socially Constructivism's main arguments are accepted, and some indicative examples explored, 'what do you do with it?'[19] In European IR, the response has been to turn to practice. In the US, the response has mostly been silence.

Charlotte Epstein has made a strong case that such moves are unnecessary or problematic, and that rather than let Constructivism die – allowing the Hegelian Owl of Minerva to take flight – a return to language will prolong the daytime of Constructivism. Acknowledging that, 'today language has largely faded out of sight as a site of constructivist theorizing',[20] Epstein urges Constructivists to deal head-on the 'radical' challenge of accepting the fundamental role of language and discourse, a starting place Constructivism shares with post-structuralism. '[P]oststructuralism always looms on the horizon of constructivist theorizing', she notes, and always will, since:

> Constructivism's founding logic, constitutivity, which also belongs to that common starting place, entails a commitment to theorizing the particular, the contingent, the historically situated. There are as many constructed worlds as there are cultures and even individualities. Constitutive theorizing, then, requires finding ways of *theorizing with* the unfixity that the focus on contingency sets into play, rather than finding ways to cut it short, which has been a recurrent move in IR constructivism.[21]

Epstein's entryway is thus the role of universals in the work of early theoretical constructivists like Wendt, who adopted structuralism's fetishization of universals, notably – for Wendt – the sovereign state with a corporate identity. For Epstein, however, Constructivism's embrace of universals went further than individual concepts, to language itself as a universal, a neutral site for the conveyance of ideas and meanings. Constructivism, Epstein notes, was more 'closely reabsorbed on the side of structuralism and its foregrounding of innate universals than may be comfortable to admit'.[22] Much Old Constructivism thus:

harbor[ed] a conception of language as the universal, fixed structures
… whose universality is founded in and guaranteed by human nature.
Reason, in this understanding, is the linchpin underpinning the
possibility of intersubjective interactions and thus social construction.
Language (or langua*ges*), for poststructuralism, by contrast, presents
open, generative structures that are always charged with relations of
domination, and temporarily fixed within historically contingent sets
of meanings (discourses), the settling of which is the outcome of a
political struggle. Discourse is the primary site for the exercise, not of
consensual reasoning, but of power.[23]

Even Onuf, Epstein shows, considered post-structuralism's rejection of
universals 'radical', and longed for something to hang on to – however
forlorn a hope.[24] The desire chimed with the twin hope of many early
Constructivists for Constructivism to *have* a centre – the constructed nature
of identity, norms, and culture in international politics – and *be* a centre in
the discipline – between naturalistic scientism and radical interpretivism.[25]

Drawing on a diverse range of thinkers, from Judith Butler to Jacques
Derrida and Michel Foucault, Epstein rejects a universalist view of language
as an adequate basis for a properly language-sensitive Constructivism.
Her aim is to find resources to straddle the post-structural/constructivist
divide, to *dwell within it*, accepting the contingency and struggle over and
through language and meaning. In particular, she foregrounds Derrida's
concept of the 'play' of language – a concept unsurprisingly also prominent
in pragmatist George Herbert Mead. In many ways, Epstein here returns
to Kratochwil's early assertion that norms and rules are counter-factually
valid – they are observed even in the breach. Constructivist accounts of
politics should thus be filled with contingency, agency, both following
and diverging from expectations as individuals and groups further their
collective projects.

Following Epstein, therefore, the New Constructivism need not resist
the siren song of language and discourse in the false belief that 'anything
goes' when that particular Pandora's Box is opened. As analyses like Patrick
Jackson's account of the 'topography' of arguments over West Germany's place
in the emerging post-war bipolar world order demonstrates,[26] 'dwell[ing]
within the divide between constructivism and post-structuralism' requires
merely resisting essentialization or substantialization of the concepts – the
'moderate sized dry goods', in Onuf's terms – we use to explore international
politics. Doing so, in turn, is furthered by a return to history to uncover the
ongoing political projects constitutive of our present, in line with the New
Constructivism's essentially historical and reflexive, sensibility.

Here the political *projects* of liberal modernity – and, indeed, IR itself come
into view. The first generation of empirical constructivists were *inside* the

project of liberal modernity, understanding and explaining world politics, accepting the system of sovereign states, specifically the United States. While not a universal, the US state – we must accept – is a very real and powerful thing. One can thus see why the early empirical constructivists were willing to accept some universals associated with US IR, which is strongly tied to the priorities and worldview of the American hegemon, as Ido Oren in particular has explored.[27] But the New Constructivism can and must go further.

The body and the birth of the state

Epstein herself shows us how.[28] Returning to the 17th-century origins of the sovereign state, Epstein offers a new account of the birth of the state, entwining conceptual history with the history of political ideas, encompassing seismic shifts in scientific cosmology, expert knowledge, and a concern for the emergence of the disciplines – discussed in the following chapter. Even when everything seems to have been written on the topic,[29] Epstein proves the value of presenting novel 'origins stories', highlighting thereby many of the core tenets of the New Constructivism.[30]

Epstein's tactic is to read the state's birth through the lens of the body, chronicling a change in perspective that took hold primarily in 17th-century England from the notion of a body politic tied to the king's two bodies – the private and public bodies of the monarch – to the individual body as the bearer of rights, property, liberty, and the consumer of security, and thereby as the 'crafter' or 'artificer' of political order produced as the state, rather than given by nature. While the epistemological disruptions caused by the Reformation and the 17th-century cataclysms – the Thirty Years' War and the English Civil War – are, to be sure, familiar, Epstein shows how the state was constructed via a multi-faceted process, conjoining political and scientific projects of an array of actors with the body at their nexus.

Beginning before Foucault's tale of the birth of biopolitics – of governance via the human body instead of the body politic – Epstein traces the change, crucially for my concern in this chapter, to jurisprudence and the expert legal argumentation of Sir Edward Coke in *Calvin's Case* (1608). The critical case concerned the question whether a new political body had been formed after the 1603 union of England and Scotland under James I and VI, respectively. Did Calvin – real name James Colville – a Scottish subject who inherited property in England – have the same protections of a 'native' English subject? The case was won by Calvin – who was judged to be an English subject, having been born after James' ascendance to the English throne. The effect was to make Scottish subjects born after 1603 natural subjects of England – to 'naturalize' them as it became in American jurisprudence and citizenship law. Coke's argumentation rooted the political bond between the subject (the individual body) and crown (the king's body) at birth and in the body rather than in the metaphorical 'realm'.

Epstein exposes what seems like common knowledge as genuinely puzzling. Avoiding the twin traps of purely metaphorical or overly real or anatomical understandings of the body – side-stepping altogether the (inappropriate) question of what the body *really is* – Epstein traces a series of key conceptual shifts in politics and society via the body as a discursive construct all the way down. She shows, first, how William Harvey's investigations into blood flow amid the ever-present 17th-century public anatomy lesson led to critical changes in the inter-related concepts of matter, space, and place. Out went the Aristotelian understandings of essences with a settled *place* to which they by nature return, and in came the early modern, de-anthropomorphized geometric *space* in which matter is constantly moving. 'Another way to understand the founding problematique of modernity', Epstein notes, 'was how to salvage a substantially reduced first law of nature from the epistemological wreckage wrought by the geometrization of space and the exogenisation of movement'.[31]

How did a geometrical understanding of matter and space shift understandings of security, liberty, and property, tying these two bodies in the modern, sovereign state? In politics, as in science – as Bentley Allan has also traced – the change witnessed a wedge driven between ontology and politics, between oughts and isses, between human nature and nature itself.[32] The body was where human nature and nature met – where thinkers from Hobbes to Locke came to believe that order was no longer yielded by nature but had to be given alternative foundations. Out went order, and in came '*ordering*: entirely voluntary, a matter of choice, to be carefully constructed, but also legitimised by reference to that indelible traits still persistently ascribed to nature, liberty'.[33] For Epstein, '*ordering* was modernity's founding problematique',[34] changing conceptions of the state its – shifting – solution.

Revisiting the familiar figure of Thomas Hobbes, however, Epstein shows how *Leviathan* is more than an elaborate justification for a return to monarchy as a form of ordering – Hobbes develops a defence of a particular form of negative liberty, one that removes external impediments to motion, strictly of the body, inseparable from his interest in geometry. 'Hobbes is the first constructivist, in that his writings contain constructivism's founding and most precious insight, that politics is collectively constructed, and therefore always, at some level, chosen, such that it can also be unchosen.'[35] If Hobbes is the first constructivist, John Locke is arguably the second, offering a morphed form of ordering as 'crafting' a liberty of the body and the mind via consciousness – reconnecting thereby human nature and nature itself, which Hobbes had separated, seeing no role for human nature in the construction of Leviathan. Locke, writing later, retrieved the mind and made it the cornerstone of modern liberty in the shape of the English constitutional monarchy, a form of ordering grounded in the natural liberty of free-born Englishmen – on which more soon.[36]

Hobbes and Locke were far more influential than contemporary academics and public intellectuals, Locke in particular, but momentous shifts in political ontology developed slowly and via more mechanisms than intellectual histories suggest. Epstein highlights once again the role of political debate and legislation – notably the emergence of a 'corpo-realised liberty in the subject's body exclusively'[37] – as security, liberty, and property enshrined as the absolute rights of the modern political subject. Such a view was enshrined in the habeas corpus act of 1640, mobilized by the parliamentary forces during the Putney debates of 1647 – where the leaders of Oliver Cromwell's army demanded universal male suffrage – and later placed central in William Blackstone's *Commentaries on the Law of England* (1765), which described how: 'The rights of personal security consists in a person's uninterrupted enjoyment of his life, his limbs, his body, his health'.[38]

Epstein is careful not to valorize these thinkers, underlining the necessary sensitivity of the New Constructivism to concerns central to feminism and post-colonial approaches. For example, Locke's corpo-realised subject was a male, White, English body.[39] Similarly, Coke's argumentation in *Calvin's Case* was used to justify expropriation of native Americans' lands in the English colony of Virginia, the native Americans' described as 'infidels' not subject to the same rights as subjects of conquered Christian monarchs. Accepting the agency of intellectuals and elites of various stripes is not, therefore, to adopt a positive or negative evaluation of the change in which they played a role – about which more in Chapter 6.

The recognition of agency, gendered and racialized as it is, however, serves to summarize Epstein's contribution to the New Constructivism. Her purpose is nothing less than to 'rejuvenate the term, because the insights it holds, and the agency it promises, are too important to give up'. Rather than have Constructivism adopt a middle position – a centre to the field, at the centre of it – however, she emphasizes how:

> the juncture of the epistemological and political is the proper locus of critique. What locks existing political, social, international structures in place are the epistemological schemes that work to render these invisible or indeed 'natural', starting with 'rights' and 'the state' ... so long as the focus is on actions, behaviours, or practices only, without attending, not just to political structures, but to the concepts, epistemological frames, and discourses that underwrite them, then the analysis will continue to remain barren.[40]

Rules

The route to a revitalized and reinvigorated Constructivism runs directly through language, and its denaturalizing and de-essentializing promise. In so doing, however, it by necessity also runs through rules – particularly, as I pick up in the following section – legal rules. Rules, Onuf explains, 'are statements that tell people *what* we *should* do'.[41] Rules provide a standard for 'people's conduct in situations that we can identify as being alike and can expect to encounter'.[42] Rules, again, communicate what actions are expected from given meanings – how, in Wittgenstein's popular phrase, individuals recognize how to 'go on'.[43]

Rules appear in the Old Constructivism, but in ways that downplay their analytical import, hence the excavatory exercise of this chapter. In the Old Constructivism, the mechanism by which individuals 'go on' was rendered as the so-called 'logic of appropriateness', following institutionalist theorizing beyond IR.[44] As James March and Johan Olsen described, individuals do not simply act on cost-benefit analyses, weighing actions against consequences – but shape behaviour to what fits social situations, what is appropriate for a given identity in a given institutional milieu.[45] While certainly insightful – particularly as a corrective to overly rationalist assumptions predominant within economics and political science, the logic of appropriateness imported its own problems and blind spots. In particular, it defers the question of *how* individuals come to know what is appropriate – how external norms, identities, and cultural meanings 'enter' the normatively-aware actor, and how appropriateness itself is constructed and re-constructed. Elucidation of a logic of appropriateness also implied an equivalence between competing logics of action, leading to comparisons that could be 'tested' against observed outcomes – such as when states are strategic versus normative, when even strategic action is based on rules and norms of appropriate conduct.

Elaboration of the logic of appropriateness thus placed into the same analytical register two distinct understandings of social action and how it should be studied. Vincent Pouliot's attempt to expand the binary view of the logics of social action as part of the practice turn to include a 'logic of practicality' faces similar difficulties – limiting the practice turn's ability to grasp the nature of rules and their centrality to international politics. Pouliot rightly shows that rule-following is often non-conscious, deriving less from conscious understandings of what is appropriate – 'fits with' – a given situation, and more from subconscious, embodied, *practical*, knowings. As Wittgenstein suggested, at the bottom of much social life lies not what individuals want to do – or think will get them what they want – or what they think they should do or have to – but simply what people *do* do, a sense rooted in who they *are*.

For Sylvia Lechner and Mervyn Frost, however, by placing the logic of practicality alongside those of consequences and appropriateness, Pouliot and the proponents of a practice turn short-circuit the critical potential of foregrounding rules.[46] For Lechner and Frost, the practice turners collapse rules into an ill-defined notion of practice. While itself misplaced in crucial respects, their analysis highlights important reasons for re-centring rules within a practice-sensitive New Constructivism.

Practice, practices, and rules in international politics

Lechner and Frost set out to develop a philosophy, as opposed to a sociology, of practices. As such, they define *a* practice or *practices*, not as a domain of action in general – the quotidian, everyday, practical – but as 'an institution which constitutes a meaningful framework for interaction'.[47] Rejecting a sociological reading of practice theory means resisting the attempt to explain practice as action from the outside of a given practice. Their aim instead – following Hegel, via H.L.A. Hart, Michael Oakeshott, and Wittgenstein – is to understand practices, from the inside. As they make clear, their practice theory is independent of and 'fundamentally critical' of the practice turn associated with Emanuel Adler, Vincent Pouliot, and others.[48]

Noting, quite correctly, that '[t]he notion of practice has been foreshadowed in the writings of some early IR constructivists', specifically Alexander Wendt and Nicholas Onuf, Lechner and Frost argue that 'those currently debating the character of social practices are prone to conflate the category of action (and interaction) with that of a practice, social activity constituted by rules'.[49] The root problem, as they see it, lies with the intellectual resources the practice turners draw upon – principally the sociology of Pierre Bourdieu and social theory of Theodore Schatzki. By drawing on Bourdieu and Schatzki, they suggest, the practice turn theorists have misunderstood rules. 'The thrust of our position', Lechner and Frost state, 'is that to be able to achieve a proper understanding of practices, it is critical to begin analysis with the concept of rules and rule-following ... before tackling the question of action as meaningful doing'.[50]

A properly rendered practice theory for IR should specify its object more accurately – not practice as a general category of action, but specific practic*es*, structured by rules and rule-following, providing thereby the most appropriate object of scholarly analysis. Lechner and Frost elaborate on two such practices operative at the international level: the practice of global rights and sovereign states. Here the distinction between constitutive and regulative rules, associated with Searle, is pivotal. Exploring state action from a practice theory perspective is not a matter of explaining the regulative rules in play – be they related to consequentiality, appropriateness, or practical action – but rather also always understanding the constitutive rules of the given practice.

63

As explored in the following section, sovereignty as a multi-faceted global practice provides an array of rules that both shape the activities of states and constitute the very actors subject to those rules.

Lechner and Frost's development of a philosophical practice theory for IR is laudable. It offers a powerful critique of practice theory à la Pouliot and Adler, especially the over-generalization of the concept of practice. But the New Constructivism does not give up on the sociological explanation of action in favour of a philosophical interpretation of understandings purely within a practice – as Lechner and Frost would have it. To that extent, their argument misses the mark for our purposes.

At the core of the disagreement is the appropriateness of 'internalist' versus 'externalist' accounts of practice. For Adler and Pouliot, delineating the logic of practicality offers a way to *explain* practice-based action in international politics, action distinct in important ways from norm-driven or strategic – that is, instrumentally rational – behaviour. Lechner and Frost, by contrast, argue that such an outside perspective is impossible to obtain, and that explanation of practice-based action is a false hope. Explanation 'tends to gravitate towards invariance, reduction and abstraction' – a 'high price, since it assumes away the distinctiveness of the diverse provinces of human activity comprising our practical life'.[51] A more appropriate aim is to understand a practice from the inside, from within. Defending an internalist perspective requires recognizing 'the language through which observers investigate (i.e. "explain") a practice is, at bottom, the same as the language of self-description its participants use in making sense of their own practice'.[52] Rather than seek generalization and abstraction, internalism 'acknowledges the distinctiveness of practices',[53] where each 'practice is a common domain of interaction constituted by [practice-specific] *rules*'.[54]

Lechner and Frost echo Bruno Latour's critique of Bourdieusian sociology – and, indeed similar objections lodged at Marxian analyses and the notion of false consciousness. The objection is to attempts to fashion explanatory categories that impute meanings and decision-making logics distinct from those actors themselves recognize.[55] Externalism's 'major defect', Lechner and Frost note, 'is that it outstrips the boundaries of what is intelligible to the agents under study'.[56] The scholar's duty, for them, is instead to *re*present faithfully the rules of practices. Lechner and Frost thus disagree with Bourdieu's attempt to impute deeper meaning to the Cabyle's rain dance – for them, it is sufficient to describe their beliefs at what the dance means, what rules they follow to practise the dance, within a particular practice.

Lechner and Frost's position is philosophically defensible, but is ultimately unsuitable as a basis for the incorporation of practice theorizing into the New Constructivism in IR. The reason is that, like Bourdieu, most Constructivists *do* want to explain social action from the outside – and, in my view at least, that is no bad thing. IR scholars *are* outside the practices they study – diplomacy, humanitarian aid, foreign policy-making, global health, or environmental governance, or whatever it may be. IR scholars are not within these practices, but within the discipline of IR and its various nationally rooted institutional and professional architectures. An externalist standpoint of some variety is unavoidable.

A deeper reading of Bourdieu's reflexive sociology, indeed, would have uncovered the sociologist's attempts to grapple with the implications of an inevitably outsider perspective. Bourdieu's work evolved from an earlier structuralist and materialist anthropology to a reflexive and relational approach. Lechner and Frost make much of Bourdieu's comment during an interview on his work where he stated 'that all of my thinking started from this point: how can behavior be regulated without being the product of obedience to rules'.[57] But a cursory look at this comment makes clear that Bourdieu meant formal and fixed rules. He means how can we explain the immense 'stickiness' of social institutions without a naïve structuralism or functionalism that suggests people *have to*, or are rule-bound to, behave in accordance with social structures. The Bourdieu of *Classification Struggles* or *Habitus and Field*, both steeped in Wittgensteinian struggles over definitions of the doxic or taken-for-granted in society, is unrecognizable in Lechner and Frost's description – as is, tellingly, the Bourdieu of *The Rules of Art*.[58]

In short, Bourdieu says much of what constructivists – and Lechner and Frost – assert: the logic of consequences does not exhaust how rules work. Rules are about practical notions of appropriateness, and are playful and contingent. Just before the aforementioned quote, Lechner and Frost consider a smoking gun, he notes the importance of distinguishing 'clearly between *rule* and *regularity*. The social game is regulated, it is the locus of certain regularities. Things happen in *regular fashion* in it; rich heirs *regularly* marry rich younger daughters. That does not mean this it is a *rule* that rich heirs marry rich younger daughters'.[59]

The real issue, as Lechner and Frost note, is externalism and the desire to understand and explain action. Again, Bourdieu, like most constructivists I wager, want more. Lechner and Frost say we cannot have it, and should content ourselves with thick internalist descriptions of the meaning of rule-following from inside a practice. 'As observers, we must go no further than describing the self-understandings of the practice participants observed: our task properly construed is not to conjure up explanations *de novo* but to describe more coherently their actually existing self-understandings.'[60] Yet, the third-party observer *is* external to practices, practically speaking – the IR scholar is *not* a direct participant in the practice of sovereign states. So the challenge, which Bourdieu and others foreground, is the one of fashioning reflexive analytical concepts able to grasp the practice rules that ground social action, objectifying at the same time the relationship between the observer and the observed. To be sure, such concepts – for Bourdieu particularly the concept of *field* – should uncover rules recognizable to practice participants. But they may also uncover 'principles of vision and division', and hence constitutive rules of social spaces participants do not explicitly recognize.

While a useful addition to the debate, and particular within the sub-field of international ethics and international political theory, giving up on the explanation of social action in favour of a philosophical practice theory is inappropriate for the New Constructivism. The New Constructivism, with rules at their heart, can do more than assess international practices like sovereignty and global rights. Mark Raymond has made a strong case that a good place to begin is to highlight the importance of processual rules in world politics – rules about when and how rules should be applied.[61]

Rules all the way down

Raymond echoes Lechner and Frost's dissatisfaction with the place of rules in the practice turn, demonstrating how the lack of attention to rule-following can either render explanations of events in world politics partial, or prevent the recognition of puzzling outcomes necessitating explanation in the first place. Raymond stresses specifically the importance of secondary or procedural rules: rules that tell actors what rule or rules should be applied in given situations.

For example, Raymond explores the recent development of behavioural norms in the cyber domain, agreed and formulated by *Group of Governmental Experts on Developments in the Field of Information and Telecommunications in the Context of International Security* (2015).[62] The puzzle is how progress was made in a domain seemingly absent all of the necessary background to agreement. Russia, for instance, was hostile to international diplomacy because of international condemnation of its 2014 incursion in Ukraine, in addition to increased contention over cyber security at the international level.[63] How was the expert group able to make progress? The answer, for Raymond, lies with recourse to secondary or procedural rules states fall back on when there are no agreed-upon primarily rules to inform practice. 'Participants', Raymond shows, 'drew on existing procedural rules of diplomacy and international law in order to advance their positions on the most desirable and appropriate rules to govern state use of ICTs'.[64]

Highlighting the importance of secondary rules, Raymond draws, in typical constructivist fashion, on resource outside IR – in his case, those of the philosopher of law H.L.A. Hart, also explored by Kratochwil – to complicate common-sense explanations that centre national interests and strategic action in world politics. Raymond shows how international law shaped the array of possible positions of the actors involved, even a United States at the height of its post-Cold War primacy. Even as President Bush sought to maintain strategic superiority in the cyber domain – as such realist-inflected accounts would suggest – US experts drew on the procedural rules of international law in their argumentation. Seeking to put off the creation of a stand-alone agreement on ICTs, the American side argued that 'the law of armed conflict and its principles of necessity, proportionality and limitation of collateral damage already govern the use of such technologies'.[65] The absence of primary rules governing the cyber domain did not, therefore, render practice rule-less.

Raymond is careful not to claim too much for his rules-based account. Interpretations of national interest – a good constructivist must re-emphasize the *interpretations* aspect here – are still crucial in presenting a full account of the struggle over the writing of rules to govern the cyber domain. But he affirms the nature of that struggle cannot be fully understood without paying attention to procedural rules.

The second set of such rules the actors seeking primary rules to govern the cyber domain drew upon are what Raymond terms the procedural rules of great power diplomacy – what he terms elsewhere 'great power management'.[66] Raymond is in good company in revisiting the concept of great power management.[67] English School theorists like Hedley Bull considered great power management a core feature of international society, as have constructivists like Christian Reus-Smit, for whom great power management is a 'fundamental institution'.[68] Kenneth Waltz himself, indeed, placed great power management as foundational in the little-read ninth chapter of his *Theory of International Politics*, 'The management of international affairs'.[69] In Constructivist language, great power as an identity – or, more accurately, a *role* – is constituted by taking part in the practice of managing the international system: avoiding crises, providing public goods, and seeking regional stability, for Bull, or maintaining the 'diplomatic pecking order' in Vincent Pouliot's insightful practice theoretic work. Contra the under-socialized view of great power characteristic of realism and neorealism,[70] which emphasizes balancing almost exclusively – managing international affairs, like rules over cyber security, is *what great power-ness is.*

Tellingly, Raymond emphasizes how even authoritarian regimes recognize the connection between great power status and the practice of management, particularly via the institution of multilateralism. Multilateralism is another international practice prominent in Old Constructivism – especially in the work of Ruggie – but sidelined to make room for norms, identity, and culture.[71] As Raymond notes:

> the irony of authoritarian regimes promoting a multilateral legal instrument is indicative of the broad legitimacy of the procedural rules of the contemporary international system. This point is worth emphasizing. Despite illiberal preferences inconsistent with prevailing

notions of thick multilateralism … authoritarian states have regularly and consistently adopted the vernacular of multilateralism and of contractual international law to advance their agendas. Far from making the claim that participation in the post-1945 rule based global order has transformed the identity of these states or that these states have internalized the norms and rules underpinning that order, I am arguing instead that, to varying degrees, these rules: (1) constrain illiberal states, requiring them to take pains to express their positions in terms at least ostensibly consistent with those rules; and (2) enable them to advance such interpretations, albeit in ways that are subject to limits and constraints.[72]

Law

Re-positioning language and rules at the heart of the New Constructivism has for each of the scholars discussed so far in this chapter meant confronting the power and prominence of international law. Not all work that follows the core tenets of the New Constructivism will foreground law to the same extent as do Epstein, Raymond, and others. Although unlikely to be entirely absent, formal international or domestic law may at times be peripheral to the stories New Constructivists tell about the constructed nature of the events, processes, and institutions of their content. However, re-forging the link between IR and international law remains a pressing task. Rules and norms are indelibly bound up with law. As Kratochwil notes, there are no clear demarcation lines between them – law is a style of reasoning with rules.[73] Attendance to the constitution of politics as a rule-governed activity, frequently resting on legal dispute, is therefore essential for the New Constructivism.

Sovereignty between politics and law

Tanja Aalberts explores the unsure intellectual terrain at the intersection of international politics and international law, unpacking the concept of sovereignty as forever suspended between politics and law.[74] Again, there are no shortage of works in IR and international law on sovereignty. Rather than adopt a genealogical approach, as do Epstein and Jens Bartelson, Aalberts depicts sovereignty's various aspects or faces. Confronting head-on the knotty problems thrown up by interdisciplinary research, Aalberts rejects the notion that sovereignty *is* one singular thing. In line with the de-essentializing core tenet of the New Constructivism, sovereignty is, for Aalberts, a relational practice. The operative question is what it *does* and actors do within it, rather than what it *is* in some essential sense. '[T]he meaning of an institutional fact like sovereignty does not reside with what it is, but rather what follows from it' – again, how sovereignty allows prescribed actors to 'go on'.[75]

To parse sovereignty as a relational practice, Aalberts examines sovereignty as an identity, a narrative, an institution, a language game, and a subjectivity, never collapsing it into any as what sovereignty 'really' is. As a narrative, for example:

> 'Westphalia' symbolizes the concomitant birth of the international society *and* sovereign states as its legitimate participants, even when its birthday is historically controversial. It subsequently entails an appreciation of international law beyond a set of rules to regulate and constrain international relations between pre-given sovereign states, to its more fundamental role in constituting international persons with rights and duties to enact on the international stage.[76]

The notion of narrative does not imply a factiousness nature to sovereignty. Rather, it highlights how argument and reasoning in international politics relies on a complex set of rules that are themselves constructed by emplotment within a story about what states can and should do qua sovereign nations. What sovereignty means as a narrative about the society of states from its – again, disputed, founding – is always under construction, drawing attention to legal and political reasoning that not only follows the rules sovereignty prescribes, but the attempt to reinterpret those rules in light of new problems.

Solving new problems in light of changed circumstances – and indeed identifying problems – highlights the connections between Aalbert's interdisciplinary exegesis of sovereignty and the Old and New Constructivisms. Practice turn theorists like Adler and Pouliot, and Christian Bueger and Tim Edmunds make much of practice theory's ability to explain change in international politics, developing similar critiques of the Old Constructivism as those I lay out in Chapter 2. Again, however, such critiques dissolve, as does the consequent need to move to 'pragmatic ordering' outside of Constructivism, with proper recognition of sovereignty as a relational practice.

Aalberts notes, however, how in the system of sovereign states some are more equal (or sovereign) than others, as the concepts of quasi- and failed states convey. As Epstein and others showed, the concept of sovereignty emerged from a particular vision of law, property, rights, from particular states, developed for particular reasons. Acknowledging the centrality of law to the New Constructivism, therefore, requires – with Onuf – not merely foregrounding rules, but power and *rule*.

From the rule of law to rule through law

In just that vein Nikolas Rajkovic draws on Foucault to reconceptualize the post-Cold War solidification of a discourse of the global 'rule of law' as instead the 'rule through law' of some – Western – states over others.[77] Noting the rule of law's taken-for-granted positive character – who could argue that more law is a bad thing in everyday society or international politics? – Rajkovic argues the rule of law is a governmentality of control, a form of 'productive power' in Barnett and Duvall's terms, one that hold immense symbolic power in international politics. One might say, following Emile Durkheim, the rule of law is held sacred, above the profane world of the law of men and nations, or the rules of the geopolitical jungle.

To the extent that the rule of law has a special status in international politics, however, it is due less to its place as a settled institution in world society and more to the activities of international jurists, supranational courts, activists – a project aimed at exporting the culture of specifically – American law. Noting the paradox whereby the American view of law is and should be the law of no one, the rule of law discourse in international politics becomes very much the law of someone. As Rajkovic notes, 'the idea that global governance should be furthered by a "global" network of courts and judges represents a departure from conventional international law as constituted by a society of states'.[78] For him, at the heart of the agenda to 'the institution of a global legal system in succession to the "old" international law of state power', is a kind of 'juridical and legal idolatry which has suggested that a new regime of "global law", furthered by a network of courts, judges, and lawyers, would mark a process where the archaic law of states was replaced by a more universal system of global judicial governance'. Missing from the triumphalist narrative is the 'recognition that law does possess a more conflicted nature: it is also an integral participant in rule'.[79]

Rajkovic's insistence on denaturalizing an accepted discourse confirms the principal point of this chapter, which is that re-engaging with language, rules, and law allows constructivism to re-engage with power and rule in world politics. Rather than a cultural, ideational approach that leaves power to materialist theories, a properly rendered New Constructivism is concerned with the nature and drivers rule. In the case of the rule of law, American post-Cold War predominance is a central driver. So too, however, is an activist legal profession underpinned by the discipline of law. Epstein too notes, if too briefly, the role of the disciplines and the legal profession as an important aspect of the birth of the state, observing how: 'The seventeenth century was also the birthplace of disciplines, now in the sense of ordering the world into distinct domains.'[80] In the following chapter, I develop this line of thinking further, as another core feature of the New Constructivism.

Re-reading Onuf's *World of Our Making*

By departing from a non-essentialist standpoint, scholars advocating a practice and relational turn begin from a more nuanced understanding of social knowledge and social action, one that foregrounds *praxis*, overturns the theory/practice divide, posits the situatedness of all knowledge claims, and replaces concerns about relativism with relationalism. However, they do it by and large without referring to *World of Our Making* and other key works from the first generation of IR Constructivism – that is, *what we already know*. A full elaboration of these claims is of course beyond the scope of this chapter. However, a case can be made that scholars new to Constructivism should revisit *World of Our Making* before engaging with recent literature.

World of Our Making is about how we construct our world. The bulk is traditional constructivist fair: the role of rules in allowing people to 'go on', linguistic rules, speech acts, and so on. But a more subtle theory of language is not its most interesting feature. Recall the book's subtitle: *Rules and Rule in Social Theory and International Relations*. This emphasizes the ever-presence of exploitation/authority/domination/power in social life. Thinking through how *rules* work was not inconsequential philosophizing, but was to better understand how *rule* works. Unlike most characterizations of Constructivism, *World of Our Making* is not just about socialization into a world of happy liberal 'ideas', but a *struggle*, with differentially endowed individuals practically engaged in conflict.

We can see then how the conflation of Constructivism with idealism, and even a rejection of 'the real world', is problematic, and in the latter case simply wrong. As Iver Neumann noted in 2002, 'A central challenge for social analysis must be how to preserve the insights produced by the linguistic turn while adding the insights promised by practice theory, to combine the study of meaning and the study of material.'[81] In *World of Our Making*, Onuf had already tried to do that. 'The Constructivism I prefer … does not attempt to draw a sharp distinction between material and social realities.'[82] As such, once again, 'To say that people and societies construct each other is not to imply that this is done wholly out of mind.'[83]

However, despite the clarity of expression here, the notion of social construction was translated unproblematically into meaning the constitution agents with interests, *without* the notion of practice and the issue of one's relation to practice, again as way of understanding social struggle, being involved. Hence the conflation of Constructivism with constitutive theorizing and hence 'interpretation' rather than explanation. Yet, once again, Onuf asserts quite plainly that rules are not enough to explain action. This was highlighted by the early constructivists but ignored by the second generation. Onuf made clear how 'rules cannot provide closure for the purposes of carrying on because rules are not the sufficient agency whereby intentions become equivalent to causes'.[84] Since following other rules or other strategies within social struggles is possible, it is not possible to attribute causality to rules. 'Rules do indeed tell us how to carry on … [but] [t]hey do not tell us everything we would like to know as we carry on. No human creation could do that.'[85] However, and crucially, that does not imply that social action can be explained *without* them, and that Constructivism can only offer only 'understandings'.[86]

This discussion takes us back to John Rawls and his separation of 'constitutive' and 'regulative' rules, which lies at the heart of these issues. Contra Peter Winch, the distinction is a false one: 'In the social reality that people construct (and constructs people), what people take to be possible and what society makes permissible depend on one's vantage point, one's relation to practice, and not practice itself.'[87] 'All rules in a socially constructed reality are related to *practice*.'[88] 'Practices are the content of carrying on' – of engaging in struggles, to rule, to dominate.[89]

The need for a notion of 'practice' and 'practical reasoning', recently being highlighted, but always there, an understanding of humans as innately capable of understanding practically, was clearly required. But what this also makes clear is the Pouliot's 'logic of practice', while an improvement on the rational actor model, focuses overly on the non-conscious or habitual.[90] It again plays down the conscious element of social life, and its role in social struggle. Onuf had already noted how this view, which draws also on Michael Oakeshott's assertion 'that most human behavior can be adequately described in terms of the notion of *habit* or *custom* and that neither the notion of rule or that of reflectiveness is essential to it'.[91] Like Oakeshott, there is too little language and conscious reflection included in the notion of the logic of practice, and hence there is actually too little struggle.

But in showing that habits do not fully explain the social, and that a concept of rules is required, Winch overreached in a way interesting for us here. 'What Winch lacked was any way to ask specific questions about rules that are not just rules governing language.'[92] Winch did not ask: '(a) Who makes the rules and how do the makers benefit from doing so? (b) Why do people follow rules without considering who makes them and how they and others are affected by doing so?' What the last chapters of *World of Our Making* do is to develop a theory of world politics that bears little resemblance to later Constructivism, where all the struggle and conflict was sucked out. Onuf focuses on what he calls 'the influential', a term strikingly similar to the 'power elite' in the sociology of C. Wright Mills.[93] What the practice turners are discovering in the social theory of Bourdieu, Foucault, and others, then, is taking on the project from *World of Our Making* that the second generation abdicated. Tying IR back in, once again rather than anew, into the rich tradition within sociology and social theory that includes Karl Marx, Max Weber, and Emile Durkheim, and many others.[94]

To take the example of the old chestnut of the ideas-material debate, Onuf stated quite clearly in *World of Our Making*, 'The constructivism I prefer … does not draw a sharp distinction between material and social realities – the material and the social contaminate each other, but variably – *and it does not grant sovereignty to either the material or the social by defining the other out of existence.*[95] Yet, as noted earlier, Constructivism made its name by stressing the causal impact of ideational factors neglected by mainstream work.[96] Of course, at the time this was a necessary move to gain a disciplinary audience, just as recourse to the language of efficient causation and hypothesis testing. But it served to undermine what was distinctive about Constructivism.

This feature of *World of Our Making* and Constructivism was downplayed, however, as 'discourse' understood mainly as words became a crucial concept for IR Constructivism. But the relational and practical aspects of discourse, and its fundamental role in social struggle, should have been clear. For Onuf, 'Constructivism begins with deeds. Deeds done, acts taken, words spoken. These are all the facts there are.'[97] Wittgenstein's notion of a form of life is crucial here – at bottom, there is just what you *do*. This is crucial for Pouliot and the practice turners. Practices are relational, both in the sense of how they impact on those taking part in them, but only exist in relation to other practices. Language itself is practical – as the concept of 'speech acts' grasps – but also relational. As de Saussure said, 'The content of a word is determined in the final analysis not by what it contains but by what exists outside of it.'[98]

World of Our Making's status as a foundational text of Constructivism is surprising; despite its popularity, it is far more cited than it is read – try buying a first edition copy! If it was more frequently read, fewer of the myths and mischaracterizations about Constructivism – and indeed many of the unhelpful concepts and false dichotomies beyond Constructivism – would hold up. And there are many dichotomies invoked to locate Constructivism: agency versus structure, and the notion that Constructivism is either all about international norms or about the agency of states or individuals to change their world; ideas versus material factors, and the suggestion that Constructivism has nothing to say about the latter; and explanation versus understanding, and the claim that the constitutive analysis put forward by constructivists are different from but as valid as the real causal stories of the neo-positivists. These misunderstandings have weakened Constructivism by allowing neo-positivism and rationalism to claim (falsely) superior to be the only truly 'scientific' approach to world politics.

Conclusion

This chapter has situated rules, law, and language at the heart of the New Constructivism, a place it should have held within Constructivism all along. The New Constructivism does not seek to avoid the rough terrain at the intersection of politics and law. It does not, consequently, rest on a distinction between Constructivism as the realm of norms and hence 'oughts', as opposed to the domain of politics, power, and what 'is'. Kratochwil has recently noted, to use only the example of law, 'law constitutes not only "the people", but it also creates the "public power" vested in the government to decide all questions of common concern, thereby solving the collective action problem in a purely instrumental fashion'.[99] Through a discussion of exemplary New Constructivist work by Epstein, Aalbert, Raymond, and Rajkovic – and the early work of Onuf – the chapter showed that language, law, and rules are political and normative through and through, a matter of convention and common agreement, very much real in their effects.

The cases looked at here are illustrative only; the breadth of possible New Constructivist work that follows the imperative to foreground rules, law, and language, is immense. Crucially, New Constructivists may not set out to work on law, rules, and language to find them. Andrew Linklater's recent analysis of the 'civilizing process' in international society is indicative.[100] Bringing to the IR conversation insights from the historical sociology of Norbert Elias – *doing Constructivism* thereby – Elias traces the growing dislike in European societies of public displays of violence, internally – as interrogated by Foucault and Giorgio Agamben – and internationally too.[101] For Linklater, such changes were tied to the growth of court society in the 17th and 18th centuries, 'where elaborate codes of etiquette and propriety separated the higher, "civilized" groups from the lower strata'. Here codes of conduct, and expectations of dress and behaviour – gendered, racialized, and embodied – function as and through rules and language. They also function as means and modes of *rule* in modernity, raising a topic picked up in the following chapter.

Acknowledgements

This chapter departs from David M. McCourt and Brent J. Steele, World of Our Making and Second Generation Constructivism, in Harry Gould, ed. 2017, *The Art of World-Making: Nicholas Onuf and His Critics*, Routledge, pp 1–16. Reproduced with permission of The Licensor through PLSclear.

4

World-Making: Experts and Professionals in the New Constructivism

Introduction

In the process of bringing to the surface the continuing centrality of law, rules, and language to the New Constructivism, the previous chapter repeatedly emphasized the pivotal role of experts and professionals in the making of contemporary global politics, notably in the legal field but in others besides. Seemingly natural, the prominence of professions and experts is – in fact – a historically contingent feature of today's international affairs and domestic life. A range of scholars – Michel Foucault only the most prominent – have traced the rise of the professions and the academic disciplines as core features of modernity, emerging alongside capitalism yet representing a distinct driver of the shift to the modern world.[1] Inseparable from the New Constructivism's interest in the problematic of *rule* in world politics is thus an interest in the individuals and groups – and the changing labels we use for them, from 'intellectuals' to 'experts' – that are the throughputs for rule's modalities and technologies.

This chapter seeks to flush out world-making in the New Constructivism, exploring a key distinction between the Old Constructivism and the New – the New Constructivism's thoroughgoing reflexivity. The Old Constructivism cemented the approach's place in the field on the back of careful empirical studies proving the impact of norms, culture, and identity in world politics. Yet those social factors were, with some exceptions, already constituted – the *constructing* was less salient than documenting the effects of the social constructions.[2] Many of the problematic intellectual binaries left over from the Old Constructivism are thus overcome by careful analysis of the role of specific agents like experts and elites in international political outcomes. Theoretically, the impetus to focus on world-makers comes from a rejection – central to a practice-relational sensibility – of accounts of political action focused on norms, cultures, and identities understood in monolithic terms.[3] One of the fundamental insights of this line of thinking is that it is not enough to account for political outcomes by citing the influence of norms, culture, and identities as ready-made artefacts, since their origins, trajectories, and differential effects must be accounted for – once again, foregrounding power in the process. Careful tracing of the impact of agents of different kinds, in other words, solves the agency-structure dilemma, not theoretically so much as practically.

Focused on process and practice, the New Constructivism places the act of constructing and its actors in stark relief. The New Constructivism is fully cognizant of the way in which social actors, including perhaps IR theorists, are not merely produced by constructed processes but are engaged in the process of construction. Practising reflexivity in IR is not, however, a straightforward exercise, as Jack Amoureux and Brent Steele have shown.[4] Reflexive scholarship is not the same as putting the author into the picture along traditional lines of race, gender, nationality, socio-economic status, and so on. Recent interest in 'auto-ethnography' has shown the promise of paying greater attention to the scholar's own role in the knowledge they produce. As Oden Löwenheim explains, the promise of auto-ethnography is that greater attention to analytical or more morally bias, IR auto-ethnographers 'become aware of and open to the importance and uniqueness of other human beings' experience and subjectivity'.[5] But the New Constructivism requires a fuller conceptualization of reflexivity, one that goes beyond putting the researcher back into the research process.[6] The New Constructivism does not, to be clear, offer a *single* answer to the puzzle of the observer's relationship to practice. ANT, social network analysis, field theory, and other frameworks each offer unique resources to face head-on the challenges of including in analysis the relationship of the observer to the observed.

The chapter first assesses two predominant ways of assessing the role of experts and professionals in the Old and the practice turn – namely via 'norm entrepreneurs' and 'communities of practice'. I then explore four key examples of work that accords with the tenets of the New Constructivism – work on, respectively, peace professionals, diplomats, terrorism experts, and piracy governance. I subsequently delve into the case of my own research on US-China expertise. The New Constructivism is a broad church, but together these works point towards a unified approach and set of problematics.

Beyond norm entrepreneurs and communities of practice

World-makers are not absent in the Old Constructivism or the practice-relational turn. However, in the former they became tied to an overly homogenous view of norms and culture, creating the manufactured 'puzzle' of normative change the practice-relational turn can 'fix' by drawing attention to the pragmatic, process-driven nature of political action. True, Alexander Wendt's structural Constructivism imported similar challenges in relation to explaining systemic change that afflicted Waltz-inspired realism. Yet, Wendt's *Social Theory of International Politics* did not reflect all there was to early Constructivism. From the outset, world-making and world-makers were a centrepiece of a properly rendered Constructivism.

While oft repeated, change *is not* and never was a true analytical puzzle in constructivist research. International politics, like domestic life, is a process of constant change – technological, moral, and cultural. As Patrick Jackson has shown, change should be a starting assumption – *continuity* or *stability* is what must be explained.[7] In this section, I revisit the main approaches to change in the Old empirical Constructivism and the practice turn, before developing a series of examples that demonstrate the promise of New Constructivist approaches to world-making.

Norm entrepreneurs and international political change

Criticisms of Constructivism's structuralism, and its alleged difficulty explaining international political change, obscures the fact that the empirical constructivist work has been, and remains, very much concerned with the activities of individuals seeking to promote norm change in global governance.[8] Taking the term 'norm entrepreneur' from Cass Sunstein to label such agents,[9] the first wave of empirical constructivist studies – particularly the work of Martha Finnemore, Margaret Keck, Audie Klotz, and Kathryn Sikkink – explored international norm dynamics and the role of transnational advocacy networks as entrepreneurs generating norm adoption, diffusion, and transformation.[10] In what must be acknowledged as a startlingly successful intervention in the field – if suffering from something of a progressive bias – their intervention allowed IR scholars to catalogue the array of norm entrepreneurial activities in international security and global governance.[11]

The problem with the dynamics of normative orders was, then, not that there were no agents, no world-makers, but rather that labelling elite promoters of norms 'entrepreneurs' does little in explanatory terms. How do norms emerge and change? When and how do some norms get picked up, while others do not? As Jeffrey Legro and Amitav Acharya asked, respectively, which or whose norms matter?[12]

In the New Constructivism, the label of norm entrepreneurs is put to one side in favour of the question of when the promotion of norms is successful and when not. In an important early move, Stacie Goddard, for example, adopted a relational approach, showing how social networks provide putative norm entrepreneurs resources, structural conditions, and means to effect change.[13] Here again, successful norm entrepreneurship is not explicable simply by reference to either interests and capacities, or to practice and practical knowledge, but by one's *relation to* practice.

In the following section, I explore other works that offer more relational understandings of world-making in international politics. First, I address the currently popular notion of 'communities of practice'.

Communities of practice

For proponents of a practice turn in IR theory – a turn to be made separately from any singular paradigm in the field – a 'practice approach in IR begs for a close scrutiny of the role of communities of practice in world politics'.[14] Emanuel Adler, for example, suggests IR theorists should 'think about our world, neither as an assemblage of states nor as divided by borders and lines of national identification, but as transnational communities of practice, based on what people actually do rather than by where they happen to live'.[15] Using examples largely from constructivist work, Adler and Pouliot suggest that doing so would highlight:

> transnational communities of diplomats sharing a diplomatic culture, common values, and interests that are intrinsic to their practice. … We might also see international and transnational lawyers trying to make human rights more legitimate, acceptable, and accessible to people on the global level. We might witness scientists and scholars organizing themselves for worthy causes, such as alleviating world hunger or banning landmines.[16]

Also tellingly, a key rationale behind the turn to communities of practice is the need to overcome problematic binaries, like agency versus structure. For Adler and Pouliot, 'Communities of practice are intersubjective social structures that constitute the normative and epistemic ground for action, but they also are agents, made up of real people, who – working via network channels, across national borders, across organizational divides, and in the halls of government – affect political, economic, and social events.'[17] However, the binaries communities of practice are meant to overcome were contingent features of Constructivism's socially constructed narrowing.

The problem with a communities of practice approach is not, therefore, as Christian Bueger has argued, its progressivist bias, ontological imprecision – that is, what are the boundaries of a community? – its neglect of power and struggle, nor the danger of being seen as a 'totalizing' argument, that the study of communities of practice is all there is to IR.[18] The problem is that world-making and the communities of world-makers *were already there* in constructivist IR and did not need to be 'brought back in'.

Rather than adopt a communities of practice approach as a theoretical starting point, therefore, New Constructivists should explore the communities of world-makers by reconnecting to broader problematic of forms of rule via epistemic knowledge, professional jurisdiction, and expert competence. Since communities are not all of a piece – economic communities, political communities, and cultural communities, as Bourdieu has shown, feature quite distinct modes of thinking and acting – the New Constructivism should not limit itself to following the practice turn's new ontology. Rather than adopt practices as a 'gluon' to hold an increasingly fragmented IR together, as a form of classic social analysis the New Constructivism instead reconnects to a longer tradition of thought and its major problematics, from the origins of the state and the nature of the division of labour, to capitalism and modernity itself.

Experts, expertise, and political interventions

The most suitable problematic for constructivist approaches to international change properly rendered is the construction, or constitution, of world politics writ large, not the processes of norm formation and diffusion only, nor the primacy of the practical. By 'writ large' I do not mean to suggest that all New Constructivists need to address the deep constitutive rules of international affairs, like state sovereignty, international law, great power management, nor capitalism and modernity themselves. The foreign policy of a single state remains an entirely legitimate research question to tackle from a constructivist perspective, for instance. However, even relatively narrow issues of concern are tied to broader shifts in the taken-for-granted norms, rules, and roles/identities that underpin action at the global level – the action of states, non-governmental organizations, corporations, and individuals. Identifying, and then theorizing these shifts is within the purview of the New Constructivism, and its toolkit of fields, social networks, assemblages, and narratives, frames, and process. All of these frameworks, and others besides, finally, can overcome the problematic binaries of agency versus structure, understanding versus explanation, constitution versus causation, and ideational versus material explanation. The following sections develop this unified New Constructivism in the case of the peacebuilding profession, diplomacy, and expertise in terrorism and counter-piracy.

The peace industry

The division of economic and social labour in modern society into an array of professionalized spheres has only rarely entered the discourse of IR theory, at least explicitly. More often, attention to the activities of diplomats, foreign policy-makers, strategic experts, and other agents has naturalized their professional training, connections, and dispositions, rendering unproblematic the contingent – and puzzling – emergence of precisely the communities of practice Adler and Pouliot are right to place at the centre of contemporary international politics.[19] In her recent 'social analysis' of peacebuilding, by contrast, Catherine Goetze epitomizes the promise of the New Constructivism by denaturalizing what seems a natural feature of today's global governance – the existence of a coherent, transnationalized, profession composed of individuals invested in the process of peacebuilding in war-torn countries around the globe.[20]

Tracing the social construction of the peacebuilding profession, Goetze begins by rejecting an essentializing or substantializing perspective that would seek to 'define terms' like peace and peacebuilding before the analysis proceeds. As Goetze makes clear from the very outset, the object of her analysis is not 'peace' nor 'peacebuilding' per se, since neither are features of the world that exist outside the terms we use for them. As Goetze notes, state-building, military intervention, civilian peace missions, democratization can all be part of the peacebuilding repertoire, but do not exhaust or necessarily make up peacebuilding.

Playing on what is perhaps Bourdieu's most famous work on the relationship between class distinctions and cultural tastes,[21] therefore, Goetze highlights the struggle within a peacebuilding profession over its core object, the boundary-drawing processes that identify an object and the professional field simultaneously. Thus, 'peacebuilding exists because it has become for a sufficiently large number of people and institutions with sufficiently important authority an unquestioned way of political action in the world, and, on a more individual level, a way of making a living (in the full sense of the word).'[22] As such, Goetze's is an analysis of 'the social structures of power in globalization processes. Peacebuilding is a globalization process, and an extremely important one'.[23]

Explicitly driven by field theory, Goetze emphasizes the approach's 'empirical' or inductive potential – guiding questioning rather than imposing any particular logic or structure to the peacebuilding profession. An inductive field approach guides the researcher to search first for the boundaries of the field, the – often-fuzzy – limits beyond which actors no longer feel the 'pull' of the field's normative expectations and incentives. In the discipline of IR, for example, the limits of the field are where individuals no longer feel bound by or indeed recognize the field's major divisions – mainstream versus critical approaches, its major stakes – publishing in recognized journals, seeking employment in recognized departments, and pushing forward prominent debates. A field approach also guides the researcher to the forms of power or 'capital' participants wield, the relationship between position and disposition, and whether fields are highly unified or dispersed, and whether fields are separate from others, or overlapping or 'interstitial'. These are empirical questions.

The counterpoint, for Goetze, is an institutionalist account of peacebuilding that takes it for granted as a natural feature of institutions like the United Nations and NGOs, an approach prominent in Old Constructivism. For Goetze, these 'are not neutral bundles of rules, norms, and decision-making procedures, as many institutionalist theories of international relations argue'.[24] Echoing Arthur Stinchcombe's classic critique of the New Institutionalism in organizational studies, Goetze emphasizes that 'institutions are filled with real people who have real ideas, interests, tastes, likes, and dislikes, and who work together to achieve not only abstract, institutional goals but also their own professional goals, furthering their own professional careers'.[25] Peacebuilding is thus a socio-professional space, in which people simultaneously push forward institutional and personal projects.

Once again, Goetze develops an origins story of the peacebuilding field, which emerged during the Congo crisis of 1960 and the UN's failed efforts to secure peace. The peacebuilding field emerged, Goetze shows 'by default', born out of the 'necessity' of involving the United Nations in the conflict but with little ability to bring about real peace. This core tension – of a field predicated on promoting, but never able to secure, peace, remains at the heart of the field – hence the label 'peacebuilding', not 'peacemaking'. As the field has expanded to include an array of organizations besides the UN, from the OSCE, UNHCR, and others, like NATO, 'The matter at stake in the Congo crisis', remains at the field's heart: 'the definition of – and the authority to establish – peace'.[26] It is therefore not surprising that the link between peacebuilding and peace is tendentious at best. As sociologist Monica Krause has also explored, the *raison d'être* of the highly rationalized world of NGOs is the product, the project.[27] 'It is the "doing well" that is questioned, not the "doing good",' Goetze notes.[28] That peace must be built, lives must be saved, is unquestioned, not just as *doxa*, or the taken-for-granted, but as part of a wider *nomos*, or 'normative belief structure that ties the field together as a coherent space of action'.[29]

Goetze's tour of the peacebuilding field passes through its structure and boundaries, the *habitus* or dispositions of its most powerful actors and the narratives they tell themselves of the field. A form of productive power, à la Foucault, the peacebuilding profession features personal networks and credentialing institutions that reflect the modalities of hierarchy in world politics. Such modalities are all the more powerful because they are hidden to IR scholars, many of whom share the same credentials and dispositions. How could one *not* have a degree from a top international school to qualify as a peacebuilder? For early peacebuilders like Dag Hammarskjöld and Ralph Bunche, however, such credentials were new, a route to success for middle-income families. Today, Goetze traces empirically, 'in every aspect cosmopolitan: [the peacebuilders] are polyglots, have frequently travelled, and are highly educated, independent, and mobile in their leisure activities and social networks'.[30]

Finally, the legal field is once again paramount, particularly Anglo-American legal studies. Sitting at the intersection of academia, international law, business, and NGOs, the field draws heavily on the legitimacy of its legal expertise. In so doing, it fosters capacities easily transferable from the classroom and seminar to the field, and back again, particularly where peacebuilding has taken over parts of civilian management that require legal advice. Here the unquestioned dominance of US legal field as a seemingly depoliticized space is apparent. The prominence of arbitration, litigation, and dispute resolution are not then natural aspects of peacebuilding as a professionalized field, but instead reflections of their prominence in common law, as opposed to civil law, traditions. The rule of law is, once again, a mode of rule *through* law.

Inventing 'terrorism'

A second example also draws on a fuller reading of Bourdieusian sociology – one where the primary concern is the empirical use of thinking in field terms, rather than the primacy of practice in world politics. Like Goetze, Lisa Stampnitzky draws on field theory, and other relational approaches, to interrogate the origins of the concept of 'terrorism'. Stampnitzky demonstrates that terrorism is not a natural feature of contemporary international politics. Like peacebuilding, terrorism is, in fact, a recent phenomenon – also dating from the 1970s or so. Defining terrorism, typically as the political use of violence in order to create fear is, consequently, an insufficient and indeed misdirected analytical starting point. Terrorism is not natural but a social invention, a creation of artifice in Hobbes' words, or 'craft' in Locke's. Stampnitzky shows how terrorism was birthed conterminously with the emergence of a new field of terrorism expertise which created the concept at the same time as the field itself – experts located in particular institutions, at particular times, for particular purposes. In so doing, Stampnitzky's *Disciplining Terror* displays the core tenets of the New Constructivism – thoroughly reflexive, anti-essentialist, practice-oriented, and necessarily historical.

Stampnitzky begins the process of denaturalizing terrorism – highlighting its socially constructed nature – using the case of an August 1961 hijacking of a Boeing 707 by an American man, Leon Bearden and his 17-year-old son. Bearden hoped to travel to Cuba, evading US sanctions of the island, but was stopped during a refuelling at El Paso airport by the FBI. Jarring to our understanding, Bearden was not alone in his attempt at the time. The hijacking of civilian aircraft is, alongside bombings, the most recognizable terrorism activity. However, in the 1950s and 1960s, Stampnitzky explains, the hijacking of aircraft was far from unheard of, for reasons far from our contemporary assumptions about terrorism. But while the consequences today would be grave for anyone trying to steal an aircraft, Bearden eventually faced the modest charge of 'interfering with international commerce'.[31]

Through the Bearden case, we see the connection between aircraft hijackings and terrorism as a matter of artifice – of taking two things that do not belong together in any natural or necessary sense and forging a connection that has since become durable, expected, *doxic*. Stampnitzky shows how 'terrorism' emerged during the 1970s, such that: 'By the end of the decade bombings, hijackings, kidnappings, and hostage-takings were melded together, conceptualized not merely as tactics but as identifying activities, and joined to a new and highly threatening sort of actor: the "terrorist".'[32] Stampnitzky thus combines, rather than counterposes, Bourdieusian field theory and Latourian ANT in analyzing the social construction of terrorism and terror expertise, highlighting again how, while not of a piece, they are both aimed at the same thing: denaturalizing the taken-for-granted. The terrorism expertise profession is an actor-network, actors reach out to events, 'enrolling' them in a social construction process. Events – like a plane hijacking – therefore have their own agency in the process, facilitating or resisting framing as a particular type of event. '[T]he thing to be known is not merely an inert object but an active participant in the process,' Stampnitzky explains.[33]

To be sure, political violence is not new. Anarchist 'propaganda of the deed' during the late 19th and early 20th centuries, for example, deployed a range of techniques for political purposes, from the assassination of political leaders, to the bombings of public meeting places and landmarks.[34] As Mark Shirk has explored, propaganda of the deed was a pivotal stimulus to the formation of modern surveillance technologies, including the passport.[35] What set the 1970s apart was the construction of terrorism as a particular framework for understanding political violence, tied to a profession-building project to conceptualize terrorism as a particular thing, a specific type of activity or set of activities, legible to those with a given set of expert competencies.

Like peacebuilding, then, terrorism evades definition. Both are objects of ongoing, and indeed necessary, struggle – well captured by W.E.B. Gallie's over-referenced notion of 'essentially contested concepts'.[36] It is through an ongoing definitional struggle over terrorism that the broad, shifting, and contested boundaries of terrorism as a particular type of act are created – a definitional struggle that creates terrorism's shifting boundaries at the same time as a certain type of expert, the 'terrorism expert'.

Tracing terrorism's origins story, Stampnitzky emphasizes the way terrorism emerged in contrast to the more recognizable activity of counter-insurgency, a mode of political action and knowledge of it capable of rational analysis within the American military-industrial-academic complex. Putative terrorism experts asked whether terrorist activity was rational or irrational? Was not 'one person's terrorist another's freedom fighter?' The question was at once political and analytical. Analytically, an affirmative answer suggested no sphere of expertise was needed separate from counter-insurgency expertise. Stampnitzky also shows how over the 1980s and 1990s the terrorism expert field struggled with the politicization of terrorism and the question of its rationality, which underpinned the emergence of the notion of irrational and illegitimate actors who nevertheless needed to be studied because of the threat of the 'mass destruction' they might cause.

Stampnitzky likens the struggle to define terrorism to the classification struggles that lie at the heart of the modern state – the struggle to define certain types of problems, issues, people, and groups in certain ways, exercising in the process immense symbolic power.[37] The terrorism expertise field is by its nature suspended between different experts and organizations who each define terrorism in distinct ways, as a legal/diplomatic problem, a problem of modelling, as at organizations like the RAND Corporation and finally as a phenomenon that can be quantified, or predicted, as practiced by risk management professionals. The essentially contested nature of terrorism reflects the 'liminal' nature of the field of terrorism expertise itself, located at the intersection of political science, international security and conflict studies, area studies and psychology, and between the academy, the world of think tanks and Federally Funded Research and Development Centers (FFRDCs) and the for-profit world of risk management.[38]

The pay-off to the historical and theoretical effort required to denaturalize terrorism is to offer a unique perspective on why and how terrorism came to occupy such a powerful place in the Western political episteme over the last half-century or so. Precisely the fuzziness of the concept, its unsettled place between rationality and irrationality, morality and evil, and the politicized nature of its study, allowed for heightened concern over WMDs, and, ultimately, the formation of a war on the abstract noun 'Terror'.

Diplomacy

Diplomacy, and the international cadre of diplomats, military attachés, and other official state representatives, have received less interest in IR than is warranted given their centrality to the practice of international politics – as Paul Sharp among others has noted.[39] A third example of New Constructivist literature that centres world-making and world-makers thus comes from the work of Iver Neumann, Vincent Pouliot, Ole Jacob Sending, and Rebecca Adler-Nissen, who together place diplomacy at the forefront of the discipline. For these scholars, diplomacy is the site of international politics where the pay-off of a practice-relational sensibility is perhaps best on display.

In an insightful early paper, Neumann challenged constructivists not to leave practice behind as the approach drew IR's attention to norms, culture, and identities. Summing up much of what the New Constructivism is all about, Neumann explained that a 'central challenge for social analysis must be how to preserve the insights produced by the linguistic turn while adding the insights promised by practice theory, to combine the study of meaning and the study of the material'.[40] For Neumann, doing so required acknowledging how rules and practices are not automatically put into action by individuals viewed as mere cultural throughputs. As explored in the previous chapter, just as 'rules do not contain rules for their use', Neumann notes, 'so practices do not contain rules for their use: "it is always necessary to ask what disposes people to enact the practices they do, how and when they do".'[41] As Emile Durkheim tells us, however, such aims and practices are *themselves* socially constructed – we explain social facts by prior social facts – necessitating focus on the broader institutional, cultural, and social construction of such dispositions.[42]

Neumann presents a study of the Norwegian diplomatic corps as a case in a specific country's diplomatic dispositions.[43] Reflecting on his time at the Norwegian Foreign Affairs Ministry, Neumann highlights the potential of ethnographic research and participant observation in IR, and again the potential of a relational sensitivity to how people, things, and stories, are held together. 'The social fact that things are ordered in a particular way and not another', Neumann notes, 'may be conceptualized as a story that tells specific people what to do in specific contexts'.[44] Neumann shows that a theoretically straightforward act of writing a foreign policy speech, for example, is in practice the result of countless day-to-day compromises between diplomats, which render what should be a unitary pronouncement of the objective national interest a lowest common denominator statement. All such texts are written in the same manner, where '[t]extual production largely determines textual output, making each text very similar to its predecessors, so that understanding ministerial textual production is key to understanding the bureaucratic mode of knowledge production at large'.[45]

Neumann came to recognize the rules of speech writing by repeatedly – and occasionally deliberately – breaking them. As he recounts, on one occasion he attempted to deviate from the Ministry's norm of speech writing by proposing a novel theme – an identity for Norway on the international stage as the promoter of 'ethical globalization'. As the speech made its way around the ministry, the unifying theme was written out of the final speech so that it would sound like prior speeches. When delivered, the Norwegian Foreign Minister's speech garnered no media attention and the ministry went on about its day-to-day business, ministers – to Neumann's surprise – pleased the speech had passed off without any attention.

Neumann's failure had unearthed the taken-for-granted logic of the ministry. He 'had confirmed that analysis was unimportant in the Foreign Ministry system, that the audience's reception was of little or no interest in the ministry, and that the established patterns were difficult to break'.[46] The reason can be rendered in institutionalist terms: the ministry is not academia. The point of speeches, from the perspective of ministers and their staff, is not to produce something new. In Bourdieu's terms Neumann's mistake was to confuse the 'logical logic' of the academy for the practical logic of the ministry. Novelty and creativity in ministry speechwriting is simply not the point. Whereas academics want novelty, diplomats are interested in reiteration of priorities. For academics, a speech – or paper, or book – that says little new is not worth the paper it is written on, a point that goes a long way towards explaining the felt need for a practice-relational turn separate from Constructivism, it is important to point out. For diplomats, if the old rules of Norwegian foreign policy are passed over, they run the risk of being weakened over time, no longer providing clear guidance for how ministers should 'go on'. For that, it is far better to have a consensus document than one with creativity and debate.

Neumann's fascinating analysis uses the 'artefact' of a speech – a material thing – to shine a light on the practical logic of Norwegian foreign policy. A boring, repetitive, speech furthers the ministry's goals by reproducing the ministry itself. In particular, it fosters the creation of foreign policy generalists rather than specific specialists – Neumann's first foray into speechwriting, he recalls, was to pen a speech about China and economic policy, of which he is admittedly no expert.[47] But the production of narrow expertise is not the point. The *re*production of the ministry also furthers its boundary work vis-à-vis other government groups with a foot in foreign policy, notably the political leadership and public relations – Neumann's conceptual speech would have transgressed the tacitly agreed distinctions between such parts of the Norwegian foreign policy establishment.

The case of the Norwegian foreign ministry opens clear potential for comparative study into international diplomatic dispositions. In the United States and the United Kingdom, for example, foreign policy speeches without the sort of unifying theme Neumann sought to develop for Sweden would appear odd. In the US case especially, foreign policy speeches would seem to require a new theme – even novel policy initiative – each time. Seemingly natural, the distinction highlights something important. Realists would suggest the difference between Oslo and Washington DC lies with national power and its relationship to national interests – that Norway says little new in its foreign policy speeches because it can do little. A practice-relational Constructivism suggests the opposite is the case, that deeply socially and culturally conditioned institutional habits determine dispositions and projects in the diplomatic and national security spheres, with effects independent of the distribution of global power.

Together with Ole Jacob Sending, Vincent Pouliot, and others, Neumann thus shows the potential to be gained from a practice and relational re-examination of diplomacy as one of the varied sites where world politics and global governance are constituted.[48] Leonard Seabrooke, for example, tracks the rise of economic consultancies as diplomatic actors around the world, actors – typically headquartered in the West – who bring with them styles of knowing, dispositions, from the NGO and for-profit consulting sectors. 'Independent Diplomat', for instance, a non-profit, registered in NYC, offers such services as helping draft aides-memoires and letters to the United Nations Security Council, working on declaring independence for Kosovo, issues relating to the Tamils in Sri Lanka, and Western Sahara. Seabrooke traces how consultants bring different frames than traditional diplomats, notably 'economic-systematic knowledge' and 'programming-managerial knowledge', acting as brokers, and 'carving out new markets for political work and who are occupying positions in political networks are engaging in economic arbitrage by drawing on different types of professional knowledge'.[49]

Together, a far broader range of questions are opened up for IR from taking a practice-relational approach to diplomatic world-making than is suggested by the narrower theoretical imperative to 'bring practices back in'. At stake is nothing less than the drivers of contemporary globalization processes, a problematique that connects Constructivism to concerns of the classic social analysts, notably rationalization processes and the division of professional labour as components of the spread of liberal governmentalities and the dynamics of Western hegemony.

The counter-piracy 'assemblage'

Christian Bueger's research on the global governance of piracy offers a powerful final example of the promise of a practice-sensitive New Constructivist approach to world-making. Theoretically, Bueger deploys assemblage theory, which, he explains, 'encourages us to study how actors establish and maintain relations, and create shared regulatory spaces and narratives'.[50] Like terrorism and peacebuilding from the previous examples, piracy would seem a long-standing taken-for-granted feature of world politics, from the Barbary corsairs to the pirates of the 17th- and 18th-century Caribbean. Yet, what ties together such 'persistent agents of transnational harm', in Oded Löwenheim's words, is less the naturalness of something called 'piracy', and more the shifting projects that construct, *relating* things that appear self-evident as the result of often-immense effort among different actors.[51] Citing anthropologist Tania Li, Bueger explains that: 'Assemblage flags agency, the hard work required to draw heterogeneous elements together, forge connections between them and sustain these connections in the face of tension.'[52] Assemblage theory thus denaturalizes the processes behind the forging of the cultural contexts and norms Old Constructivism seemed to take for granted, appearing as relationalism,[53] international practice theory,[54] and ANT:[55] in other words, the *New Constructivism in IR Theory*.

Bueger's case is the rapid emergence of a counter-piracy assemblage after 2008. How did a web of understandings, narratives, and a diverse array of agents – including the strange sight of European Union, Chinese, American, and Indian navies cooperating to stem pirate activity off the coast of East Africa – come about? What made it hang together, in Ruggie's (via Durkheim) formulation? The first analytical step, Bueger urges, is what in other guises might be termed 'thick description'. 'Assemblage theory … follows a distinct style of analysis primarily interested in empirically describing practices of assembling.'[56] The primacy of description follows the nature of assemblages:

> An assemblage depends on the relations that it maintains. This relational logic implies that elements of an assemblage (actors, objects, practices) are seen as having no essence or particular identity prior to entering the assemblage. Assemblages, moreover, have no fundamental organizing principles, such as the balance of power or a prescribed hierarchy. This does not exclude the possibility that assemblages reach a form in which they are organized by one principle, are institutionalized or are structured hierarchically. Assemblage research, however, does not presume *a priori* that assemblages are ordered and structured, but leaves this question open to research. Structural stability is seen as the exception rather than the norm.[57]

Here many New Constructivists – myself included – push back. I agree that order is emergent, emerging to form a territory or space through processes of sorting, dividing, grouping, on the back of relations of authority, control, power, expertise. However, the insistence that practices can only be described, not explained, is misplaced, an effect of a form of hostility towards stability that seems to be the price of accepting the flux of social life. In different ways, Ayşe Zarakol and Vincent Pouliot, for example, both show how international hierarchies *are* highly stable.[58] It is possible, therefore, to retain the puzzle of how such orders, hierarchies, structures are created, via the thick description of assembling processes, and consider this an explanation of the production and reproduction of broader international orders.

Nonetheless, Bueger's account of the counter-piracy assemblage represents a key advance in theorizing in global governance, pushing beyond first-generation state-centred accounts and second generation where transnational networks and non-state actors centred towards a third, practice-relational generation where states, navies, industry, and global governance organizations each feature as important actors. These unnatural partners, Bueger shows, were tied together by a specific artefact, the handbook of Best Management Practices (BHM), which codified a set of agreed-upon rules for anti-piracy activity available to all mariners. Following assemblage theory's 'sensitiv[ity] to mundane matters of international cooperation, the role of objects and things, the importance of territories of governance, the vitality of expert knowledge, and the instability of governance arrangements'[59] – Bueger shows how a specific artefact – the 'High Risk Area' (HRA), a swathe of ocean intersecting an imaginary line from Tanzania to the south of India – created a new social space within which its rules held sway. Here again, the 'how' of international political interaction *is* the 'why' – the interest in suppressing piracy tells us far less than how piracy is defined, by whom, through what means. Bueger's account shows us how, illustrating the power of assemblage theory as a resource for New Constructivists along the way.

Framing China's rise in the United States and the United Kingdom

The four examples discussed earlier highlight the diversity of theories and perspectives available under the heading of the New Constructivism. In this section, I extend their collective demonstration that experts and professionals lie at the heart of the New Constructivism using the case of the United States' changing strategy towards China since approximately 2016. The official American view of China's rise has shifted in recent years from an economic opportunity to be 'engaged' to a rival challenging 'American power, influence, and interests', with which the US is locked in 'strategic competition'.[60] Carried out under President Trump, the transformation sets the frame under which the Biden administration has addressed the question of relations with Beijing.[61] What accounts for, *explains*, this change?

My aim is not to present a full accounting for changes in US policy, but rather to highlight the value added of the sort of anti-essentialist, reflexive, and historically sensitive perspective offered by the New Constructivism. The usefulness of this case for the purposes of this book is rooted in the seeming primacy of changing power balances, threat perception, and the taken-for-granted capacity of the state to profess the national interest when it comes to an increasingly authoritarian and self-confident Beijing – as securitization scholars have long held.[62] Downplayed by practice theorists in their desire to foreground the 'practical' vis-à-vis Constructivism, the main counter-argument to a constructivist account of changes in US national security policy towards China rests on objective national interests. In other words, the cause of the shift in US policy towards China appears clear – it is a response to changes in China, including crackdowns on democracy in Hong Kong, the mass internment of Uighur minorities in Xinjiang, provocative actions in relation to Taiwan and continued build-up of military capacity in the South China Sea. The argument that what appears natural is, in fact, socially constructed is here weak – both analytically and, more importantly, politically. Changed circumstances in relation to China have necessitated a changed strategy. What else needs to be said?

Offering a powerful New Constructivist account is thus a serious challenge. A first step is to denaturalize the taken-for-granted. Early constructivists did this primarily by implying counterfactual worlds. Why during the Cold War were Russian nuclear weapons aimed at the US from Siberia viewed as threatening, when British nuclear submarines able to operate off New York viewed as part of common Western deterrent?[63] Others stress historical change to achieve the same effect. In the case of US-China relations, for example, scholars and commentators – John Mearsheimer only the most prominent within IR – have warned that post-Cold War US primacy would prove short-lived.[64] Why did it take US strategists until 2016 to address the China challenge?

Here I address a comparative case – that of the United Kingdom's evolving relations with China. The logic of 'structure, focused, comparison' is sometimes eschewed by constructivists – especially within security studies – who instead often deploy in-depth within-case process-training techniques, which do indeed follow from the inductive and interpretive constructivist approach, as well as the rejection of states in world politics as genuinely like cases. Nonetheless, comparison can be a powerful tool with which to objectify the institutional and cultural factors that underpin seemingly objective outcomes. Contra the United States, the UK government has not completely rejected cooperation with Beijing, nor adopted a clear competitive focus in its relations with China. Nonetheless, a long-standing economic opportunity interpretation of China's rise is increasingly challenged by a national security-dominated understanding. While many in London see positive relations as central to Britain's post-Brexit global role, concern over developments like crackdowns on democracy in Hong Kong suggest a possible permanent shift in the UK's China frame.[65] What explains these differential outcomes, if not objective national interests and the different power positions of Washington and London vis-à-vis Beijing?

The second analytical step is to attain some precision regarding what, precisely, is being compared. Interpretations, meanings, policies, and strategies are each distinct objects. Here the objects are foreign policy *frames*. Frames are an appropriate analytical focus because they are broader than individual policies, yet more concrete than foreign policy traditions and state identities constructivists might address.[66] Frames provide the conceptual resources for governmental action, defining the bounds of thinking on a given topic, within which policies cohere.[67] As such, tracing changes in framings of China offers the potential to identify possible and even likely future policies, without implying determinism.

Bringing these themes together, the question is why the US' and Britain's framings of China differ, and how are differential frames related to the individuals involved – China policy-makers and professional experts, in the two countries? To answer this question, I too draw on Bourdieusian field theory. Fields structure contestation along principal divisions and distinctions, producing a limited number of credible positions, and at times a strong common sense or *doxa*. National security fields are composed of actors including political parties, lobbyists, and decision-makers – typically highlighted by foreign policy analysts – but also academics, business leaders, and think tankers, evading a singular logic of competition. Field theory views foreign policy frames as the outcome of ongoing field-based struggles to interpret international objects as certain types of issue – be it a problem, opportunity, or something in between. Frames are shaped by the structure of fields understood as the distribution of influence, the rules and norms by which the struggle is carried on, and the distribution of worldviews and dispositions. The operative question, in short, is how the respective structures of given fields promote individuals with certain views and dispositions in relation to China, and not others.

Drawing on a set of 133 original interviews,[68] I highlight three key features. First, the US field features a belief that China's rise can be either arrested or prevented, absent in the UK, which gives rise to intense framing contestation and occasional frame turnover. I root this dynamic in the system of professional appointments and a large and intense 'marketplace of ideas'. I then identify the key positions or 'stances' produced by each field, the positions from which key actors have shaped the differing interpretations of China and its meaning. The election of Donald Trump – strongly critical of overreliance on China – empowered key individuals across government who shifted the predominant framing of China from potential challenger to current threat. The smaller field Britain features fewer and less intense voices. In the UK, finally, a handful of MPs took up the cause of changing British minds on China's rise.

The US and UK national security fields and China

The first salient difference between the US and UK national security fields is that in the latter, China's rise is as an inevitable feature of 21st-century world politics, whereas the US field features an assumption, a *doxa*, that China's rise is a problem in search of the correct US response.[69] The May 2020 *Strategic Approach to the People's Republic of China* reflects how 'Americans feel that they can do something about China's rise'.[70] Although it asserts that America 'does not seek to contain China's development',[71] nor change China's 'domestic governance model',[72] it mirrors the Engagement frame it replaces. Laying out 'Beijing's challenge' to America's 'way of life',[73] it details how strategic competition can 'compel Beijing to cease or reduce actions harmful to the United States' vital national interests'.[74]

Again, accepted wisdom suggests that power differentials lay at the heart of this difference – that the US simply *can* do more than Britain. From a field theory perspective, however, taken-for-granted agency is a contingent feature of the US national security field, a field of unparalleled size and intensity, where an intense struggle among multiple stakeholders frames issues like China's rise as actionable for policy-makers.[75] On any given day, a 'permanent conference on China' in Washington features speeches, panels, congressional testimonies, and myriad other events.[76] The UK national security field is smaller and less geographically concentrated, and the debate over foreign policy less intense. Moreover, organizations like the Royal United Services Institute (RUSI) and Chatham House are part of an international 'marketplace of ideas',[77] deeply interconnected with the US national security conversation.

Thus, while government and private US funding is far more substantial than in the UK,[78] economic power fails to explain the intensity of the US field. Rather, the root cause is a feature central to the US state – namely, the system of political appointments to policy-making positions.[79] The expansive ecology of national security organizations acts as a holding place for those hoping to enter, or having just left, government. From there, the struggle over influence is at once professional and deeply political,[80] as individuals hoping to enter government seek influence via forceful claims to expertise and the maintenance of prominence and relevance in matters of national security.

A signature artefact of the US national security field is thus the tendency towards often-sizeable swings between engagement or toughening with respect to certain issues and regions like China, as incoming administrations bring in new approaches and energy.[81] The issue is partly one of party politics and a politicized think tank space, as Republican administrations draw more heavily from conservative establishments – like Heritage and the American Enterprise Institute (AEI) – and Democrats their own sources – Brookings, the Council on Foreign Relations, and so on. Foreign policy often goes beyond partisan divisions, however, demonstrating that the tendency towards framing turnover reflects the broader dynamics of the 'revolving door' in and out of government.

The same dynamic is not operative in London, which features greater separation between the government, universities, business, and think tanks. If the 'UK government has a China crisis … it turns to its own resource base'.[82] In Britain, moreover, China expertise is a matter of party affiliation: 'China hands … are neither labor people nor Tory people. … We talk to both'.[83] Separation between the government, universities, and the business world is both reflected and furthered by aspects of the British national security context typically little mentioned, especially the high cost of living in London, which severely hinders the formation of a community of similar intensity to the 'Beltway'.[84] The China sector of the national security fields in the UK reflects this separation. A standout feature of each is the predominance of unique forms of China expertise, notably political risk advisors and corporate consultants in Britain.[85] Without the array of think tanks and research institutes in Washington, the British equivalent is the prominence of 'Little niche organizations below the radar … discreet offices in the city or West End or Mayfair … doing due diligence [and] corporate risk'.[86]

Ending engagement in the United States and Britain

The aforementioned presents in broad brushstrokes the unique structural dynamics of the US and UK national security fields. How does this matter? The major aspect of a field theory of differential framings of China's rise is the set of possible stances and counter-stances the respective fields produce, shaping the struggle to frame China as an international issue.

Trump's election brought to the centre of US policy a view of China gaining in popularity in certain sectors in the national security community: that Engagement had been a failure, and a new frame was needed for a CCP bent on global hegemony. Elements of the case long preceded Trump, resonating through DoD-funded organizations like the Center for Strategic and Budgetary Assessments,[87] human rights groups,[88] and the annual reviews of the twin congressional commissions established in 2000 as part of China's accession to the WTO – the US-China Economic and Security Review Commission and the Congressional-Executive Commission on China.[89] Offering no top-level direction aimed at preserving good relations with China, as had his predecessors – as the president's early phone call to Taiwanese leader Tsai Ing-Wen indicated – Trump empowered a group of strong China sceptics to fundamentally reframe Sino-US relations.[90]

Rhetorical reframing found support – and inspiration – from conservative Congresspeople, commentators, and experts previously considered radical in China. Notable among these were former Trump advisor Steve Bannon, the reformed Cold War *Committee on the Present Danger-China*,[91] Newt Gingrich, and Gordon G. Chang, who each promote the ideological view echoed in administration justifications for strategic competition.[92] As Pompeo noted: 'We have to admit a hard truth … if we want to have a free 21st century … the old paradigm of blind engagement with China will not get it done.'[93] A group of strongly anti-CCP Republican Congresspeople, including senators Marco Rubio (R., Fl) – chair of the human rights-focused CECC – and Tom Cotton (R., Ark), have used ideological language, language also evident in a Republican Party memo on how to use China to electoral advantage.[94]

The weakening of countervailing, that is, pro-Engagement, constituencies facilitated the framing shift. Trump largely excluded business groups like the US-China Business Council,[95] with many large businesses in any case welcoming of a new approach – at least initially – in response to increasingly unfavourable business conditions in China.[96] The absence of China-expert financial figures such as Henry Paulson in the Trump administration is thus telling, although Treasury Secretary Mnuchin found himself cast into the role of the Engager on account of his concern over souring relations on the markets.[97] Other constituencies isolated as Trump 'drained' the Washington 'swamp' were the main foreign policy think tanks, prompting organized pushback in the form of op-eds and open letters[98] – initiatives prompting their own counter-arguments.[99]

Criticism of Engagement therefore came from beyond the Republicans' right wing, preventing the politicization of China policy – as failed attempts to paint Biden as 'Beijing Joe' demonstrate.[100] In addition to human rights groups, with significant support from key congressional Democrats, Engagement was also criticized by former government officials and typically pro-Engagement sectors of the national security field. An influential early article by former insiders Kurt Campbell and Ely Ratner proclaimed America 'got China wrong',[101] signalling an important shift in the centre of gravity on China in the US national security field. Together with a military establishment after 2015 no longer preoccupied with counter-terrorism and small wars, the weight of the national security field tended towards a tougher line. Even those calling for a more restrained policy towards China had to acknowledge Beijing's deeply troubling behaviour.[102]

The UK national security field has not replicated the type of China stances seen in the US, nor, consequently, a paradigmatic frame change. The debate over Huawei is indicative. Unlike in the US, until January 2020 the Huawei question remained narrowly defined as about control over critical national infrastructure rather than as tied to the CCP and China's rise. Recommendations from the National Cyber Security Centre – part of the UK signals and intelligence services – drove government policy, doubtless with background input from the City of London conscious of Brexit.[103] There have thus been fewer loud voices calling for either allowing Huawei's participation as part of an overall strategy of courting China, or banning it as part of a broader narrative of the Chinese threat.[104]

The UK field thus features a relatively narrow set of China-sceptic stances. One stance draws explicitly on the importance of US views in Britain. Pompeo's visit in January 2020 to lobby for a ban on Huawei amplified the views of a number of concerned parliamentarians, raising doubts about post-Brexit trade relations with Washington. In addition to Iain Duncan Smith, Conservative MP Bob Seely and former head of MI5 Sir Richard Dearlove prominently dissented from the government, contributing to a HJS report that warned of the risks of Huawei's participation, featuring input from American analysts, including Rubio.[105] Illustrative of connections between the populist right media, *The Daily Mail* has adopted a well-defined China-sceptic position.[106]

Another stance emerges from a position similar to a group of self-labelled 'Wolverines' in the Australian parliamentary debate on China.[107] The *China Research Group*, for example, set up by Conservative MPs Tom Tugendhat and Neil O'Brien to 'promote debate and fresh thinking about how Britain should respond to the rise of China', seeks a broader view of 'the longer term challenges and opportunities associated with the rise of China'.[108] An early report by Charles Parton frames UK-China relations as a 'values war', featuring 'some divergence', rather than 'decoupling'.[109] The China Research Group's values-centric approach has found a sympathetic hearing with new Opposition Leader Keir Starmer, who has sought to define a Labour Party position on China closer to those of Tugendhat than Johnson and the previous coalition government.[110] Yet, the group also emphasizes its aim to 'explore opportunities to engage with and work with Chinese people, companies and government'.[111] In so doing, the group highlights the narrow range of possible positions on China, rendering unlikely the sort of cross-field coalition in support of a paradigmatic reframing of Sino-UK relations witnessed in the United States.

Conclusion

This chapter has further developed the core concerns and analytical foci of the New Constructivism by demonstrating the importance of experts and professionals as the makers of the social worlds on whom constructivists pin their accounts of international politics. It began by showing how world-making is far from absent in the Old Constructivism, and makes a strong appearance in the practice turn as well, but is underdeveloped in each. The notion of 'norm entrepreneurs' – individuals pushing norms that subsequently socialize international actors – tells us little about who they are, how they think, and the social dynamics underpinning their success or lack thereof. In addition to a progressive bias, the concept also fails to emphasize professionals as a recent feature of world politics. Similarly, the concept of 'communities of practice' represents a useful empirical object, but a limited guide to theorizing, since communities are not all of a piece.

In their place, the chapter highlighted the power of a set of fully relational and practical works, deploying a range of complementary theoretical frameworks including field theory, ANT, and assemblage theory, to account for the how of social construction. In so doing, these approaches offer the larger pay-off of the turn to practice-relationalism, beyond the narrow intervention that practice matters, to foreground the dynamics of power and *rule* in contemporary international politics. Finally, contra Owens, the point is not to resolve into sociolatry, since the approach is necessarily historical and reflexive, and able thereby to denaturalize sociolatry in IR and political life.

New Constructivist Methodology and Methods

Introduction

What methodological commitments does the New Constructivism entail? What methods can Constructivists deploy, and which ones must they eschew? The aim of this chapter is to debunk two popular myths about constructivist *methods* and Constructivism's *methodological implications* – a useful distinction introduced by Patrick Jackson: first, that Constructivism is an interpretive approach only focused on the reconstruction of intersubjective meanings; and second, that analysis of texts – speeches, strategy documents, newspaper articles, memoirs, and so on – is therefore the singular way of 'doing' Constructivism.[1] Counter to this common wisdom, I make the case that, instead, as a form of classic social analysis, constructivists are much freer in terms of the methods they can and, indeed, should use to substantiate their claims than is captured by the focus on interpreting texts. I illustrate using a computational approach – MCA – which would typically be seen as 'quantitative' and therefore beyond the constructivist pale.

I first reflect on my own adoption of a constructivist approach, which, while unique, might read as familiar to others or prompt a useful reflexive thought process for the reader. I then further explore the concept of classic social analysis, particularly its implications for method. In short, I urge constructivists to adopt whatever methods allows them to best answer their research question, rather than assume certain methods are off-limits. I subsequently illustrate with the case of MCA – a computational method the logic of which is fully in accordance with the practice-relational sensitivity of the New Constructivism. After briefly exploring practical questions raised by adopting the approach, a short conclusion considers the potential pay-off for constructivists willing to take the risk.

Becoming a Constructivism user

Unlike sociologist Howard Becker, who famously became a marijuana user for the purposes of research, I was a constructivist from my IR 'birth'.[2] My doctoral supervisor was an early constructivist, Friedrich Kratochwil, so I was unlikely to become a realist or rationalist. Other constructivists likely feel similarly – either because they are on the constructivist 'family tree' – or because Constructivism had become by the early 2000s an attractive theoretical approach to adopt.

Being born a constructivist came with rather opaque instructions when it came to methods, however, – about how to *do* Constructivism. Methods training varies widely and generalizing is difficult. But my suspicion is that other constructivists might have had a similar experience to mine: a combination of some exposure to interpretive political science methods and some Ludwig Wittgenstein and J.L. Austin on language games and speech acts. The result has been an ongoing reflection about how to do Constructivism properly, a search which has spanned both methods writing in IR and political science, but also philosophy and social theory on the nature of knowledge, action, and science itself. Again, I would be surprised if my experience is unique; in simple terms, while many political scientists read the Stata manual, many constructivists read philosophy.

Following Patrick Jackson, much of the reason is that Constructivism entails no specific methodological commitments.[3] Constructivism is a claim about the nature of reality: that it is made up of individuals creating the meaning of their shared world(s) through their associations. The upshot is that Constructivism is a meaningless category in terms of methods. The method/methodology distinction made by Jackson helpfully distinguishes between specific techniques, like statistical analysis, and the broader accounts we hold about how knowledge is made. Again, Constructivism is a claim about reality, not the general or specific ways in which it should be studied. It follows that there is no good *philosophical* reason that Constructivism should be understood as requiring a 'qualitative' or 'interpretive' approach at the level of method – even though we may have been taught it that way.

Why then *is* Constructivism seen as a necessarily qualitative/interpretive approach? The typical answer is that because meaning is principally conveyed through language, constructivist research tends to focus on interpreting meanings through things like speeches, interviews, strategy documents, oral histories, and memoirs. Consequently, constructivist research tends to be in the form of prose where such meanings are quoted to back up assertions that some particular actor understood a situation in a postulated way and acted accordingly, thus explaining – or allowing us to understand, if the term explanation is rejected – that action.

However, there is more to the equation of Constructivism with so-called interpretive methods than this. Part of the issue is that constructivist scholars who want to engage with other mainstream approaches are forced to speak the language of science. The rise of terms like 'process-tracing' and 'discourse analysis' can in this sense be explained by the anxiety around 'naming' what constructivist scholars do to give it some legitimacy in the eyes of proponents of more naturalistic methods.

Less commonly discussed is the extent to which the choice to become a constructivist is a reflection of the position of researchers in the field of IR, such that scholars with less social capital, and those at lower ranked institutions, are (self-)selected into constructivism. Sociologist Andrew Abbott argues that Constructivism is a weapon of the weak, 'often employed by those who lack certain kinds of knowledge resources: young people who lack senior positions, researchers lacking money to do expensive kinds of work, outsiders attacking culturally authoritative definitions of social phenomena, amateurs who lack certain kinds of technical skills'.[4]

Abbott's is an unpleasant assertion, and would need to be proven rather than asserted. But the point is that there may well be social forces that lead some junior scholars to adopt Constructivism and others to reject it. One of these, certainly, is that new researchers interested in specializing in IR often choose quickly whether to do quantitative work or react strongly against it, becoming de facto constructivists. Both theoretically and methodologically, therefore, constructivists – especially in the US academy – fight on the terrain of others. Yet rather than decry this state of affairs, constructivists should embrace it. To see why, we should turn to sociologist C. Wright Mills.

Constructivism as classic social analysis: implications for method

Mills' *The Sociological Imagination* is foundational for any trainee sociologist, but Mills has much to offer IR constructivists too.[5] The main take-homes are these: if we accept that (1) IR Constructivism is a form of what Mills terms 'classic social analysis', then (2) we can also accept that each scholar should be their own methodologist, designing methods to fit problems rather than restricting themselves to standard methods. Constructivists can and should look far and wide for techniques and methods that help them analyze the social construction of world politics.

I am not, I should stress, the first to point out the affinities between constructivism and classic social analysis. Justin Rosenberg for one has urged IR scholars to develop a fuller form of 'international imagination', a sort of 'classic social analysis'.[6] Mills traces such thinkers as Herbert Spencer, August Comte, Emile Durkheim, W.E.B. Du Bois, Karl Mannheim, Karl Marx, and Max Weber.[7] As Ruggie has shown, constructivism had its antecedents primarily in Durkheim and Weber. Tellingly, bringing Mills' list up to date would have to include Michel Foucault and Anthony Giddens – both influences on early constructivists – and Pierre Bourdieu and Charles Tilly – each influential more recently.[8]

The case for viewing Constructivism as classic-social-analysis-in-IR need not be pressed. Its usefulness is to set up the argument that constructivism understood as a space within US IR and political science for doing something different from the mainstream, this is a *positive* condition. As heirs to classic social analysis, the type of knowledge aimed at by constructivists is different from the timeless, general, abstract, and context-free knowledge aimed at by the scientistic mainstream. As Friedrich Kratochwil in particular has stressed, Constructivism is or should be *problem-driven* and attuned to the practical and not merely theoretical nature of political knowledge.[9] The consequence is that questions of method – of what counts as data or evidence – cannot be determined before research is designed. Indeed, deciding *of what something is a case* and therefore what counts as evidence is always part of the challenge.

As such, a second important implication follows. As Mills noted, 'every working social scientist has to be his [*sic*] own methodologist and his own theorist, which means only that he must be an intellectual craftsman'.[10] The constructivist should resist, therefore, adopting wholesale available methodologies or methods, and *must craft their own depending on the question at hand*. The rise of interpretivism in political science, although a welcome development in many respects, should not then be seen to exhaust the types of methods a constructivist can deploy.[11]

Where, it might be asked, does this leave methods training? For Mills, the type of course graduate students take in regression analysis, for example, has value: 'Every craftsman can of course learn something from over-all attempts to codify methods.'[12] But he cautions that what such courses convey is 'often not much more than a general kind of awareness. That is why "crash programs" are not likely to help social science develop'. Mills further warns 'The Methodologist' to '[a]void the fetishism of method and technique'.[13] In the rest of the chapter, therefore, I offer an overview of – rather than a crash course in, and still less a fetishization of – one technique constructivists might find useful in their research: MCA.

Constructivism and computational social methods: the example of Multiple Correspondence Analysis

The foregoing reflection suggests that constructivists are not limited to a narrow form of research design centred on interpretive methods; this is not to say that interpretive methods are inappropriate, only that Constructivism is a broader tent than commonly recognized. To give an illustration from my own work, my previous research on UK foreign policy since 1945 aimed to shift constructivism away from the notion of *identity* towards the more relational and processual concept of *social role*.[14] I showed how in repeated interactions between Britain and the US and France, Britain was constructed as a *residual great power*. While I believe the account is persuasive, I came to realize it lacks a sense of the wider world of UK foreign policy – the people who have done the constructing of Britain's role in the world: diplomats, policy-makers, think tank analysts, even IR scholars.[15] Who are they? How do they come to speak authoritatively in the struggle over UK foreign policy? In the wake of Brexit, these questions have become even more pertinent, as a domestic discourse of national sovereignty pushed aside a long-standing and powerful discourse of great power politics. In designing a new study, I am exploring ways to pose and answer these questions. MCA is one way.

The following introduction does not aim to show the reader how to use MCA, but rather to introduce MCA's logic, show how it meshes with a constructivist perspective, and ideally convince readers to investigate further.[16]

Multiple Correspondence Analysis: the basics

MCA is a form of geometric data analysis (GDA) that can be used to construct a graphical representation of a social space – like the worlds of foreign policy-making noted earlier, or the social space of diplomats at the UN recently analyzed by Pouliot.[17] A statistical technique, MCA takes a dataset of information about a set of actors, whether individuals or groups, and uncovers the latent relationships between them. A dataset analyzed might include biographical data such as age, race, gender, nationality, education level, earnings, and level of experience, if the actor is an individual, to organizational data on the size and make-up of organizations. Data might also cover subjective information, such as personal tastes, habits, opinions, or policy preferences, again both for individuals and groups. Using either R or a software package called SPAD, MCA then measures the degree of social distance between the actors in the dataset on the basis of their information. Two female individuals aged 30 with the same level of education and earnings have a social distance of 0 from one another; two individuals of varying characteristics on these variables move further towards a social distance of 1. By measuring such distance across multiple variables, MCA identifies the principal axes of difference and thus uncovers the structure of a social space. MCA then displays that structure graphically as an aide to interpretation.

There are two tendencies when it comes to the use of graphical and mathematical techniques we need to be wary of if we are to understand what is distinct and therefore powerful about MCA, and its affinities with Constructivism. The first tendency is to assume that statistics covers only methods that search for probability – in other words, that the aim in statistical social science is to sample from a population to find the probability that two variables – the independent and the dependent – are sufficiently correlated to make causal claims about the relationship. For the creators of GDA, the equation of statistics with probability is incorrect, as statistics is not in the first instance about the discovery of probable relationships in a dataset but actual ones. The conflation of statistics and probability still characterizes much of the academic study of statistics, but proponents of a geometric approach, which originated in France, have developed a set of approaches that have a different – geometric – conception of statistics that now occupy a clear niche within the broader statistics field.[18]

Here long-standing debates in the philosophy of social science raise their heads: disagreements about the nature of explanation and causal inference, and the difference between explanation and interpretation. These debates need not be rehashed here. What must be highlighted is the distinction between regression analysis and geometric analysis. Whereas standard regression analysis is quantitative (that is, the data analyzed is in numerical form), driven by standard matrix procedures (for example multiplication, division), and sampling oriented, the logic underpinning MCA is geometric or spatial, formal (that is, mathematical procedures are guided by the geometric structures uncovered, not the other way around), and description-oriented.[19] These distinctions underpin the affinities between GDA and constructivism.

First, like Constructivism, MCA is inductive rather than deductive. Is it the case, for example, that the social space of foreign policy-making is split into two, between insiders with certain characteristics, and outsiders with other characteristics? Or is it divided in different ways? Which views and dispositions of foreign policy-makers actually go together? Whereas standard statistics tries to uncover the likelihood of, say, social class, age, or party affiliation correlating with hawkishness, from a sample to a population – which is always tricky in the small-N world of international politics, leading to often meaningless inferences – MCA describes the actual relations between individuals in a population, in terms of what makes them similar and different.

The second, related, tendency to be wary of, is to read graphs as a mode of data *presentation*, rather than as an aide to the *interpretation* of data. In simple terms, we tend to assume that information presented in a graph can be read off by looking at where points fall along the graph's axes, where axes measure certain things – age, GDP, percentage of a given measure, and so on. By contrast, the graphs produced by MCA are a guide to interpretation, and the points' location on an axis does not correspond to absolute values of anything. The axes on MCA graphs represent the amount of the overall variance in a dataset that is captured by two axes of differentiation. What the axes represent, then, is *precisely what has to be interpreted*.

An MCA has two principal graphical outputs: a so-called 'cloud of individuals', which plots on a series of 2D spaces each individual in a dataset in terms of their relations to every other individual; and a 'cloud of categories', which plots the variables put into the dataset, such as education level – for example PhD – or age. The axes on Figure 5.1 thus do not do what axes on graphs typically do – display known characteristics, such as age, wealth, sex, plotted against the individuals with those characteristics. Rather, the axes represent the amount of difference captured by the social distinction the MCA has uncovered – the content of Figure 5.1 does not concern us for now. The aim, when reading an MCA graph, then, is to begin the interpretive process by which social divisions can be understood. In simple terms, how is a given social universe structured?

A further advantage of MCA is the recovery of individuals. A common criticism of variable-based methods is that the individuals in the data are replaced by numbers.[20] Again, the logic of regression analysis is quantitative ('Numbers are the basic ingredients and end products of procedures.')[21] In MCA, the dots represent real individuals in the dataset. While not reducing the power of regression analysis, it provides further evidence of the potential of MCA and its elective affinity with meaning-centred approaches like Constructivism.

Through the use of computing power, MCA can handle larger amounts of data than the historically minded social scientist. Each datum of information provided in a dataset represents a dimension of difference among the individuals. The 2D images an MCA produces then are representations of n-dimensional space. Again, far more complex than the historically minded social scientist can handle.

Using MCA: the field of American political consultants

Figure 5.1 comes from a study conducted by political sociologist Daniel Laurison on the field of political consultants in the United States.[22] Typically graphed separately, Laurison combines the clouds of individuals and categories. The small dots represent the actual individuals in Laurison's dataset. The squares represent the average position in a social space of the individuals with characteristics covered by that category – job type, position, level of experience. The space is constructed using the measures of positions or capitals, not tastes or dispositions.

While the MCA plots a potentially large n-dimensional space, when it comes to interpreting an MCA the task is to analyze only those axes of difference identified that capture the most variance in the dataset. The amount of the total variance or 'inertia' is captured by the percentage figure next to each axis. Laurison retains two principal axes of division within this group of individuals for his analysis of what social divides structure political consulting in the US. The operative question, then, is what the axes mean.

Figure 5.1: A standard cloud of individuals and categories (from Laurison 2014)

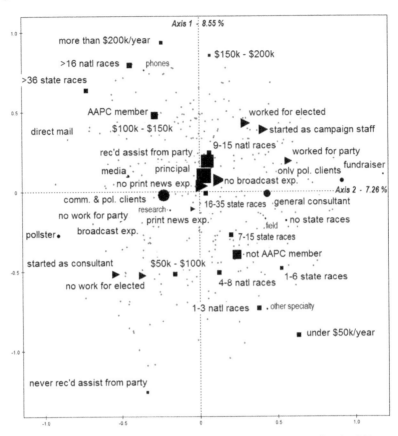

Source: Republished with permission of Peter Lang, from Michael Grenfell and Frédéric Lebaron, 2014, *Bourdieu and Data Analysis: Methodological Principles and Practice*, permission conveyed through Copyright Clearance Center, Inc.

As Laurison notes, the 'first axis [the vertical axis] describes an opposition between the dominant and the dominated or aspiring political consultants'.[23] Those at the top of Figure 5.1 are the dominant members of the field. They 'earn the most money, work on the most races, and possess key field-specific capitals in the form of experience working for elected officials, having started out working on campaigns, and membership in the American Association of Political Consultants (AAPC)'.[24] The bottom of the graph is essentially the negative position: consultants located there earn less money, have participated in fewer races, and hold lower positions within consulting firms. This axis is thus a combination of economic and social capital in the world of US political consultants. The second, horizontal, axis 'describes an opposition between the more politically-oriented consultants, on the right, and more commercially-oriented ones on the left'.[25]

Recall that the main aim of GDA is to explore the locations of individuals in social space – what traits they share, and crucially also what differentiates them. Here Laurison's finding that there are broadly two groups: the experienced, wealthy, and primarily politically oriented, on the one hand, and the less experienced, lower earners and corporate-focused on the other, is interesting in and of itself. But the construction of the space also facilitates investigation of other aspects of the field, in particular the identification of what differences structure that social space (see Figure 5.2).

In Figure 5.2, Laurison highlights the average position of all the people who answered certain questions in a particular way: how old were you when you went into consulting? Do you have a PhD? What is your age and gender? Inclusion of these so-called *structuring factors* – which were not used in the MCA to construct the social space of political consultants – is both an aide to interpretation, and represents a move in MCA towards more familiar understandings of causal analysis, as the method uncovers statistically significant relationships between these attributes and the way the social space is structured.

From Laurison's analysis, it is clear that there are obvious relationships between the age at which an individual enters the social sphere of political consulting and where they end up, and that women and people of colour are generally located in the dominated – that is, less powerful segments – of the field. By further 'projecting' into the social space constructed by MCA the responses of political consultants on questions of the ethics of consulting, Laurison also shows that the most powerful members of the field are most likely to view as acceptable some of the more morally circumspect polling techniques.

Some of Laurison's other findings are less expected, however. Laurison shows for example that education does not ensure success in the world of political consulting. In fact, having a PhD is a marker of dilettantism: real commitment to the cause means having been in the game since college – of course, easier for those of independent means and pre-existing political connections. This finding highlights the power of MCA: common sense might suggest that in a technical field like political consulting holding a high credential like a PhD would translate into higher earnings, which turns out not to be the case.

Like standard statistics, MCA – and GDA generally – is advancing in sophistication and analytical power. It is an ever-moving target. To name one example, MCA can be profitably combined with cluster analysis.[26] This allows for the further analysis of sub-clouds produced by the MCA, which can address questions of the degree of separation between sub-clouds and the homogeneity or heterogeneity of parts of social spheres, again with the aim of aiding inductive interpretation.

Figure 5.2: Structuring factors and the field of US political consultants (from Laurison 2014)

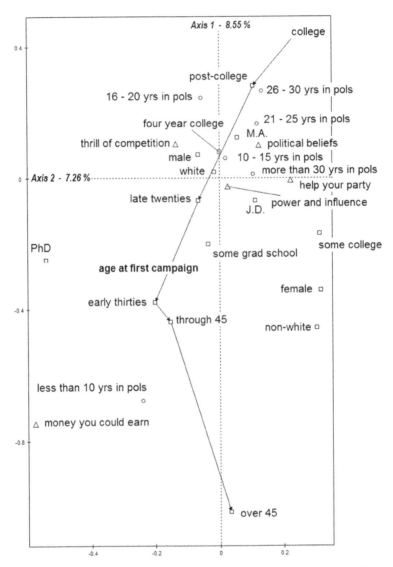

Source: Republished with permission of Peter Lang, from Michael Grenfell and Frédéric Lebaron, 2014, *Bourdieu and Data Analysis: Methodological Principles and Practice*, permission conveyed through Copyright Clearance Center, Inc.

Deploying computational social relational methods

The final task is to give a sense of the steps involved in using MCA and the challenges it poses. Although specific to MCA, similar practical issues will arise in relation to other computational social relations methods. Best known outside of statistics as 'Pierre Bourdieu's method' – the French sociologist saw the affinities between MCA and his own theoretical perspective, deploying it in his *Distinction* – MCA brings with it a set of biases about the value of Bourdieu's corpus, as well as the implication that MCA means adopting a Bourdieusian approach.[27] Only a minimum theoretical commitment is required for using MCA, however: namely agreement with Bourdieu and other classical social analysts, notably Weber, who see society as separated into relatively autonomous social spheres in which the construction of reality occurs.

For Bourdieu and Weber, spheres like the cultural and economic are conceptualized as *social fields* and *value spheres* respectively. Other examples include sociologists Neil Fligstein and Doug McAdam's own field theory,[28] or Andrew Abbott's employment of the concept of social *ecologies*.[29] In other words, using MCA implies only a willingness to move beyond the traditional state-centric approach in order to identify the social spheres that drive foreign policy behaviour. These spheres might be limited to the government, as with the bureaucratic politics model of foreign policy-making, but often an issue area extends beyond the state, into civil society and transnational relations.[30]

MCA is thus useful if a deeper account of the social construction of policy is the aim, which brings into the foreground the institutions, organizations, and individuals involved. Note: If no struggle is taking place, MCA is not needed – the analyst can simply read off from the participants their rationales, interests, or motivations, as fits with the analyst's theoretical commitments. In most settings of interest to a social constructivist, however, social struggle will be taking place. From the outset of the research design process, then, there is an assumption that certain social realms have separated themselves off sufficiently to be understood as something like a field. Beyond that, however, the scholar should make as few assumptions as possible about how a given space is constructed: its size, who is or is not a participant, the forms of power that decide who wins and who loses, the perspectives of any participants, and the relationship between the site of struggle and other institutionalized settings such as the governmental bureaucracy. The aim of MCA is to answer these questions inductively.

An MCA could be run on institutional- and individual-level data. The collection of data follows a simple rule of thumb which separates information on the positions of the participants and their dispositions. The reason for this, in field theory terms, is that the structure of social space should be constructed either out of the forms of social capital participants hold, or information on the types of individuals that are involved and their dispositions or tastes. Constructing the social space out of both types of data would not only mix up different forms of information, but it would also make it difficult to use the structure to uncover relationships between positions and dispositions. The orthodox approach is to let MCA construct the space from disposition variables by designating them 'active variables'. This allows the analysis of positions as supplementary variables.

Much work using MCA uses survey data from individuals. IR scholars have a traditional handicap in this regard, however, as interviewing elites is often difficult and costly, and few sources pre-existing datasets exist. One solution is to engage in what is termed 'prosopographic research', which focuses on the biographical characteristics of individuals. Prosopography can be done either by interviewing or by accessing varied sources such as memoirs, biographies, obituaries, and résumés contained on personal and organizational websites. As much information – both positional and dispositional – is collected as possible, with the aim of enabling the MCA to uncover the latent relationships in the dataset.

Summary: what does MCA get us?

The start-up costs to using methods like MCA are considerable. There are few shortcuts to in-depth training, ongoing self-education, and significant time spent in trial and error. Since it is unlikely that any time soon doctoral methods training will automatically include methods like MCA, like they do regression analysis using Stata, interested students will have to attend one of a few specialized courses – which are far from free. Such practical issues are in addition to the standard problems of data collection.

Another set of obstacles will be persuading interlocutors from both sides of the methods divide. Constructivists can be the harshest critics of other constructivists' work. They may misrecognize MCA and similar techniques as incompatible with Constructivism, perhaps deploying the problematic terms 'quantitative' and 'positivist', despite the aforementioned arguments about their inappropriateness. On the other side, the typical and often wrong-headed objections raised against constructivist work by non-constructivists – generalizability, unclear causation, and so on – will continue to be raised against work using MCA.

The reader persuaded to take on the task of engaging computational social science methods has their work cut out for them. Why then should students convinced of Constructivism's value bother? One reason, tied primarily to the norms and incentives structure of the US academy, is that MCA represents a particular *tactic* for younger scholars who hope to work within the American academy as constructivists – whether they self-consciously adopt that label or not. To that extent, it should be supported by all constructivists – whatever their career stage – because it represents a viable strategy for continuing the constructivist research programme in US IR by getting jobs for young constructivists.

The tactic of MCA responds to an important element of hiring decisions in US social science departments, namely the issue of whether an applicant has developed some methodological prowess through their graduate studies, as evidenced by having engaged in a significant new data collection exercise. Colloquially, this is the answer to the question, what did the applicant *do*? Reading books, newspapers, memoirs, and speeches, when faced with that question, look less impressive than developing a new dataset with the universe of cases of X, Y, or Z.

Readers will bristle at this statement, and they are right to do so. Why is large-N or formalized rational choice work so respected when it may be a very problematic way of understanding international politics, as decades of constructivist and critical research has shown.[31] Why should constructivists *have to* be the ones to change?

The answer is that the norms and incentive structures of US political science cannot be ignored and for younger scholars have to be negotiated.[32] The alternative is to leave the academy, leave the US in search of work, or move on to lower prestige tracks. MCA, I suggest, is one way for high prestige-oriented younger scholars to try to have their critical/constructivist cake and eat the US political science department job too.

Another – and more important reason – is that adopting MCA, or other computational methods like topic modelling and network analysis, is not in the last analysis only a matter of professional tactics. Adopting MCA is not a concession to the quantitative side, not a cynical move. Using methods MCA means taking a wager that traditional constructivist methods of discursive analysis might – in fact – missing some of the crucial unobservable social structures affecting outcomes in international politics. A best-case scenario of the use of MCA is that axes of social opposition common sense would not suggest will be identified, meaning less intuitive accounts can be developed. In the worst case, MCA merely confirms divisions that might be expected from the outset.

Conclusion

If this chapter has been successful, it has done two things: first, if it has persuaded the reader that Constructivism is the IR heir to what C. Wright Mills terms 'classic social analysis', a core feature of which is to design methods that fit research problems, rather than vice versa. Constructivists are not only free but in some sense required to look far and wide for the most appropriate methods in their work from this perspective. Constructivists certainly should not adopt a method because it is what constructivists are 'supposed' to do.

Second, the chapter will have achieved its purpose if it has piqued some readers' interest in the potential of new computational methods consistent with Constructivism's core philosophical premises. The chapter has outlined MCA as one such method, but it will have been just as successful if the reader decides to investigate other methods like Network Analysis, Latent Class Analysis or Qualitative Data Analysis. Again, for many constructivists, it may not be deemed feasible or necessary to learn such methods. But it is appropriate on philosophical grounds and should not be prevented by disciplinary norms.

6

Politics, Ethics, and Knowledge in the New Constructivism

Introduction

The following two chapters address two lingering questions from this book's exploration into the New Constructivism in IR theory. First, what is the New Constructivism's politics or ethics? Put differently, should Constructivism operate in a political, normative, or ethical register? If so how? If not, why not? Second, and relatedly, the chapter asks what form of knowledge Constructivism offers. Suspended between the positivist mainstream and various modes of critical and post-positivist theory, what type of knowledge – *exactly* – does the New Constructivism represent? How can the knowledge the New Constructivism offers be justified as comparable or even superior to alternatives, both mainstream and critical?

Scholars like Jason Ralph, Martin Weber, Silviya Lechner, and Mervyn Frost have recently posited the question of Constructivism's stance vis-à-vis politics and ethics. Together, these scholars, and others, have argued that practice-relationalism, and the pragmatist dispositions much of it builds upon not only assist the New Constructivism in offering thicker accounts of the social construction of world politics vis-à-vis Old Constructivism, but also allow constructivists to interrogate the ethical content of norms and culture in ways previously downplayed.[1] Armed with pragmatism and practice-relationalism, it is suggested, the New Constructivism can bridge the gap between the 'is' and the 'ought' in world politics.

In this chapter, I assess their arguments, and others who seek to place ethics and Constructivism into dialogue. I argue that the New Constructivism struggles – without different degrees of success – to move beyond a core tension from the Old Constructivism when it comes to the issue of ethics and normativity. In many ways, a problem with Old Constructivism was not the lack of norms and normativity, but an over-abundance, which led many realists and rationalists to characterize Constructivism as a 'soft' approach based on norms and taboos, rather than the 'hard' matter of power and interests. The Old Constructivism was normative by definition, and scholarly disposition. But at the same time, a critical engagement with ethics and politics was absent, as Old Constructivists sought to keep the approach within the modernist project of a social science of IR, remaining true to Max Weber's plea for a fact-value distinction in theorizing. Can the New Constructivism generate a real *via media*, and should it?

I do not seek to settle these debates. Such tensions will continue to shape the New Constructivism and neither can be, nor should be, avoided. Various 'posts' – post-structuralism, post-positivism, and postmodernism – are in Constructivism's philosophical background, and their critical, political, and ethical consequences need to be addressed head-on. As Laura Sjoberg and Samuel Barkin note, moreover, there are no *necessary* philosophical commitments that follow from claims of the political world's socially constructed nature – there is, in short, no reason one cannot be a conservative constructivist.[2] But as Martin Weber and Richard Price both argue, such a conviction is difficult to encapsulate in the same scholar-citizen, since 'the historicist underpinnings of constructivism would seem to make its proponents hard-pressed to maintain a strong view of its alleged neutrality, given the premise that all theories as cultural artifacts embody a perspective from somewhere and for something, as put famously by [Robert] Cox'.[3] Unsurprisingly, therefore, IR scholars – constructivists included – are frequently liberals or Leftists, many wearing their progressive creed on their sleeves.

I put forward an understanding of the New Constructivist as having pluralist ethical commitments that follow from carefully tracing the social and historical origins of contemporary problems in world politics. Rather than diagnose specific solutions to be applied, like theoretical knowledge is supposed to do in common understandings, this chapter sets up what follows in Chapter 7, where I explore the form of knowledge the New Constructivists aim for via an engagement with the ongoing debate over history and historical knowing in IR.

The first section poses the question of constructivist ethics, outlining Price's challenge to the Old Constructivism, before exploring two literatures that have responded – respectively, via the role of mutual recognition in world politics, and via the notion of a pragmatist constructivist ethics. The chapter then addresses the question from the angle of politics, and Constructivism's relationship to critical theory, including post-colonialist and feminist theorizing. The second half of the chapter switches tack to the relationship between historical knowing and the form of knowledge offered by the New Constructivism, which – I believe – offers one way the New Constructivism can have its ethically and politically sensitive social scientific cake and eat it too.

The question of Constructivist ethics

What are the New Constructivism's ethical and normative commitments? Can and should Constructivism operate in an ethical register? If so, what exactly does that look like? If not, what should the relationship be between the 'is' and the 'ought'? Questions like these went unasked in constructivist circles for the first decade and half or so of Constructivism's time in IR. They were not posed in large part because the answer seemed self-evident. As Kathryn Sikkink later explained, 'When I started working on human rights in the late 1980s, the choice of topic alone was a sufficiently normative signal that I felt obliged to spend the rest of my time demonstrating that I was being rigorous in my theory and method.'[4] The first empirical generation of constructivists felt it largely unnecessary to delve deeper into the relationship of the new approach to matters of ethics. Again, Constructivism arose in response to a conservative mainstream debate over the fundamental nature of the international system, baked into which was a serious pessimism over any sort of system change – I hasten to avoid here the terms 'progressive' or 'positive' change. Constructivism was a breath of optimistic fresh air. If the structure of the international system was not solely a reflection of anarchy, as structural liberals and realists held, but was filled with norms and legal expectations, then change was possible. The Old Constructivism was seemingly normative from the get-go.

Sikkink's confession encapsulates the built-in assumptions, incentives, and biases of the US political science profession, and the American academy more broadly, as the social space within which Constructivism emerged. As noted earlier, just as important as what Constructivism has done in IR is *what has been done to it*, within the various professional contexts in which it appears. US political science strives for scientific objectivity, following fads and fashions as to what 'science' means – from systems thinking in the 1960s and 1970s, through various strands of rational choice theory, game theory, and statistical modelling, to the more recent predominance of experiment-based methods. Constructivists seeking to engage the mainstream, like Sikkink, have had to respond to these trends, with deep empirical knowledge of topics of interest to the US state – including the American military – an important source of disciplinary capital.[5]

Those scholars that explored Constructivism's place in US political science consequently downplayed the approach's ethical and political implications. Constructivism, famously, was to be a *via media*, a middle road to be taken by scholars hoping to avoid the 'dangerous liaisons' promised by critical and normative theories.[6] The early statements of Emanuel Adler, Ted Hopf, Jeff Checkel, and Alexander Wendt are crucial here, as explored in Chapter 1 – especially the latter's attempt to defend a 'rump materialism' to the international system.[7] David Dessler's defence of Constructivism 'within a positive social science' is less often cited than Adler's in particular, but is a useful reference. Dessler made the case that Constructivism sat squarely within positivist social science since it offered 'particularizing' positivist explanations, in contrast to the covering-law 'generalizing' explanations more commonly linked to positivism.[8] Remaining on ontological, rather than epistemological terrain, and expanding rather than challenging the main norms of positivist political science thus promised for constructivists like Sikkink the twin advantages of avoiding ethics and politics while highlighting the empirical pay-off of their investigations into little-studied areas of international politics, such as human rights.

Moral possibilities in world politics

Although a central voice in early empirical Constructivism, Richard Price quickly came to question Constructivism's silence on the normativity of norms. As he urged in an influential article published in 2008, the next stage of Constructivism was to go beyond chronicling the empirical effect of norms, to evaluate normative change and norm-governed behaviour. Constructivism, Price noted, 'demonstrates the possibilities of progressive moral change in world politics such as the movements to end slavery and apartheid, the rise of human rights norms, humanitarian intervention, and the effects of humanitarian norms of warfare to name a few'.[9] It was natural therefore that Constructivism should also have something to say about the 'what to do' question. However, 'for the most part this literature has not offered its normative defenses of particular changes as being in fact good – such positions are often not explicitly articulated let alone rigorously defended'.[10] Price thus laid down the gauntlet, pointing out 'explicit engagement with the relation between the "is" and the "ought" as an important next stage of the constructivist agenda, and of IR debate more generally'.[11]

Price suggested the potential of combining, or folding in, normative assessments derived from approaches like communitarianism and cosmopolitanism to constructivist accounts of what is empirically possible in concrete situations in global politics. Through such a 'division-of-labour' approach, constructivists could, according to Price, empirically show that non-instrumentally rational state behaviour is still rational, only in pursuit of other, normative ends; highlight hypocrisy on the road to norm compliance; describe the constitutive as well as regulative effects of norms; identify forms of co-optation and complicity in the formation and maintenance of normative orders; and finally defend the role of power to Constructivism in the form of normative persuasion, as Neta Crawford in particular showed.[12] Together, Price demonstrated, IR constructivists were in a unique position to identify alternative possibilities and the potential for progressive change, leaving analysis of what to do in any concrete case to decision-makers or normative IR theories.

Price's challenge struck a nerve, stimulating an ongoing debate featuring a variety of reactions and rejections of his framing of the problem of constructivist ethics, including a book-length treatment. For Tony Erskine, 'A self-sufficient "constructivist ethics", or one that relies on constructivism's empirical strengths and interpretive methodology to arrive at a critical, evaluative criterion for making moral judgments, is an intriguing possibility.'[13] But few, Erskine included, have accepted Price's middle-of-the-road solution to *Via Media* Constructivism's ethical commitments.

Jack Snyder and Leslie Vinjamuri, for example, mounted a strong defence of explanatory constructivist norms research. In their opinion, the 'project of some prominent constructivists, to show how the "ought" becomes the "is", risks the conflation of "is" and "ought" in ways that can confound its explanatory and prescriptive analyses, diminishing the potential of a social constructivist approach to develop a theory of moral progress'.[14] In the place of a division-of-labour approach, they argue instead for 'a strong "firewall" between the explanatory and the prescriptive role of norms in constructivist analysis'.[15] A firewall, rather than a bridge, would allow constructivist explanatory norms research to show, for example, that decision-makers might need to adopt flexible pragmatic approaches to secure the best outcome, which may include tough ethical trade-offs, like dealing with the perpetrators of violations in relation to compliance with human rights.

For Nicholas Rengger, Price's division of labour – much less Snyder and Vinjamuri's 'firewall' – is an appropriate basis for a constructivist engagement with ethics. In ways echoed later on, for Rengger, at issue in the relationship between Constructivism and ethics is the relationship between theory and practice. Normative theory is what Rengger calls 'world-disclosing' rather than, or at least as much as, 'action-co-ordinating'.[16] Rengger revisits Kant's 'Theory and Practice', where Kant suggests that 'As long as we can say that human progress is possible in principle (i.e. is not obviously impossible) … we have a moral duty to work for it.'[17] The issue, then, is less the creation of criteria to prove moral progress, but to be sure of its possibility, and the role of Constructivist theorizing in recognizing such a possibility.

While a useful intervention, Rengger's still leaves open the question of *how* a properly ethical Constructivism would, practically, assist in identifying the possibility for moral progress. Two more recent literatures in different ways address the same basic question. The first draws on philosopher and social theorist Axel Honneth on the moral grammar of recognition in IR and international law, falling more on the 'isses' side of the equation. A second outlines a pragmatist constructivist ethic, displaying a clearer normative – 'oughts' – bent.

Identity and recognition in international politics

Much of the conversation about the ethics of Old Constructivism has highlighted its limited engagement with the normativity of norms, beyond empirical descriptions of norms they shape and shove state behaviour in world politics. A second literature, however, moves the focus to the way in which the first empirical wave of Constructivism also played down normativity when it came to how identity works in international politics. This approach catalogues the normative power enmeshed in the struggle between states and other international actors for recognition as having certain statuses in international politics, notably – although not exclusively – sovereign statehood.[18]

The literature draws principally on the work of social theorist Axel Honneth. Honneth revisits Hegel on the nature of mutual recognition, seeking to place recognition back at the forefront of social and political theory. For Honneth, cursory readings of Hegel's reflections on the master-slave dialectic as the basis for claims about the relational constructedness of social identities misses his earlier, deeper, discussions of the centrality of mutual recognition to the development of the subject. Put simply, it is not merely the existence of entwined entities – like the master and the slave – but the *recognition* of relational subjectivities that is at issue, that is, neither slave nor master can enjoy their subjectivity within a relation that denies one the very ability to be subject. Furthermore, for Hegel, as for Hobbes, a fundamental struggle lies at the heart of human nature, but it is a struggle over recognition as a full human subject within society, not merely a struggle over material resources.

The work in IR flowing from Honneth's insights spans the line between the more descriptive and more normative. In the former domain, Thomas Lindemann and Richard Ned Lebow deploy the concept of mutual recognition to analyze the role of recognition struggles in the causes of international conflict. As they demonstrate, the search for status is as much, if not more, the trigger for inter- and intra-state violence as is the struggle over material power. Given widespread concern over the rise of peer challengers to the United States and new regional powers even staunch realists like William Wohlforth have accepted that status-seeking is a major cause of conflict in world politics. Elsewhere Mikulas Fabry and Christian Reus-Smit explore the power vested in international organizations and the international community in their ability to bestow recognition on states and other actors, or to prevent such recognition. For Reus-Smit, the struggle to have individual human rights recognized at the supranational level has been an important driver of international society.[19]

The acknowledgement of recognition's importance in international political life raises the question of the relationship between 'isses' and 'oughts' in world politics in ways that prompt a much-needed dialogue between the disciplines of IR and international law. As Jens Bartelson explains, does recognition bring into existence something new or merely 'recognize' something that already exists? IR brings to the table, Bartelson explains, empirical proof that sovereignty is performative, a product of speech acts that create sovereign statehood, an artefact of declaration and constitution.

Contra Hegel, and Honneth, however, Bartelson lacks confidence that recognition, *necessarily*, represents a mechanism for transforming international orders in a more peaceable manner. While 'further inquiry into the theory and practice of recognition can provide important insights into the nature of this relationship', for Bartelson, we should 'regard recognition less as a solution to a series of problems – such as the formation, reproduction, and transformation of the international system – but more of a problem integral to that system'.[20] This means going beyond, or before Hegel, to ask how – intellectually and practically – the problem of recognition appeared to the philosopher:

> Doing this would compel us to inquire into the prehistory of the international system, and describe how the anterior conditions of recognition first evolved, until it became possible to look back upon and reconstruct the historical trajectory of that system precisely as an outcome of practices of recognition. In that regard, we would perhaps be better off no longer taking Hegel as our starting point, but rather – and true to the spirit of his work – as the point of emergence from which it becomes possible to narrate the past, present, and possible future of the international system in terms of recognition.[21]

In just such a vein, Xavier Mathieu has powerfully demonstrated the limits of a racialized Eurocentric international society to extend sovereign recognition to non-Europeans, and the power of exclusionary practices and discourses as a means of constructing sovereignty within Europe itself.[22] Returning to 16th-century French politics, including colonial encounters in the Americas, Mathieu chronicles the mutual construction of sovereignty internally with the depiction of colonized peoples as 'savages' and uncivilized, and hence unsuitable for recognition. In line with the New Constructivism, state identity – here sovereignty – for Mathieu, is less an essence than a performance, one undertaken using shifting discursive tools to draw a line between 'us' – and different possible 'us's' – and 'them's'. In the context of religious turmoil after the accession of Protestant Henry of Navarre in 1584, Catholic opponents deployed images of savagery to describe conditions in France, while the monarchy deployed civilization and sovereignty as the solution to the state of nature caused by its opponent's attempts to de-stabilize the succession and the country.

The case for pragmatist constructivist ethics

Jason Ralph develops perhaps the most direct and forceful response to Price's initial challenge by outlining what he terms a *pragmatist constructivist ethics*.[23] For Price, Constructivism 'had to engage normative theory to distinguish good progressive norms from bad regressive ones and – on the other side of the same coin – normative theory had to engage constructivism to distinguish idealism from utopianism'.[24] In Erskine's words, Ralph faces Price's challenge head-on – to find within Constructivism 'the evaluative criteria necessary to judge and to champion alternatives to the moral norms they currently map'.[25]

Ralph notes that: 'While certain strands of constructivism might share with critical theory a normative commitment to bettering the human condition, constructivism generally focuses on the "is" without commenting on the "ought".'[26] In terms of particular responses to, for example, human rights abuses, 'constructivists would not advocate a particular to atrocity, nor would they judge state practice. That task is left to normative theorists'.[27] While Ralph affirms that Constructivism cannot provide a real outsider position – a 'view from nowhere' that can offer some ultimate judgement about right and wrong conduct – what does follow from Constructivism's ontology is the ability to assess norms in use. How well, constructivist research can answer, do certain norms help solves real lived social problems?[28]

Ralph follows a number of scholars who plumb the affinities between pragmatism and Constructivism – a core feature of the practice turn, as Chapter 2 explored.[29] For Ralph, norms are not fixed rules – structures that make or force actors to obey their dictates. Rather, they can be likened to *hypotheses*, tools that can be pragmatically useful, or not, depending on circumstance and context. 'The constructivist emphasis on the historical and social contingency of a norm does not rule out ethical standpoints but suggests instead a "pragmatic" ethic,' Ralph explains. 'Rather than fix one's ethics to moral foundations, this approach finds value in social norms that ameliorate lived social problems, which normatively "anchors" constructivists to useful beliefs without fixing them to positions their epistemologies cannot sustain.'

Viewing norms – and other normative rules in world politics – as pragmatic hypotheses that *may* be useful in practical decision-making scenarios, but need not be, connects the empirical and normative aspects of constructivist research more integrally than Price's division of labour. 'From this perspective', Ralph explains, 'constructivists can trace the "life cycle" of a norm (e.g., the Responsibility to Protect), examine the effects of its various "meanings in use," and assess the usefulness of those meanings'. To illustrate:

> pragmatic constructivists can commit to R2P as a useful hypothesis for addressing the social problems that were exposed by the

1990s experiences in Rwanda, Bosnia, and Kosovo. ... Pragmatic constructivists can interrogate how various meanings of R2P are used discursively to make possible certain practices. And, building on that, they can normatively critique those practices by 'weighing' the consequences of those meanings for threatened populations and international society both at a particular moment and in the future.[30]

A pragmatist constructivist ethics thus collapses the division of labour between theory and practice that Erskine identified in Price's challenge, and others have situated in a 'wider modernist frame of knowing' of which mainstream Constructivism forms part. As Matthew Hoffman explores, the power of pragmatism lies with its faith in the scientific enterprise, wherein knowledge is tested against lived experience, answerable to the community of practice.[31] 'What pragmatism adds is an argument that the normativity of those ideas rests not on a priori foundational knowledge, nor on communitarian claims to authenticity.'[32] Instead, in pragmatism, 'ideas can claim normative authority by proving their worth as "intellectual" instruments to be tested and confirmed – and altered – through consequences effected upon them'.[33] As Ralph explains, 'Pragmatism emphasizes the "ought" that is immanent within the "is" of the specific situation (what Dewey called "ends in view") ahead of the "ought" that exists in the abstract.'[34]

Ralph thus makes clear that the relationship between the 'is' and the 'ought' is ultimately more a practical than theoretical issue, making the connection in so doing between pragmatism and the recovery of 'prudence' and practical wisdom, recovered by a variety of scholars in IR over the last decade or so. For Ralph, echoing the discussion of Hegel and mutual recognition discussed in the previous section:

> pragmatic constructivism shares with classical realism an emphasis on practical judgment and the ability to decide well by weighing the consequences of acting according to a norm. However ... classical pragmatism emphasizes these skills in the context of a commitment to ameliorating the shared social problem, which means those skills should be put to use in ways that are other- as well as self-regarding."[35]

Constructivism and critical theory: or, does the New Constructivism have a politics?

Price's challenge to constructivists to engage normative theory and develop the normative implications of the approach mirrors another debate in Constructivist circles over the relationship between the 'is' and the 'ought'. That second debate is about the points of connection or disconnect between Constructivism and critical theory. To what extent can, or should, the New

Constructivism be seen as a contributor to the critical project in the broader social sciences?

As noted throughout, a common way of characterizing Constructivism is as an approach born at the intersection of critical and positivist theorizing – again, a *via media*. I have emphasized the need to be more accurate in associating such a position with the first empirical constructivist works – rather than the early theoretical treatises of Onuf and Kratochwil especially – and the secondary works that sought to introduce the new approach to the wider field. Here the seemingly off-hand comment by Alexander Wendt and Ron Jepperson that Constructivism is not a form of 'exotic, presumably Parisian social theory' is telling; Old Constructivism was developed by scholars inclined neither by disposition nor professional incentives to situate their work within the critical theoretic tradition. The opting-out of the constructivist project of self-described 'posties' of various stripes, like Richard Ashley, V. Spike Peterson, and Michael Shapiro, together with the opting-in of scholars like Jeffrey Checkel and Kathryn Sikkink who had earlier been engaged in the 'ideas' debate in political science, provided further evidence for Old Constructivism's via media credentials.[36]

For Martin Weber, Old Constructivism's separation from critical theoretical approaches to the study of global politics is both philosophically misguided and theoretically counter-productive. Mainstream Constructivism, in Weber's view, was co-opted by essentially behavioural account norms and identities in world politics. Weber focuses his critique of the separation of Constructivism and critical theory on Frankfurt School Critical Theory, acknowledging that while Frankfurt School theory is not all there is to critical approaches, it has a useful centrepiece in its '*critique of domination*'.[37] Citing Honneth, Weber notes that the:

> 'grammar' of social and political power is *always* normatively inflected; the struggles of those excluded, denigrated, or subjected to abuse have normative substance, therefore, not least because they constitute a challenge to prevailing normative arrangements, which either justify and legitimize the experienced offenses, or render them invisible and beyond reproach, reform, or resistance.[38]

Mainstream norms constructivists 'attempt to settle the question of validity essentially empirically: norm entrepreneurs propose and promote a norm, its gradual acceptance leads to normative change, and subsequent to norm internalization by a sufficient number of significant actors, settles the norm as valid, proven by its capacity to circumscribe normalcy and deviancy'.[39] Critical theory, by contrast, operates with the tension between the facticity and validity of norms as a constitutive problem ... and demonstrates in detail that the unconditionality of validity claims is an indispensable component of norm contestation. For Weber, the implications are clear: constructivists should get on board with the critical project, or get out of the way.

Before challenging constructivists to engage fully with the ethical, Richard Price – together with Christian Reus-Smit – had already questioned the emerging common sense on where Constructivism sat vis-à-vis critical theory. For Price and Reus-Smit, liaisons between Constructivism and critical theory were less 'dangerous' than mutually productive.[40] For Price in particular, however, it was critical theorists who should 'get out of the way' if an approach was not reciprocated. As he explained, critical theorists should get on board with the constructivist project in order to overcome the tension in critical theory that renders critique never-ending. From a critical theoretic perspective:

> every new social formation [i]s yet another form of domination, because relations of domination can never be eliminated. ... To the extent that this is so leaves critical theorists so inclined in something of a bind. Since there must be some hidden agenda of complicity with domination in every political practice – for power is everywhere – it is almost as if progressive developments that have been achieved, because they have become reality, cannot be praised, because their very realization then resets the ethical bar of possibility.[41]

In an extended and forceful engagement, Laura Sjoberg and J. Samuel Barkin explore 'IR's last synthesis' – that, in Weber's view at least, between critical theory and Constructivism. Sjoberg and Barkin refute Weber's claim that Constructivism and critical theory are typically seen as separate. From their American, rather than European, perspective, Constructivism and critical theory are often seen as one and the same – the disciplinary Other to rationalism and realism, previously realism and liberalism. For them, the 'Constructivism-Critical Theory synthesis is the "direct descendent" of the "radical paradigmatic other",' exemplified most starkly in Robert Keohane's analysis of two approaches to institutions, the 'rationalist' and the 'reflexive', meaning a broad swathe of work from Marxism to post-structuralism.[42]

While Weber, and Price and Reus-Smit, each advocate forms of a Constructivism-critical theory synthesis, for Sjoberg and Barkin, such a synthesis is a bad idea. They take issue both with arguments that position Constructivism and critical theory as intellectual siblings and those that see the two as separate. In much the same way practice theorists have sought to separate themselves from the Constructivism they rebel against, for them, calls for a synthesis are *professional* moves or tactics within the field of IR, not in the first instance intellectual arguments about the affinities between Constructivism and critical theory. They insist, most starkly, that one can be a conservative constructivist. Constructivism and critical theory should be thought of 'as *different* tools that *can* but sometimes *should not* be deployed for common analytical causes'.[43] No *necessary* politics follow.

Both sets of debates – over Constructivism's politics and ethics – thus arrive at a similar point: the question of the relationship between theory and practice, between analysis and decision. Both Weber and Sjoberg and Barkin are correct in important ways: the latter rightly point out that it is possible to be a constructivist by professional inclination and, say, a committed White nationalist. But the former is also right in insisting that, practically, such a position would be difficult to embody in someone committed to denaturalizing social formations and the discursive and performative power of which they are constituted.

The institution of gender and colonial hierarchies represent two prominent examples of such social formations, raising the question of the New Constructivism's relationship to feminist theory and post-colonial scholarship. In similar ways its position vis-à-vis critical theorizing, is the New Constructivism an impediment or complement to these approaches? In this section, I defend contingent connections between the New Constructivism and feminist and post-colonial theories, highlighting their synergies, while rejecting the disciplinary move to coin a 'New Constructivist feminism' or 'New Constructivist post-colonialism'. As Sjoberg and Barkin note, the emphasis should be on empirical insight not disciplinary gate-keeping.

Post-colonialism and Constructivism

As a distinctly liberal internationalist research agenda, early empirical Constructivism was noticeably not post-colonial.[44] Amitav Acharya soon questioned the universality of the norms researchers catalogued, while Charlotte Epstein later asked, was constructivist norms research truly about socialization or infantilization? For many non-Western states liberal norms upheld stigmatized identities that sustained hierarchies placing Western states at the top of the international 'pecking order'. Ayşe Zarakol, in the case of Turkey, and Iver Neumann, using the case of Russia, reflected a New Constructivist research agenda more attuned to questioning dominant Western norms and hence the analytical concerns of post-colonial theorists.[45]

In an insightful evaluation, Robbie Shilliam explores the synergies between Constructivism and post-colonialism, making a strong case for a fuller engagement with the 'lay' voices of colonialized subjects as the route to a more post-colonial Constructivism. Connecting the present discussion of the New Constructivism's politics and ethics with Chapter 4's concerns with 'internal' and 'external' modes of explanation, Shilliam argues that the Old Constructivism's commitment to explanation, rather than understanding within practices or communities, renders the approach unable to recognize lay knowledge as 'real' knowledge. In terms later echoed by Lechner and Frost, Shilliam highlights 'a fundamental tension … between the strong hermeneutical proposition that all social beings interpret their reality and the epistemological qualification that some social beings can provide a superior interpretation of the reality of others'.[46] As Shilliam rightly notes, built into constructivists' scientific pretensions is the view that 'one group in an interpretive relationship has the power to de-value the explanations of another group's experiences' and 'that social scientists can arrive at a superior interpretation of reality to those who directly inhabit it'.[47]

Constructivists, to illustrate, have used the case of the abolition of slavery as an example of progressive social change based on normative argumentation. 'Constructivists in IR overwhelmingly represent the abolitionist project as a decisive and progressive transformation in international norms from practices of legal bondage to human rights.'[48] Such is not the view of many descendants of slaves, such as the Rastafari – the subject of Shilliam's intervention – who interpret themselves still enslaved in Babylon, their label for the West. Can constructivists fully incorporate – *recognize* – the Rastafari's understanding of their history in their accounts?

To answer this question, Shilliam begins by following sociologist John Holmwood,[49] who argues that social scientists should, in practice, aim for a form of scholarly 'symmetry' rather than hierarchy in the knowledge they produce. Scientific knowledge, from a symmetrical perspective, is not better than lay knowledge, but *different* and equally useful. Aiming for symmetry in this way offers a powerful response to the problem Shilliam identifies precisely in that it does not suggest an intellectual solution, but instead a disposition, a way to live within a tension that remains central to the scientific episteme. As expanded upon in the following sections, the aim of symmetry recognizes that knowledge and political action – or the application of different knowledges – are not coterminous. One can thus believe one's scientific knowledge – broadly defined – is valuable, without, in practice, silencing those it seeks to understand. Such a disposition, it would seem, is particularly important in international politics.

In this vein, Shilliam draws on the work of Jamaican scholar and writer Erna Brodber.[50] Trained as a sociologist, Brodber rejects the field's essentializing tendencies, such as, for example, its tendency to see 'slaves' rather than 'enslaved persons',[51] and its problematic relationship to history – a critique that extends to IR and political science, as elaborated upon later. For Brodber, a more appropriate starting point is one that denaturalizes – 'provincializes' in Dipesh Chakrabarty's words – the Western episteme, its fetishization of abstraction and of writing the 'I' out of research. Deploying fiction to explore lay knowledge in her native Jamaica, Brodber shows the power of being more inventive in assessing the lives and experiences of former enslaved populations.

For Shilliam, consequently, 'Brodber's hermeneutic knowledge, rather than relativist, is an ethically, politically, and intellectually engaged attempt to decolonize the knowledge of the lifeworlds of descendants of enslaved Africans.'[52] Brodber's work has 'general implications' not despite but because 'its pursuit might produce different affects and effects on participants/ interlocutors who engage with the project from different positionalities'.[53] In relation to history, once again, 'Broder has written of her own village, Woodside ... [and] maintains that the core audience are the inhabitants of the village whom she wishes to link to their enslaved ancestors so as to give present generations "a sense that we are part of a process from slavery to freedom and [that] will lend us a greater measure of responsibility".'[54] The 'is' and the 'ought', at least as potentialities, are brought to the surface in light of the radical situatedness in time and space of Brodber's writing.

Gender in the New Constructivism

A final disciplinary encounter raising the question of the relationship between the 'is' and the 'ought' for constructivists is that between Constructivism and feminist theory. As mentioned earlier, the question raised is whether Constructivism is a complement or obstacle to feminism. Does one need to 'get out of the way' of the other for its full potential? If so, which of the two approaches needs to depart stage left?

The question is not newly posed to the New Constructivism. It was first raised by Birgit Locher and Elisabeth Prügl, who entered a stalling debate in the 1990s over how feminism could engage other IR theories by suggesting that feminism and Constructivism offered particular potential for cross-fertilization.[55] Specifically, Locher and Prügl argued that 'constructivism shares ontological grounds with feminism and thus provides a unique window of opportunity for understanding'.[56] The Constructivist and feminist ontology is one of becoming – the world is not made up what *is*, but one that is in the process of emerging. Gender and gendered hierarchies are not natural or essential features of social life and international politics, but social constructions. Locher and Prügl thus disavow the then-emerging positioning of Constructivism as a new middle ground, noting the power of the post-positivist critique for both approaches.[57] The challenge is, rather, 'to stake out a middle ground that does not obliterate feminism and to search for a terrain that enables engagement on equal terms'.[58] To that extent, 'constructivist ontology forms a "planet" on which both feminists and (at least some) IR theorists could live and talk'.[59] Outlining the mutual complementarities contained within 'feminist constructivism', Locher and Prügl highlight how Social Constructivism provides feminism a theory of agency – as a product of structures – while feminism provides Constructivism a theory of power in the form of power-laded, masculinized hierarchies.

While some work within Constructivism has centred gender, notably that of Ann Towns on the spread of norms of gender equity in national legislatures around the world,[60] and Laura Sjoberg's gendered structural theory of the international system,[61] feminism and the Old Constructivism remained largely separate, with many potential complementarities unexplored. Not surprisingly, therefore, Catriona Standfield has recently – and convincingly – argued that gender is also missing from the practice turn.[62] Of course, from the perspective taken in this book, the debate is a replay of Locher and Prügl's discussion. Nonetheless, Standfield's represents an insightful example of work situated at the intersection of gender and practice-relationalism, and hence a fully gendered New Constructivism.

Standfield's argument foregrounds the role of women in diplomacy, a choice of subject right at the heart of the New Constructivism, showing how women in their various roles as decision-makers, diplomatic wives, embassy staff, and activists, are central rather than peripheral to diplomatic practice. Also drawing on the sociology of Pierre Bourdieu – but on writing under-represented in the current practice theory literature – Bourdieu, Standfield demonstrates, was a theorist of power sensitive to its gendered nature, notably in his 2001 *Masculine Domination*.[63] Gender is like class for Bourdieu – gender does not constitute itself a 'field', but like class operates within fields, as both a form of capital, or lack thereof – and hence in part structures one's position in a field – and as a key part of individual's embodied *habitus*.[64]

Standfield shows how diplomatic practice reproduces patriarchal structures. Returning to previous social formations of diplomacy, Standfield traces the way gender did not recede as a feature of diplomacy after the rise of the nation-state rendered marriage diplomacy obsolete, but morphed into new gendering processes. Diplomacy became on the one hand a more masculine field, occupied by bourgeois males 'sent to lie for their country'. The role of women did not diminish, however, as the foreign embassy became a 'family', with key tasks for women to create and run the family.[65] As a practice based on the feminized attributes of patience, listening, compromise, and social grace, a tension emerged within diplomatic practice between the masculine and feminine.

The feminist and New Constructivist contributions are clear. The tale is sensitive to gender in ways distinctly practice-relational, anti-essentialist, historical, and at least, potentially, reflexive. To illustrate the latter, Felix Rösch has recently highlighted the role of affect in world politics – typically underplayed in IR theory, with its emphasis on either material or symbolic power – by exploring the implications of shifting modes of dancing in diplomatic circles during the Congress of Vienna.[66]

Once again, Rösch frames his argument as seeking to bring affect to the practice turn to help practice approaches with change. In my view, this framing is unneeded. Change should be the default view of international politics; *continuity* is what needs to be explained. Rösch surely makes the move to answer the 'generalizability question'; why should anyone care about dancing at the Congress of Vienna? In my view, the case is strong enough. Rösch shows quite clearly that diplomatic practice is not all at the conference table – as anyone who has ever been to an academic conference knows. The bar, or dancefloor in Rösch's case, is key. The dancefloor and salon, not the negotiating table, was where diplomats tried out – *performed* – communities of diplomatic practice and, indeed, new geopolitical orders during the crucial transformations of the 19th century.

Dancing was ubiquitous at the Congress, Rösch tells us. In fact, 'so much dancing was going on that the Austrian field marshal Charles-Joseph de Ligne feared that the Congress would end up in failure, allegedly complaining … "the Congress dances, but it does not progress".'[67] Dancing was not merely a pastime for diplomats in Vienna. Rather, through dance different 'world political imaginations could be enacted'.[68] Moving beyond the polonaise, the quintessential diplomatic dance in the period, Rösch analyzes the effects of the shift from the minuet to the waltz as the second major dance at Vienna.

As a well-structured dance, involving multiple changes of partners, and little physical contact, the minuet offered little chance for affect to play a key role in diplomatic interaction. Instead, the minuet, Rösch insists, upheld a particular aristocratic European order. '[S]trictly defined movements reassured dancers of their position within a European aristocratic order, while at the same time it embodied collective public approval of this order and its members.'[69] Dancing helped to establish with the Concert of Europe a relatively long-lasting system of conflict resolution. 'Like the polonaise, the minuet could fulfill this purpose, as it allowed dancers and observers to communicate directly.'[70] In a community of diplomatic practice grounded in a broader European aristocracy, 'the minuet was affectively powerful, dancing was a central practice to sustain a transboundary aristocratic network that existed until the nineteenth century. Epitomized by the minuet, the nobility's nocturnal encounters helped to form affective communities'.[71]

But the times, as they are wont to be, were a-changing, with the rise of liberalism and the consolidation of bourgeois capitalism, with concomitant changes in the community of diplomatic practice. The diplomatic effects were felt – performed – at Vienna, in an important way, through the rise of the Waltz, as a freer, more expressive – *affective* – dance. As Rösch explains, 'While the rise of the Waltz created barriers between dancers, it helped to reduce them between classes, as dancing skills became more important than the performers' status … the aim [being] to outperform other couples on Viennese dance floors.'[72] Alongside the shift from official occasions to informal dancing in salons and private residences, a key shift was underway, bringing into question who represented the nation-state: the aristocratic elite, via the minuet, or the virtuoso bourgeois nation-state official, via the waltz? This change was crucial. 'Prior to the French Revolution, such intimate encounters were unthinkable. While this physical contact did not erase class differences, it still normalized contact between them and Congress participants started to develop emotional allegiance to the states they represented and no longer to a European cosmopolitan elite.'[73]

The connection between Rösch's historical investigations and Standfield's account of the gendered practices of diplomacy is strong. Is dancing not an essentially feminine pursuit? Not so, sociologist Maxine Craig has shown.[74] Prior to the 1960s men danced in public spaces as much, if not more so, than women. But in *Sorry, I Don't Dance*, Craig shows how sub-urbanization, the rise of homophobia, and the fragmentation of musical cultures, pushed White men in particular away from dancing. Returning to diplomacy, as Ann Towns describes, therefore, contemporary diplomacy is gendered in complex, often cross-cutting ways, that reflect its genesis and history. Taken-for-granted as a masculinized arena, it is actually not so, as 'soft-talking' feminine. 'Masculinised representations of the diplomat and diplomacy are contested and unstable,' Towns tells us. 'In US foreign policy discussions, diplomacy is regularly differentiated from the military as a "soft" and putatively "feminine" alternative to military force. US policymakers and political pundits seeking to sideline diplomatic solutions recurrently disparage diplomacy through feminisation, drawing connections between denigrated allegedly "feminine" traits and diplomacy and diplomats.'[75]

Conclusion

The stories Rösch, Towns, and others recount demonstrate the power of recovering the – historical – formation of diplomacy, as one important arena of international politics. The imperative is not just to push along the practice turn – like the Constructivist before it – but rediscovering things lost about world politics. In the following chapter, then, I approach the question of the relationship between Constructivism and practice another way, via the question of Constructivism's relationship to history and historical knowing, hopefully tying together the discussion hereto by painting the New Constructivism as what I, and others, would term a *phronetic social science*. Constructivist theory offers a different type of knowledge to the mainstream, a type that can be termed a *phronetic*, a form fostering 'prudence' and prudential political action. Here the reflexive move of the New Constructivism is key – the practical relationship of the scholar to the world. IR scholarship is part of the world, but separate to varying degrees. As such, all scholarship is *potentially* political, but not necessarily so. The relationship between theory and practice is practical, not theoretical, in the first instance.

Acknowledgements

This chapter further develops an argument made in David M. McCourt, Constructivism and Computational Social-Relational Methods, in Brent J. Steele and Harry Gould, eds. 2019, *Tactical Constructivism, Method, and International Relations*, Routledge, pp 1–13. Reproduced with permission of The Licensor through PLSclear.

The New Constructivism as a Phronetic Social Science

'Political understanding ... teaches us that the political order is articulated through its history; *the past weighs on the present, shaping alternatives and pressing with a force of its own.*' Sheldon Wolin[1]

'It is one thing to *perfect* an instrument; it is another to ensure that it is *put to use* in just, virtuous, or even rationally discriminating ways.' Stephen Toulmin[2]

'The underlying issue is not, as it is usually professed to be, the status of truth and objectivity in first order activities such as politics ... but rather the cognitive, and practical, authority, of metapractical claims.' John Gunnell[3]

In this book's Introduction, I emphasized historical sensitivity as a core feature of the New Constructivism. But what *is* history in IR? Why does the New Constructivism have to be historical?

Beginning in around 2000, a historical 'turn'[4] witnessed a proliferation of reflections on the relationship between IR and history, including assessment of IR's historical consciousness,[5] advocation for a dialogue with international historians,[6] lobbying against interpretive closure of historical events,[7] rediscovery of the historical orientation of the English School,[8] identification of narrative as an inherent feature of explanation,[9] reconsideration of the assumptions about temporality embedded in different IR theories,[10] examination of IR's historiography,[11] and outlining of the potential of historical sociology,[12] to name just a few contributions. Most of the debate's participants supported a historical turn. As Duncan Bell observes, 'History, in its various manifestations, plays an essential, constitutive, role in shaping the present'; in mainstream IR, he goes on, 'this has often been disregarded'.[13]

The debate continues.[14] But what, precisely, is at stake in the debate over history in IR? And why does it matter for the New Constructivism? What is at stake is the type of knowledge IR scholars should aim for, and, indeed, the relationship between theory and practice in international affairs. The surge in interest in history is part of the wider movement in the social sciences away from neo-positivism[15] – a broad philosophical position on human knowledge and its creation that views deductive analysis of empirical sense-data as the sure road to *scientific* truth, as opposed to knowledge gained through argumentation, belief, faith, and so on, often equated with non-science.[16] Neo-positivism's dominance has clear disciplinary consequences, one of which is to relegate history to a storehouse of context-free 'data' and historical knowledge to second-class status. Also at issue is the type of knowledge IR scholars should produce – specifically, de-contextualized and general versus particular and contextual – and what role historical analysis should play in its creation.

To that end, I trace a strand of thought in social theory associated with the work of Hans Georg Gadamer[17] that has sought to restore to a position of prominence within the social sciences a different type of knowledge than the objective generalizable knowledge associated with neo-positivism – namely practical knowledge, or what Aristotle called *phronēsis*. *Phronēsis* is defined in explicit contrast to *technē*, or technical know-how, and *epistēmē*, scientifically reproducible knowledge. The importance of history for *phronēsis* lies with how *phronēsis* is oriented towards acting in a just, wise, and appropriate manner in specific contexts, unlike the generalizable and context-free knowledge directed towards instrumental action that is the domain of neo-positivism. *Phronēsis* is therefore better nurtured by historical approaches to the study of politics than the technical and scientific modes utilized by neo-positivists.

However, taking this line of thought to its logical conclusion highlights the fact that the stakes of the historical turn ultimately lie beyond IR and the social sciences, in the relationship between academic knowledge production and the world of politics. This is because there is no final *philosophical* answer to the question of what type of knowledge IR scholars should aim for, and therefore no answer based on whether disciplinary IR is adequately 'historical'. The theory-practice relationship is as much a *practical* as a *theoretical* or *philosophical* problem, being primarily concerned with how expertise is created in a given polity, the dominant forms of knowledge, and the structural links between knowledge producers and political power. These issues can – and indeed should – be studied by the social sciences, but cannot in the end be resolved by them.

In the remainder of this section, I first explore the historical horizons of neo-positivism, which also characterizes much mainstream research in political science, whether or not a neo-positivist methodology is adopted explicitly. I then trace these historical horizons to a stubborn anxiety over the validity of the knowledge the social and political sciences can provide if they fully accept the implications of constructionist argumentation. I subsequently make the case that the New Constructivism should be considered a phronetic social science, 'world-disclosing' rather than problem-solving in Martin Weber's fruitful terms.

The historical poverty of neo-positivism

Dissatisfaction with the relationship between IR and H/history is at base a reaction against the impoverished conception of 'history' characteristic of neo-positivism – which still dominates IR, particularly in the US.[18] For neo-positivists, history is a repository of de-contextualized 'data' against which hypothetical propositions can be tested. For Bruce Bueno de Mesquita, 'history is primarily a laboratory by which to test both [social scientists'] claims about how variables are associated with other and their propositions about causation'.[19] Scholars have sought to correct the IR-H/history relationship, therefore, because the deficiencies of this history-as-dataset position are manifold, as are its disciplinary consequences.

The importance of neo-positivism in the historical turn has remained hidden, however, because the original target was not neo-positivism itself, but the dominance during the 1980s and early 1990s of Realism, particularly Waltzian Neorealism,[20] which has frequently been considered coterminous with 'science' and 'positivism'. The initial impetus for a turn then was a call for dialogue between historians and political scientists[21] spurred by the failure of the dominant theories to predict the end of the Cold War[22] – and in the case of neorealism even to conceive of its possibility.[23] The debate thus began over empirical and theoretical issues, like how to explain international change, with metatheoretical reflection coming only later. The real target of the turn, therefore, and the approaches with truly deficient historical sensibilities, remain those underpinned by neo-positivism.

The history-as-dataset position is not an arbitrary choice on the part of philosophically naïve neo-positivists. It follows directly from the central tenets of neo-positivism as a set of commitments drawn from the philosophy of science – imported into political science in specific historical circumstances for progressive political purposes[24] – and as a set of scholarly conventions. As Jackson has shown,[25] neo-positivism is based on two core commitments, 'mind-world dualism' and 'phenomenalism',[26] according to which the world exists independently of our minds, and the problem of knowledge creation is about finding direct experiential proof of hypothesized causal connections in it. For neo-positivists to be satisfied that they have uncovered, for instance, the causes of great power wars, requires the formation of hypotheses such as 'great power wars begin when state A feels threatened by State B', which can then be operationalized through the derivation of observable indicators of threat perception and the start of wars. These indicators are tested against data from the great power wars that have occurred hitherto, often using statistical techniques to back up assertions of the existence of correlations considered sufficiently significant to suggest causality.

Scholars working within the neo-positivist tradition would no doubt accept that they must radically oversimplify the very nature of 'history' and uniqueness of knowledge of the past in their work – just as many formal modellers acknowledge the necessary simplification of the models they create. Yet what they would also likely acknowledge is that such simplification is a necessary price to pay in order to reach adequately scientific conclusions in their research.

Nonetheless, that price is high. History is not a ready-made dataset. History is constructed through remembering certain aspects of the past while forgetting others.[27] Paraphrasing Robert Cox, like theory, history too is always *for someone* and *for some purpose*;[28] it is always bound up with present political purposes and projects.[29] Historical writing is also dependent on the availability of sources and subject to their biases, and its value is underpinned by cultural modes of remembrance that view the meaning of past events as worth remembering, which is of relatively recent origin.[30] In addition, as philosophers such as Collingwood and Oakeshott make clear,[31] what history *is* is very much the result of the practices of those who write it.

The use of history as a repository of facts for theory testing thus leads to a number of serious analytical problems for the neo-positivist: like secondary selection bias,[32] as scholars choose to back up their arguments with the work of historians who implicitly share their understanding of the events; primary selection biases and the danger historians themselves face of repeating only what they uncover in the particular archives they consult;[33] and the tendency to limit international history to the state's system after 1648,[34] and to reify a particular European experience.[35] Moreover, these problems are not easily avoided. The naturalistic methods associated with neo-positivism *creates* historical facts at the same time as they use them as data.[36] The popular 'democratic peace thesis', for example, rests on a reading of the meaning of 'democracy' *back into history*, thereby ordering the historical record in such a way as to lead to clear contemporary lessons.[37]

International Relations, the philosophy of science, and the Cartesian anxiety

If the poverty of neo-positivism's vision of history is very real, as are its disciplinary consequences, what has prevented neo-positivism's replacement with forms of political inquiry that try to overcome the problems associated with gaining adequate knowledge of the past? In short, downplaying the problems associated with history and historical knowledge in IR, and the social sciences in general, has been a way of easing what Richard Bernstein calls the 'Cartesian anxiety':[38] a sense of deep foreboding that follows from the either/or choice between ultimate objective foundations upon which competing claims to knowledge of the social and political world can be rationally judged – under the umbrella of social *science* – , and an acceptance of relativism, the view that our knowledge can only be deemed true within particular frames of reference, such as a historical context – associated with non-science.[39] What is at stake in the historical turn then is nothing less than the nature of science itself and its relationship to knowledge when it comes to the study of politics. The historical turn, therefore, must be viewed as a part of and not separable from the recent turn to the philosophy of science in IR.

The issues the turn raises are consequently numerous, as the many contributions to the 'second second great debate' suggests: these include the role of the observer in research – is the scientist objective, or is s/he an active part of the scientific process?;[40] the notion of theory and cumulative knowledge; the relation of theory to practice – what is theory and when and how should it be 'applied'?; the role played by method; the nature of truth; and the place of philosophical foundations in political science.[41] These questions have been debated at length within IR, as scholars have drawn on the philosophy of science in search of answers to them, and in so doing to widen IR's scientific imagination. It is impossible to review these contributions here.[42] Instead, I will trace one line of thought in recent social theory on these issues, one that has particular prescience in relation to history, in order to assess the light it sheds on the history and philosophy of science turns.

This line of thought begins from Richard Bernstein's interpretation of recent social theory, which he views as going 'beyond objectivism and relativism'.[43] As Bernstein notes, like the other binaries that have emerged during the debate over an historical turn, the 'objectivist/relativist' dichotomy which often frames the debate over the meaning of science in the social sciences is in fact an entirely false one, and obscures as much as it reveals.[44] Neither genuine objectivism nor pure relativism are, in fact, philosophically tenable, and are hence inappropriate means of distinguishing 'science' from 'non-science', and more useful from less useful knowledge when it comes to politics.

The indefensibility of pure objectivism is uncontroversial: the scientist is always conditioned by his or her social location. For us here this refers to his or her historical context, but an array of other social factors also have greater and lesser impacts on scientific research – including nationality, age, scientific culture, generation, and so on.[45] The inherently social bases of science and changes in scientific knowledge was then Thomas Kuhn's key insight.[46] He showed that whether in periods of revolution of scientific thought or settled periods characterized by 'normal science', all discoveries were made in relation to the work of others. The attempt to step outside of the social context of scientific research is doomed to failure. Objectivism is therefore better thought of as an *ideal*, as sociologists in particular, from Max Weber to Pierre Bourdieu, have made clear to great effect.[47]

The rejection of relativism is significantly more controversial, but relativism too is incoherent as a philosophical notion regarding the nature of truth claims. The core of relativism then is the idea that claims to truth are to be judged against the particular conceptual scheme – such as a historical era – in question, and not against some universal or transcendental standard. Relativism can take cultural, moral, or epistemological forms, and has been advocated by thinkers like Paul Feyerabend,[48] and often applied to others like Richard Rorty[49] and, crucially, Kuhn himself.[50] It is not to be equated with scepticism: the sceptic denies the possibility of knowing truth at all, while the relativist merely suggests that all truth is relative to a particular social space, cultural milieu, or historical period, and so on;[51] and should also not be equated with subjectivism, since one can be a subjectivist – and believe in the primacy of subjective personal experiences of the world – and not a relativist, and vice versa.[52]

Pure relativism of whatever form, however, is a position few if any contemporary philosophers of science defend, not least because the truth of the relativist position breaks down as soon as its claim to validity is brought into question: 'implicitly or explicitly, the relativist claims that his or her position is true, yet the "relativist also insists that since truth is relative, what is taken as true may also be false".'[53] Since it cannot be true and false at the same time, 'One cannot consistently state the case for relativism without undermining it.'[54] A pure relativist position is thus ultimately a contradiction.[55] Even Rorty, who often appears to be a prominent defender of relativism, is largely 'concerned to show that relativism is the epithet misapplied to pragmatism by [philosophical] realists'.[56]

The upshot of dissolving the objectivist/relativist binary is that the association – direct or implied – by neo-positivist scholars that non-neo-positivist IR knowledge claims are 'relativist' is not only unfounded, but intellectually pernicious. Non-neo-positivists may be more comfortable with historically and culturally bounded understanding than neo-positivists, but no one argues that when it comes to social science, 'anything goes':[57] truth claims must be backed up with evidence, even if it does not fit the neo-positivist mould, while systematic research is still undertaken, even if it falls short of neo-positivist understandings of 'rigour' and avoids questions of ultimate 'foundations'. We should therefore dismiss the association of non-objectivist knowledge with relativism and the downgrading of its prestige.

Specifically in relation to history, this task entails accepting the consequences of our inescapable embeddedness in certain historical contexts and historiographical traditions. The neo-positivist history-as-laboratory position should be replaced with a vision of social science that accepts the essentially hermeneutic aspect to all scientific work Kuhn stressed – in other words, one that recognizes the historically conditioned nature of not only world politics itself but also the concepts and methodologies IR scholars themselves use to study it. This conclusion raises, however, the fundamental issue of both the historical turn and the wider movement beyond neo-positivism in the human sciences: what *type* of knowledge is this non-neo-positivist scientific knowledge?

History, political knowledge, and phronēsis

Characterizing non-neo-positivist social science and understanding its relationship to history can begin by noting that since non-neo-positivist knowledge rejects the belief in objective timeless knowledge, and is therefore inherently tied to present political contexts, it is also by necessity *practical* in nature. As such, the links between the historical turn and the practice-relational turn in IR come into full relief. Both rest on a rejection of core aspects of neo-positivism and a reconsideration of the nature of theory and practice. Revisiting the theory-practice divide therefore sheds further light on the stakes of the historical turn.

Our common-sense understanding of the relationship between theory and practice mirrors that held by neo-positivists, and views practice as a form of action characterized by the *application* of knowledge learned from theory.[58] This follows from the neo-positivist notion of scientific knowledge: if hypotheses drawn from abstract sets of propositions are confirmed in objective, repeated, and rigorous tests, they can be assumed to hold in application. Whether that knowledge is applied is not the concern of theory itself. But this view of the theory/practice is partial: 'One of the classical functions of theory', Bernstein notes, 'was supposed to be its practical efficacy – its ability to help distinguish appearance from reality, the false from the true, and to provide an orientation for practical activity'.[59] This sounds odd to our modern ears because of the distinction we make between theory, practice, and action. Theory is supposed to provide knowledge when used in practice; again, the decision to apply it is not a function of theory. Thus, this 'modern conceptual revolution has led to a forgetfulness about the classical – especially the Aristotelian – understanding of politics and praxis', Bernstein explains.

> The discipline of politics was once conceived of not as a theoretical study of how the political system works, but as a discipline that has as

its *telos* a practical end: the leading of a good and just life in the polis. For many social scientists this conception of politics, however noble and inspiring, now seems apocryphal.[60]

What was lost in IR with the rise to disciplinary hegemony of neo-positivism certainly was the link between international theory and the *problems* of international politics;[61] the *ends* of international politics were not deemed the proper site of *theoretical* inquiry within the social science of IR. Yet, the theoretical concerns of IR scholars have mirrored international affairs closely:[62] consider the emergence of neoliberal institutionalism amid fears of US decline,[63] or the birth of Realism at the onset of the Cold War.[64] Neo-positivism's strong position then has weakened the traditionally intimate association between theory and practice as theory has moved away from practice towards the creation of knowledge 'for its own sake'.[65]

However, according to Aristotle, whom Gadamer draws on at length,[66] a narrow focus on the means of political behaviour leaves out much that should be the proper concern of the scholar of political *praxis* properly understood, namely the ends of (international) political life.[67] Following Gadamer's recovery of an Aristotelian understanding of *praxis* is therefore instructive.

In his *Ethics*, Aristotle distinguishes the intellectual virtue of *phronēsis* – usually translated as 'prudence' or 'practical wisdom' – from *epistēmē* – scientific knowledge – and *technē* – technical, skill-based knowledge. Aristotle even grants *phronēsis* a higher standing when it comes to the conduct of politics, because *phronēsis* is the type of knowledge which takes both the ends and the means of political life into account.[68] Whereas *epistēmē* is characterized by the understanding of what is universal and *is* by necessity,[69] what is able to be demonstrated as such from first principles, *phronēsis* is a form of knowledge in which no such first principles can be assumed to exist. It is concerned with what is context-dependent and particular, rather than what is abstract and universal. The *phronimos*, the one who exercises this practical wisdom, as Aristotle tells us, is he or she 'who is able to deliberate rightly about what is good and advantageous for himself; not in particular respects, e.g. what is conducive for good health, but what is conducive to *the good life generally*'.[70] Pericles was such an individual; he understood what it meant to practice good management of the state.[71]

Some illustrations help to clarify the nature of *phronēsis*, how it differs from technical knowledge, and its relationship to history. First, translated as 'prudence', *phronēsis* has made a strong reappearance in IR recently through a recovery of the early Realists like E.H. Carr and Hans Morgenthau.[72] These scholars were less interested than their Neorealist successors in formulating timeless laws to test in the laboratory of history than in nurturing prudential statecraft within a particular 'tragic' reading of human nature and history.[73] In the case of George Kennan, the need to contain Soviet influence around the world followed from a careful historical assessment of the Russian tradition of international engagement.[74] Beyond these early Realists, Macchiavelli is another key reference, with the Italian political philosopher drawing throughout *The Discourses* and *The Prince* on specific instances of Roman history as examples of prudent and imprudent political action.[75]

Second, practical knowledge is often invoked as characteristic of jurisprudence. Both Gadamer and Friedrich Kratochwil note how judges use good judgement within the particular context of the case to reach their conclusions.[76] In so doing, they 'do' history, and in different ways: they emplot the case within a narrative to discern its rights and wrongs; they turn to history in the form of relevant legal precedents; and they deliberate between the particular need for justice and the universal aspects of setting precedents. Again, the issue of what history *is* is less important than what the historical sensibility *does* when thinking about what can be gleaned from the past about present political concerns. Beyond jurisprudence, in politics too it is often practical understanding of the particular situation faced that is the type of knowledge required.[77] Abstract theoretical understanding, of political institutions, for example, is far from irrelevant, but it must reside alongside a nuanced appreciation of the rules of the political game and the ability to judge correctly the best course of action.

The relevance of the distinction between *phronēsis* and *epistēmē* in relation to the 'Second Great Debate' in IR needs little elaboration. A recovery of *phronēsis* has the potential to provide a unifying theme to the calls for a turn to the historical by giving name to the type of knowledge of international affairs that many scholars working in the 'classical approach'[78] have sought from a return to history: it is by necessity contextualized, playing off particular and universal, or idiographic and nomothetic forms of understanding, in the search for good political judgement, while not identical to the work of historians themselves. Not surprisingly, for these reasons *phronēsis* has gained interest from non-neo-positivist social scientists beyond IR.[79]

What does phronetic IR look like? A brief comparison of two recent publications is instructive. Charles Kupchan[80] and William Wohlforth[81] both take up the issue of the effects of shifts in the global balance of power on great power politics. But while Kupchan's contribution can be considered to foster *phronēsis*, Wohlforth's seeks more traditional neo-positivist style knowledge claims, and therefore remains within the realm of *epistēmē/technē*.

Kupchan asks how once bitter enemies can become friends. Developing an abstract description of the stages through which zones of war within international anarchies become zones of stable peace within international societies, he assesses the suitability of that framework in a wide variety of narrative case studies, from Anglo-American rapprochement during the late 19th century to the rise and demise of Senegambian confederation during the

1980s.[82] What is important here is not Kupchan's argument itself, but rather that his aim is not to 'test' his framework in a historical dataset, but to develop a greater understanding of the processes of pacification among potential rivals through historical study. Crucially, Kupchan is able to conclude with a clear ethical finding relevant to the contemporary post-American world: 'Stable peace *is* possible. Enemies *do* become friends. When international societies form, they succeed in transforming the world and enabling states to escape geopolitical rivalries that have so darkened the course of history.'[83]

Wohlforth, by contrast, asks whether unipolarity promotes peace among the major powers, and whether the return of multipolarity will increase the likelihood of war. Drawing on the social psychology of status conflict, he argues: 'Unipolarity … generates far fewer incentives than either bipolarity or multipolarity for direct great power positional competition over states.'[84] His concern then is to develop and test hypotheses concerning the workings of causal mechanisms of when actors are likely to seek to translate material power into social status, again with implied relevance for the post-American world. But this time the findings have less apparent ethical-moral implications: because 'status competition is more likely to plague relations between leading states whose portfolios of capabilities are not only close but also mismatched',[85] Wohlforth concludes that: 'With two or more plausible claimants to primacy, positional competition and the potential for major power war could once again form the backdrop of world politics.'[86]

This necessarily brief comparison shows that what is important in the recovery of *phronēsis* is not the truth or otherwise of scientific work: both Kupchan and Wohlforth are doing social science and my aim is not to critique the work of either. Rather, it is to show that there are nonetheless different *types* of knowledge of international politics equally scientific approaches can aim to produce: one more contextual and directly relevant to current problems, the other abstract and with less clear lessons for policy. Importantly, they use history in different ways, one (Kupchan) more adequately historical than the other (Wohlforth).

This contrast leads on to a final critical point concerning Aristotle's three intellectual virtues and the urgent need to recover *phronēsis* for our present predicament. For Gadamer, the contrast Aristotle draws between *phronēsis* and *epistēmē* is not as important as the one he makes between *phronēsis* and *technē*, or between practical and technical forms of knowledge. Gadamer views *technē* as a far more frightening threat to modern life than he does science.[87]

In order to understand Aristotle's conception of *technē* and why Gadamer views it as a threat it is important to clarify the distinction Aristotle draws between production or making (*poiēsis*) and acting. Both *phronēsis* and *technē* are practical virtues, but whereas *phronēsis* is invoked in the particular sense of activity directed towards living well in the *polis*, *technē* is a productive state concerned with bringing an object into being, be it a building or a piece of artwork. Acting and making are therefore different in crucial respects: *phronēsis* is fundamentally about acting upon the existing world, not bringing a new world into being. Yet, since it is abstract in nature, technical knowledge does not deliberate over ends in the same way as *phronēsis*. As the type of knowledge of one skilled in a particular craft, moreover, *technē* can be learned and forgotten; as the exercise of proper moral and practical judgement, *phronēsis* cannot. What concerns Gadamer then is that: 'Where there is techne, we must learn it and then we are able to find the right means.'[88] The existence of this type of knowledge portends his greatest fear: the domination of Method over contextualized, practical, and moral knowledge, which inheres only in acting well as the situation requires. Under the dominance of *technē*, politics becomes little more than 'social mechanics'.

Before concluding that this means that we must reject neo-positivist work in its entirety, however, it is important to heed Bernstein's warning that 'despite contemporary transformations of the meaning and scope of the practical and the technical, the point that we need to be aware of is this: the danger for contemporary *praxis* is not *technē*, but domination (*herrschaft*)'.[89] It just so happens that the contemporary threat most clearly comes from *technē*. In other words, it would be as worrying if *phronēsis* dominated political life. The rejection of the claim that *technē* and *epistēmē* are the only valuable forms of knowledge within social science does not then do away entirely with the importance of abstract knowledge in either politics or other spheres of life. The use of scientific polling data in modern democratic elections is the most obvious case here. Information gained through polling is a crucial part of political strategizing, from the actual content of policies, to the rhetoric used to sell it. Politics is replete with examples of abstract and generalizable data underpinning practical political judgements. But acknowledging with Stephen Toulmin that: 'It is one thing to *perfect* an instrument; it is another to ensure that it is *put to use* in just, virtuous, or even rationally discriminating ways,'[90] the important question raised is not whether scientific and technical knowledge can be useful, but how, when, and for whom? How is a judicious balance between objective knowledge and the use of more contextual political judgement in decision-making to be struck?

In light of these remarks, what is at stake in the historical turn is nothing less than the need for a (re)turn to the practical aspects of political action, and to *phronēsis* as a form of knowledge that places historical understanding central. If the quality of our political and moral life is not to suffer, and if we are to come together to address the very great problems of our age, we must defend within a concern for *phronēsis*, together with a space for the exercise of phronetic IR that is its prerequisite.

Conclusion: on the limits of phronetic IR

While this recovery of *phronēsis* reaffirms the importance of practical knowledge alongside scientific and technical forms of understanding of politics, the aforementioned quote also reveals that *phronēsis* as a tacit form of 'knowing-how' is situated within practical contexts that are structurally separate from the spheres within which theoretical or scientific knowledge is created: be it in academia, think tanks, the media, and so on. It thereby betrays the fact that at the same time as the historical turn leads us to question the strict *conceptual* separation of theory and practice, the logical end point of the historical turn in IR at the recovery of the notion of *phronēsis* also highlights another aspect of the theory/practice binary: namely the *structural* relationship between practical political knowledge in international affairs and knowledge about international politics generated outside the political world. Crucially, this issue ultimately takes the turn beyond IR itself, whether adequately historical or not.

The existence of a structural divide between the world of politics and the world in which politics is studied has bedevilled discussions of post-positivist social science because most philosophers and social scientists have sought theoretical rather than practical answers to the problems it poses.[91] Gadamer himself is vague on the proper place of technical knowledge in his philosophical hermeneutics. As Bernstein notes:

> There is a fundamental unresolved ambiguity in Gadamer's philosophy concerning the social sciences. ... Sometimes ... he writes as though they are like underdeveloped natural sciences, implying that it is essential for us to realize their 'limited relevance', because they never tell us how they are to be applied. *Phronēsis* is always required to apply the results of the social sciences. But at other times he writes as if all the social sciences, when properly understood, are to be assimilated to practical philosophy as a model of the human sciences.[92]

Although Gadamer is explicit in his warning against method: 'The search for method (... as a set of permanent, unambiguous rules) needs to be abandoned,'[93] he does not discriminate when and where technical knowledge is appropriate from when it is not. Bernstein's assessment that '*technē* without *phronēsis* is blind, while *phronēsis* without *technē* is empty',[94] is similarly vague. These authors are therefore left with the open question of how best to position technical skill alongside practical wisdom, knowing only that neither must entirely dominate the other.

What has been frequently overlooked, however, is that the question of the relationship between theory and practice in this sense is not a theoretical one that can be given a final answer through philosophical reflection. Rather, the relationship between the different forms of knowledge Aristotle delineates is a practical issue of how what John Gunnell refers to as 'first order' and 'second order' discourses are arranged with respect to each other.[95]

For Gunnell, science and politics are first-order discourses that construct their objects of inquiry through their practices. Science makes intelligible the natural world for humans through its classificatory schemes and analytical categorizations. In a similar way, political practices also construct the world through the enacting of political activities. By contrast, philosophy and social science are second-order discourses – that is, they are discursive spaces and sets of institutionalized practices that exist by dint of reflecting upon first-order practices such as science and politics. To make this distinction clearer, it can be pointed out that conceiving of politics without higher order discussions of it, such political science, is difficult, but far from impossible; conceiving of the existence of political science without politics as a practice is, by contrast, unthinkable.

The upshot of Gunnell's important argument is that the relationship between the knowledge produced by the disciplines, such as IR, and the social world they study, here international politics, is essentially a *sociological* and not a *philosophical* one. It revolves around the particular practical relationship between the sites within which knowledge of politics is produced – the academy, think tanks, the media, and so on – and the political world. It rests on issues like how separate the academy is to the political sphere. What function do academics fulfil: are they critical voices or rationalizers of the governmental line? Are scholars listened to or ignored? And which disciplines hold the most weight in political argumentation?[96] Crucially, such relationships vary dramatically over time and between countries. Recently, for example, in a number of Western countries the rise of think tanks with more direct links to politics than the academy has been a noted feature of the political landscape, changing the bases within which legitimate knowledge for politics and about politics is produced.[97]

The proper relationship between theoretical and practical knowledge, therefore, cannot be answered in any final way simply by moving from one discipline to another, or from one order of discourse to another, in search of ultimate foundations for knowledge claims. As Gunnell notes, 'Only when the metatheoretical search for transcontextual certainty is abandoned and the problem of relativism is dissolved can social science confront in an authentic manner the issue of its cognitive and practical relationship to politics.'[98]

The links between the Ivory Tower and politics are particularly relevant in relation to the historical turn because scholars have so frequently sought a solution to IR's historical poverty through the metatheoretical work of both various philosophers and methodologists of history. Indeed, my own investigation began in a similar way, drawing on the work of philosophers Bernstein and Gadamer in particular, which proves the strength of the tendency within post-positivist IR to look to philosophy in particular for some ultimate grounding for knowledge, even when the response from philosophy has been to give up on ultimate grounds. Yet, acknowledging that the theory and practice divide in IR and social science is a practical and not merely philosophical issue shows that the relevant issues opened up by the historical turn ultimately cannot be resolved *by* or *within* IR, nor by social science, History, or philosophy.

The foregoing comments are not meant to suggest that an IR more sensitive to history and the historicity of international politics is not to be desired, rather that there are few reasons to believe that less 'scientistic' and more humanist approaches to the study of IR automatically bring with them a more efficacious and just global political order. That depends on the actions of decision-makers themselves, and secondarily on the practical relationships between the creators of knowledge and its consumers in the political world. There are thus opposite dangers to those posed by *technē* and *epistēmē*: namely elitism and an unwarranted faith in the faithful use of history in political judgement. Once again, 'history' must not be equated with ethics, since there is nothing at all to stop historical examples being used for evil ends.

Indeed, Aristotle believed that since the *activity* of politics was not to be conflated with knowledge generated from the *study* of political science, young men were unfit to study political science since prudence cannot be taught but only be acquired over time.[99] This aspect of practical wisdom has led philosophers themselves to criticize *phronēsis* for its inherent elitism,[100] and the reliance on the good judgement of individuals can also be criticized as leaving the door open to populism. There is almost a belief that only some individuals will be naturally predisposed to display the kind of practical wisdom appropriate for politics, while others will not – that there is in any generation the *phronimos*, like Pericles. For Clausewitz too there seems to be implicit in his argument concerning history and theory a particular sociology of the relationship between the production of knowledge and its contextualized use in the training of the general, particular to the elite German military academies of his era. This forgets that the meaning of history is not fixed, and that history is not the same as ethics; there is no guarantee that deep immersion in history will naturally lead to practical wisdom.

However, before we are tempted to return to the sure world of *technē* and *epistēmē*, it is important to recall that there is no *philosophical* answer to the dangers of elitism that emerge with a call to *phronēsis*, just as there is no sure defence against the dominance of any form of technical knowledge or the misuse of historical understanding. While unable to achieve that task alone, an IR more sympathetic to non-neo-positivist and hence more historically sensitive modes of political analysis can surely help more than an IR that seeks only technical political knowledge.

Conclusion: The Space of Constructivism

This book should not have needed to be written. As I explore further in this concluding chapter, the seeds of the practice and relational turns, the New Constructivism's reflexivity, and its advancement of a phronetic social science, are written all over Constructivism's DNA. Many of the early constructivist theoretical treatises placed heavy emphasis on practices and relations – in some cases, more than norms, identity, and culture – as well as reflexivity and history.

For Wendt, for example, what was 'so striking about neorealism was its total neglect of the explanatory role of state *practice*'.[1] Noting how 'social structures are not carried around in people's heads but in their practice', he stressed that international anarchy was not sufficient to lead to a self-help world.[2] If IR displayed self-help characteristics, this was due to process.[3] For Wendt: 'Security dilemmas are not acts of God; they are effects of practice.'[4] For Onuf, similarly, constructivism at base was an approach that studied how people in practice create the rules by which they live. As a consequence, 'Constructivism begins with deeds. Deeds done, acts taken, words spoken. These are all the facts there are.'[5] While Onuf's interest lay with language and the construction of rules, he noted approvingly Michael Oakeshott's reminder that 'most human behavior can adequately be described in terms of the notion of *habit* or *custom* and that neither the notion of rule or that of reflectiveness is essential to it'.[6] Finally, Kratochwil has also consistently placed political practice at the forefront of his constructivist theorizing as social norms, rules, and conventions emerge and have their effects in the specific practical context of individual reasoning and decision-making.[7] As Ruggie explained, 'Constitutive rules define the set of practices that make up a particular class of consciously organized social activity – that is to say, they specify *what counts as* that activity.'[8]

Hand in hand with a concern with practice went a thoroughgoing relationalism in early Constructivism. Onuf, for example, cited approvingly

Michel Foucault's exhortation 'to dispense with "things". To "depresentify" them. ... To define these objects without reference to the ... *foundation of things*, but by relating them to the body of rules that enable them to form as objects of a discourse and thus constitute the conditions of their historical appearance'.[9] Again, the relationalism of early Constructivism should be unsurprising. Not only are practice and relational arguments mutually imbricating conceptually, as noted earlier, but the early constructivists were drawing on many of the same intellectual sources, in social theory and in sociology, as now underpin the turns to practice theory and relationalism. Yosef Lapid, for example, drew from relational sociologist Margaret Somers and John Shotter in making the claim that: 'Embracing the idea that cultures and identities are emergent and contested (rather than fixed and natural), contested and polymorphic (rather than unitary and singular), and interactive and process-like (rather than static and essence-like), can lead to pathbreaking theoretical advances.'[10]

Recovering the practice-relational turn as part of the New Constructivism is to draw attention to the rich array of conceptual resources for theorizing world politics in suitably anti-substantialist ways. However, the aim of the book has not been to reveal a true form of Constructivism that can be recovered following its narrowing. The aim rather is to grasp what Constructivism *is* in IR by understanding what it *does*, practically and relationally, for the field. In this sense, the practice-relational turn and the first constructivist turn are structurally similar movements. The purpose of each is to open up a space in IR for sociological and interpretive approaches that engage with the mainstream by striving for positive social scientific knowledge of world politics. I call this the *space of Constructivism*.

The argument that Constructivism was originally intended as a space in IR not a coherent approach, much less a theory, was also made explicitly by Ruggie and Kratochwil.[11] Their target was the regimes debate, which they showed was hamstrung by a disjuncture between ontology and epistemology: whereas regimes have a fundamentally intersubjective component – they communicate shared expectations – the predominant conceptualization treated regimes as objects only. Relying on revealed preferences as a way to get at the question of *why* an actor adheres to a regime is therefore unsatisfactory, requiring insights from the interpretive sciences.[12] Non-constructivists like Katzenstein, Keohane and Krasner also recognized that constructivism was a space not a theory: 'The end of the Cold War ... opened up space for cultural and sociological perspectives, often referred to as "constructivist".'[13]

The chief benefit of recognizing that Constructivism is a social space is that it forces us to recognize that like any approach, Constructivism was not meant to be closed off theoretically, in Constructivism's case as the study of norms, identity, and culture, associated exclusively with interpretive methods. Like the first waves of constructivist work in the late 1980s and 1990s, the proponents of the practice-relational turn are drawing on developments in cognate social sciences – typically but by no means necessarily from sociology and social theory – to widen IR's conceptual lenses. They are doing Constructivism, whether or not they couch their interventions as constructivist.

The space of Constructivism in contemporary US International Relations

A healthy social science of IR needs the space of constructivism. It is a physical and intellectual space in which the scope and purpose of IR as a social science is kept open. However, the space of Constructivism is fragile – especially in the United States, but beyond also. Constructivist research is pulled between the competing demands of science and the search for strongly generalizable theoretical conclusions, on the one hand, and the critical and more contextually specific impulse of the humanities, on the other.

Although the constructivists already made many of the insights of the practice-relational turn, therefore, the disciplinary context in which practice-relationalism has emerged is different to 20–25 years ago. Constructivism emerged to offer a more social approach vis-à-vis neorealism and neoliberalism. But already by 1998, Helen Milner was identifying an emerging synthesis in American political science on the twin bases of rational choice institutionalism and non-cooperative game theory.[14] She gave no justification for why rational choice and not historical and sociological institutionalisms should provide a common basis for political science. But hers was an empirical statement not a normative one, and the emerging synthesis she observed has come to pass.[15] As the TRIPS survey demonstrates, although a 'hundred flowers still bloom' in US IR,[16] it is dominated by a positivist epistemology, typically accompanied by rationalist assumptions.[17]

The claim that US IR is predominantly rationalist and positivist is difficult to fully support. The labels positivism and rationalism are largely unhelpful in categorizing IR scholarship.[18] Rationalism spans the more to the less formalized, while positivism is largely a distillation of received wisdom based on logical empiricist philosophy.[19] Not all positivists employ the rationality assumption, and not all rationalists are positivists. More importantly, the claim that IR's conceptual and methodological lenses have narrowed places into question IR's boundaries. It is not the case that constructivist work is losing momentum internationally. The TRIPS survey under-samples non-US IR where Constructivism is powerful.[20]

However, the TRIPS survey makes clear that compared to non-US IR, and US IR historically, contemporary IR in America is dominated by a convergence of rationalism and positivism. This paper is a practical intervention targeted here. It follows Katzenstein, Keohane, and Krasner in identifying rationalism versus constructivism as the primary dividing line in the field.[21] But it goes beyond them in recognizing the unbalanced nature of the rationalist-constructivist dichotomy. As the TRIPS survey reported, in 2006 constructivist article accounted for approximately 15 per cent of the field's top-ranked journals, whereas liberal and non-paradigmatic articles – generally positivist and/or rationalist – accounted for over 90 per cent.[22]

The emergence of OEP in IPE provides a good illustration of the stakes of the narrowing of the space of Constructivism.[23] The narrow vision of politics underpinning OEP stands in stark opposition to both constructivism and practice-relationalism. The sphere in which the rationality model is directly applicable in the study of politics is smaller than often proclaimed, being most applicable in areas of social life that resemble market conditions since 'in a market the problem of rights and contract have been solved and when all participants have agreed to a minimum of exchange'.[24] These conditions are not met in most areas of political life, where inequality and disenfranchisement are the norm.

It is noteworthy therefore that prominent rationalists have reservations about OEP. For Keohane, 'there is little emphasis [in OEP] on how "interests" are constructed – how the ideas that people have in their heads, and that they share collectively, affect their preferences'.[25] Here is another re-running of an old debate: Keohane's concerns are precisely those early constructivists had about the Neo-Neo consensus. Checkel stressed that the constructivist critique concerned not what neoliberalism and neorealism did, but what they ignored: 'the content and sources of state interests and the social fabric of world politics'.[26] IR still needs constructivist and practice-relational work because the now-dominant rationalist and positivist approaches lack sensitivity to the social fabric of international politics. As Tilly noted, in the background of every rationalist analysis, therefore, there is 'allocative structure that is external to the choice-making individual'.[27]

Allocative structures, or in constructivist terminology constitutive rules, are a chief concern of both neo-classical constructivists and practice-relationalists. Neither reject rationalist or models of social action; they are concerned with 'what happens *before* the neo-utilitarian model kicks in'.[28] But practice-relationalists add new ways to understand the production and functioning of constitutive rules in world politics in response to a changed disciplinary context. Whereas neoliberal institutionalists and neorealists took the sovereign state as their starting point, contemporary rationalists do not, dropping down a level of analysis to groups and individuals viewed as strategic utility-maximizing actors.[29] This responds to Ruggie's critique of neo-utilitarianism in that it allows rationalists to explain a larger array of actions and outcomes, including the thick institutional environment of contemporary global politics.[30] In response, practice-relationalists repeat the initial constructivist critique at a lower level of analysis, stressing the often habitual nature of political action by individuals in specific contexts.

However, with this move the question of epistemology and the most appropriate form of social science can longer be avoided. While behaviour can be *modelled* in rationalist terms, the issue is whether practical action is accurately *described* as such, and whether this matters. The aim is not to decry rationalism or IR's predominant understanding of science. It is to recognize the historical specificity of their predominance, how 'the mainstream has become so narrow in its understanding of what constitutes social science that on the dominant conception today [Max] Weber might no longer qualify – his approach to concept formation, method of theory construction, and model of explanation all fail to conform to the norm'.[31]

The science question, pragmatism, and the tragedy of the Constructivism

One explanation for IR's mistrust of Constructivism is that rationalism embodies 'American culture's strong ideology that "this is the way people really are"'.[32] Individuals *do* weigh costs and benefits and choose options based on what is best in the circumstances. OEP thus 'resonates in the US academy with sweet common sense'.[33] However, rationalism's predominance is a relatively recent development, raising the question of why it emerged. Moreover, individualism exists alongside another tradition in American culture that has at times balanced out its atomizing tendencies: pragmatism. As Robert Keohane recently noted, 'I am very American Mid-Westerner, pragmatic to the core.'[34] Whereas liberal economics represents the scientific distillations of individualism, American pragmatist philosophy serves as an important source of inspiration and legitimacy to constructivism and practice-relationalism.[35]

Indeed, the rationalist-constructivist debate in contemporary IR has important precursors in much broader debates in the human sciences in America over the last 150 years that have pitted pragmatism against different challengers over the nature and scope of science. Between the civil war and the 1960s pragmatists defended a publicly engaged science in which normative questions were viewed as within the bounds of scientific inquiry.[36] Ultimately, however, the vision of these *scientific democrats* was defeated by an understanding of science as a value-free enterprise, concerned with the means and not the ends of the public good.

During the 1930s and 1940s, pragmatists like Dewey, Bentley, Franz Boas, and Max Otto offered critiques of the supposedly objective nature of scientific inquiry.[37] While well received, they compared unfavourably to the abstract work of the logical empiricists like Rudolf Carnap and W.V. Quine. As historian Andrew Jewett argues, 'postwar philosophy of science focused closely on causation, imputation, and other elements of scientific reasoning, saying little about the social and cultural settings in which that reasoning took place'.[38] In the academy, it was the humanities, not the historical social sciences, which became the mouthpiece of society's values, leaving 'a stripped down social-scientific enterprise' where scholars increasingly 'emphasized their disinterestedness'.[39]

What gave these debates purchase were large-scale shifts in the relationship between science and society associated with the New Deal and the War and its aftermath. While the period saw unparalleled expansion in science, powerful forces were arraigned in favour of a narrow understanding of science, separate from society and sceptical towards the social science. Much of this story – the role of McCarthyism,[40] the rise of the military-industrial complex, and rational choice theory's origins in the RAND institute – are well known.[41] Other aspects are worth highlighting, however, like the debate over the creation of the National Science Foundation in 1945.[42] The debate saw influential figures in post-war science policy, like Harvard president James Bryant Conant and Johns Hopkins president Isaiah Bowman, win massive government investment in science, but without government oversight. Scientific research would remain university-based, separate from the direct concerns of citizens. At the same time, Conant, Bowman, and others successfully argued against strong NSF support of social science.[43]

By the 1960s, C.P. Snow's notion of the 'two cultures' represented an accurate depiction of the relationship between sciences and the humanities, with the sciences physically and normatively held separate from the values of society supposedly given voice by the latter.[44] But as Jewett notes, while to Snow social science was capable of occupying the space between the sciences and the humanities, in the event: 'To that extent that social scientists would find a place for themselves in American intellectual culture in the 1950s, they would do so largely by wedging their work into the narrow vision of the scientific enterprise forged by physical scientists and humanistic and religious critics.'[45]

The New Constructivism is cast in a different light by placing it into a longer clash between pragmatist-inspired thought, with its broad understanding of science, and a narrower account, with rationalism as it apogee. Crucial here is the role played by the sociology of scientific knowledge in the practice-relational turn and the place of Thomas Kuhn's pioneering work.[46] Kuhn is celebrated by post-positivists for placing social and historical factors back into the practice of science, and the trailed he blazed has been followed by Latour and Knorr-Cetina.[47] But as Steve Fuller has argued, Kuhn's sociology of scientific revolutions served to finalize a split between the practice of science and the history of science.[48] By the time Kuhn was writing, in other words, the idea that scientific disciplines would contain within them a historical and sociological imagination was unthinkable.

In this context, the viability of a contextually and historically rich form of social science like constructivism is difficult to maintain. Constructivism is fated to periodic bursts of popularity, punctuating general marginalization.[49] This is not because the mainstream rejects social construction, nor because constructivists deny the existence of a world 'out there', but because Constructivism is a weapon of the weak. Internally, 'Constructionist arguments are often employed by those who lack certain kinds of knowledge resources: young people who lack senior positions, researchers lacking money to do expensive kinds of work, outsiders attacking culturally authoritative definitions of social phenomena, amateurs who lack certain kinds of technical skills.'[50] Externally, efforts to broaden the meaning of social science to include neo-classical constructivist and practice-relational work, like those of Jackson, face stronger social forces working to narrow science's scope and keep them separate from the shifting concerns of society.[51]

The path ahead

The New Constructivist's task, therefore, is nothing less than to keep the space of Constructivism open by offering such insightful accounts of important features of world politics that their research, and the constructivist community, cannot be ignored. Here the crucial word is 'important'. Who decides what is and is not important? Here the reflexive gaze of the New Constructivism is essential. Turning the scholarly gaze back on the researcher can help identify how the priorities of the consumers of knowledge – be it the state, the media, funders, or the profession – shape what is considered important. Armed with such knowledge, integrated into the very formation of research design, New Constructivists can better navigate a world already divided into the important – war, geopolitics, economic conflict – and the seemingly frivolous – like dancing at the Congress of Vienna. Such reflexive knowledge cannot weaken the grip of the power structures that determine what is important to research, but it can trace their origins, emphasizing once again the historically constituted nature of the seemingly natural.

Notes

Preface

1   See, among others, Adler, Emanuel. 1997. Seizing the Middle Ground: Constructivism in World Politics. *European Journal of International Relations* 3 (3): 319–63; Kubálková, Vendulka, Paul Kowert, and Nicholas Onuf, eds. 1998. *International Relations in a Constructed World*. Armonk: M.E. Sharpe; Ruggie, John Gerard. 1998. What Makes the World Hang Together? Neo-Utilitarianism and the Social Constructivist Challenge? International Organization 52 (4): 855–85; Wendt, Alexander. 1995. Constructing International Politics. *International Security* 20 (1): 71-81; Finnemore, Martha, and Kathryn Sikkink. 2001. Taking Stock: The Constructivist Research Program in International Relations and Comparative Politics. *Annual Review of Political Science*. 4: 391–416; Guzzini, Stefano. 2000. A Reconstruction of Constructivism in International Relations. *European Journal of International Relations* 6 (2): 147–82; Zehfuss, Maja. 2002. *Constructivism in International Relations*. Cambridge: Cambridge University Press; Klotz, Audie and Cecilia Lynch. 2007. *Strategies for Research in Constructivist International Relations* New York: Routledge; Bertucci, Mariano, Jarrod Hayes, and Patrick James, eds. 2018. *Constructivism Reconsidered: Past, Present, and Future*. Ann Arbor: University of Michigan Press; Hayes, Jarrod. 2017. Reclaiming Constructivism: Identity and the Practice of the Study of International Relations. *PS: Political Science and Politics* 50 (1): 89–92; Srivastava, Swati. 2020. Varieties of Social Construction. *International Studies Review* 22 (3): 325–46; Steele, Brent J. 2017. Introduction: The Politics of Constructivist International Relations in the US Academy. *PS: Political Science and Politics* 50 (1): 71–3; Subotic, Jelena. (2017) Constructivism as Professional Practice in the US Academy. *PS: Political Science and Politics* 50 (1): 75–8; Zarakol, Ayşe. 2017. TRIPping Constructivism. *PS: Political Science and Politics* 50 (1): 75–8.

2   Lake, David. 2011. Why 'Isms' Are Evil: Theory, Epistemology, and Academic Sects as an Impediment to Understanding and Progress. *International Studies Quarterly* 55 (2): 465–80.

3   Lake 2011: 465.

4   See Sil, Rudra and Peter J. Katzenstein. 2010. *Beyond Paradigms: Analytical Eclecticism in the Study of World Politics*. New York: Palgrave.

Introduction

1   See Emirbayer, Mustafa. 1997. Manifesto for a Relational Sociology. American Journal of Sociology 103 (2): 281–317.

2   Hayes, Jarrod. 2017. Reclaiming Constructivism: Identity and the Practice of the Study of International Relations. *PS: Political Science and Politics* 50 (1): 89–92.

3   Mills, C. Wright. 2000 [1959]. *The Sociological Imagination*. Oxford: Oxford University Press.

4   Ruggie, John Gerard. 1998. What Makes the World Hang Together? Neo-Utilitarianism and the Social Constructivist Challenge? *International Organization* 52 (4): 855–85.

5   See respectively Onuf, Nicholas Greenwood. 2012 [1989]. *World of Our Making: Rules and Rule in Social Theory and International Relations*. Columbia: University of South

Carolina Press; Wendt, Alexander. 1992. Anarchy is What States Make of It: The Social Construction on Power Politics. *International Organization* 46 (2): 391–425; Pouliot, Vincent. 2011. *International Security in Practice: The Politics of NATO-Russia Diplomacy.* Cambridge: Cambridge University Press; Nexon, Daniel H. 2009. *The Struggle for Power in Early Modern Europe: Religious Conflict, Dynastic Empires, and International Change.* Princeton, NJ: Princeton University Press.

[6] Rosenberg, Justin. 1994. The International Imagination: IR Theory and 'Classic Social Analysis'. *Millennium: Journal of International Studies* 23 (1): 85–108.

[7] See, for example, Standfield, Catriona. 2020. Gendering the Practice Turn in Diplomacy. *European Journal of International Relations* 26 (S1): 140–65.

[8] Sellar, Walter Carruthers and Robert Julian Yeatman. 1930. *1066 and All That.* London: Methuen.

[9] Kratochwil, Friedrich V. 2006. History, Action, and Identity: Revisiting the 'Second' Great Debate and Assessing Its Importance for Social Theory. *European Journal of International Relations* 12 (1): 5–29.

[10] This is particularly the case for handbook chapters and review articles. See Hopf, Ted. 1998. The Promise of Constructivism in International Relations Theory, *International Security* 23 (1): 171–200.

[11] As prominent constructivists have maintained, see Adler, Emanuel. 1997. Seizing the Middle Ground: Constructivism in World Politics. *European Journal of International Relations* 3 (3): 319–63. Typically, the point has been downplayed if not ignored altogether.

[12] See Adler, Emanuel and Vincent Pouliot. 2011. *International Practices.* Cambridge: Cambridge University Press; Kustermans, Jorg. 2016. Parsing the Practice Turn. Practice, Practical Knowledge, Practices. *Millennium: Journal of International Studies* 44 (2): 175–96; Bueger, Christian and Frank Gadinger. 2018. *International Practice Theory: New Perspectives*, 2nd edition. Basingstoke: Palgrave.

[13] Kratochwil, Friedrich V. and John Gerard Ruggie. 1986. International Organization: A State of the Art on an Art of the State. *International Organization* 40 (4): 753–75.

[14] Adler 1997: 323.

[15] Finnemore and Sikkink 2001: abstract.

[16] Abdelal, Rawi, Mark Blyth, and Craig Parsons, eds. 2011. *Constructing the International Economy.* Ithaca: Cornell University Press, 2.

[17] Kratochwil, Friedrich V. 1989. *Rules, Norms, and Decisions: On the Conditions of Legal and Practical Reasoning in International Relations and Domestic Affairs.* Cambridge: Cambridge University Press; Wendt 1992; Ruggie, John Gerard. 1993. *Multilateralism Matters: The Theory and Praxis of an Institutional Form.* New York: Columbia University Press; Onuf 2012 [1989].

[18] Grieco, Joseph M. 1988. Anarchy and the Limits of Cooperation: A Realist Critique of the Newest Liberal Institutionalism. *International Organization* 42 (3): 485–507; Baldwin, David. 1993. *Neorealism and Neoliberalism: The Contemporary Debate.* New York: Columbia University Press.

[19] Klotz, Audie. 1995. *Norms in International Relations: The Struggle against Apartheid.* Ithaca: Cornell University Press; Finnemore 1996b.

[20] Reus-Smit, Christian. 1997. The Constitutional Structure of International Society. *International Organization* 51 (4): 555–89; Bukovansky, Mlada. 1999. *Legitimacy and Power Politics: The American and French Revolutions in International Political Culture.* Ithaca: Cornell University Press.

[21] Price, Richard. 1998. Reversing the Gun Sights: Transnational Civil Society Targets Land Mines. *International Organization* 52 (3): 613–44.

22 Katzenstein, Peter, ed. 1996a. *The Culture of National Security: Norms and Identity in World Politics*. New York: Columbia University Press.

23 Katzenstein, Peter J., Robert O. Keohane and Stephen D. Krasner. 1998. International Organization and the Study of World Politics. *International Organization* 52 (4): 645–85.

24 Hall, Rodney Bruce. 1999. *National Collective Identity: Social Constructs and Internationlal Systems*. New York: Columbia University Press.

25 Katzenstein, Peter, ed. 1996b. *Cultural Norms in National Security: Police and Military in Postwar Japan*. Ithaca: Cornell University Press.

26 See, for example, Szent-Iványi, Balázs and Pēteris Timofejevs. 2020. Selective Norm Promotion in International Development Assistance: The Drivers of Naming and Shaming Advocacy Among European Non-Governmental Development Organisations. *International Relations* 35 (1): 23–46.

27 Jackson, Patrick Thaddeus. 2011. *The Conduct of Inquiry in International Relations: Philosophy of Science and Its Implications for the Study of World Politics*, 1st Edition. New York: Routledge.

28 Maliniak, Daniel, Amy Oakes, Susan Peterson, and Michael J. Tierney. 2011. International Relations in the US Academy. *International Studies Quarterly* 55 (2): 437–64.

29 See Jackson 2011: 201–7.

30 Klotz and Lynch 2007.

31 Wendt, Alexander. 1998. Constitution and Causation in International Relations. *Review of International Studies* 24 (5): 101–17.

32 Drawing on Hollis, Martin, and Steve Smith. 1991. *Explaining and Understanding International Relations*. Oxford: Clarendon Press.

33 For example, Ross, Andrew A. G. 2006. Coming in from the Cold: Constructivism and Emotions. *European Journal of International Relations* 12 (2): 197–222.

34 Tickner, Arlene B. and Ole Waever, eds. 2009. *International Relations Scholarship Around the World*. Abingdon: Routledge. For a manifesto for a truly global IR, see Acharya, Amitav. 2014. Global International Relations (IR) and Regional Worlds: A New Agenda for International Studies. *International Studies Quarterly* 58 (4): 647–59.

35 Kratochwil and Ruggie 1986.

36 Klotz 1995; Finnemore, Martha. 1996a. *National Interests in International Society*. Ithaca: Cornell University Press.

37 See https://trip.wm.edu/ for the research results of ongoing research into Teaching and Research in International Politics. Also Maliniak et al 2011.

38 Milner, Helen. 1998. Rationalizing Politics: The Emerging Synthesis of International, American, and Comparative Politics. *International Organization* 52 (4): 759–86.

39 Hyde, Susan D. 2015. Experiments in International Relations: Laboratory, Survey, and Field. *Annual Review of Political Science* 18: 403–24.

40 Fearon, James D. and Alexander Wendt. 2002. Rationalism Vs. Constructivism: A Skeptical View. In Walter Carlsnaes, Thomas Risse, and Beth Simmons, eds. *The SAGE Handbook of International Relations*. London: SAGE, pp 52–72.

41 Johnson, James. 2002. How Conceptual Problems Migrate: Rational Choice, Interpretation, and the Hazards of Pluralism. *Annual Review of Political Science*. 5: 236.

42 Friedrichs, Jörg. 2004. *European Approaches to International Relations Theory: A House With Many Mansions*. London: Routledge.

43 See, for example, Onuf 2012 [1989].

44 Reus-Smit, Christian. 2008. Constructivism and the Structure of Ethical Reasoning. In Richard Price, ed. *Moral Limit and Possibility in World Politics*. Cambridge: Cambridge University Press, pp 53–82, p 72.

[45] For other takes along these lines, see Hayes 2017; Onuf, Nicholas. 2017. The Bigger Story. *PS: Political Science and Politics* 50 (1): 93–6; Subotic, Jelena. 2017. Constructivism as Professional Practice in the US Academy. *PS: Political Science and Politics* 50 (1): 75–8.

[46] Maliniak et al 2011: 10.

[47] See Subotic 2017. Subotic's figures are now some five years old, but there is no reason to think the trends will have shifted substantially or at all in constructivism's favour.

[48] See Wendt, Alexander. 2006. Social Theory as Cartesian Science: An Auto-Critique from a Quantum Perspective. In Stefano Guzzini and Anna Leander, eds. 2006. *Constructivism and International Relations*. New York: Routledge, pp 181–219; Wendt, Alexander. 2015. *Quantum Mind and Social Science: Unifying Physical and Social Ontology*. Cambridge: Cambridge University Press.

[49] Struett, Michael J. 2017. Reading and Writing Constructivist Research in American Political Science. *PS: Political Science and Politics* 50 (1): 80.

[50] Hayes 2017: 90.

[51] Or similar words. Personal communication with the author.

[52] Bertucci, Mariano, Jarrod Hayes, and Patrick James, eds. 2018. *Constructivism Reconsidered: Past, Present, and Future*. Ann Arbor: University of Michigan Press.

[53] Barder, Alexander D. and Daniel J. Levine. 2012. 'The World Is Too Much With Us': Reification and the Depolitising of *Via Media* Constructivist IR. *Millennium: Journal of International Studies* 40 (3): 585–604.

[54] Ruggie 1998: 871.

[55] In the words of Emanuel Adler, see 1997.

[56] Onuf, Nicholas Greenwood. 2018a. *The Mightie Frame: Epochal Change and the Modern World*. New York: Oxford University Press.

[57] Onuf 2012 [1989]. The label 'Constructivism' is unique among the social sciences, where thee same perspective is typically termed *Constructionism*, which some in IR have tried to reclaim, see Patrick Thaddeus Jackson and Daniel H. Nexon. 2009. Paradigmatic Faults in International-Relations Theory. *International Studies Quarterly* 53 (4): 907–30.

[58] Onuf 2017: *xiv*.

[59] See the special issue International Institutions and Socialization in Europe, *International Organization* 59 (4) (2005); Bearce, David H. and Stacey Bondanella. 2007. Intergovernmental Organizations, Socialization, and Member-State Interest Convergence. *International Organization* 61 (4): 703–33.

[60] Risse, Thomas. 2000. Let's Argue! Communicative Action in World Politics. *International Organization* 54 (1): 1–39; Dietelhoff, Nicole. 2009. The Discursive Process of Legalization: Charting Islands of Persuasion in the ICC Case. *International Organization* 63 (1): 33–65.

[61] Acharya, Amitav. 2004. How Ideas Spread: Whose Norms Matter? Norm Localization and Institutional Change in Asian Regionalism. *International Organization* 58 (2): 239–75; Bush, Sarah Sunn. 2011. International Politics and the Spread of Quotas for Women in Legislatures. *International Organization* 65 (1): 103–37; Towns, Anne E. 2012. Norms and Social Hierarchies: Understanding International Policy Diffusion "From Below." *International Organization* 66 (2): 179–209.

[62] This was the problematic of the regimes debate under new terms, see Crawford, Neta C. 1994. A Security Regime Among Democracies: Cooperation Among Iroquois Nations. *International Organization* 48 (3): 345–85.

[63] Abbott, Andrew. 2001. *Chaos of Disciplines*. Chicago: University of Chicago Press.

[64] Abbott 2001: 10–15.

[65] Abbott 2001: 11.

66 Checkel, Jeffrey T. 1998. The Constructivist Turn in International Relations Theory. *International Security* 50 (2): 324–48.

67 Katzenstein, Keohane and Krasner 1998: 649.

68 Checkel 1998: 325.

69 See Hynek, Nik and Andrea Teti. 2010. Saving Identity from Postmodernism? The Normalization of Constructivism in International Relations. *Contemporary Political Theory* 9 (1): 171–99.

70 It was facilitated by an expansion in job and publication opportunities overseas, with *Millennium* and *European Journal of International Relations* (founded 1995) particularly influential.

71 I thank Ido Oren for drawing my attention to this point. See also Maliniak et al 2011: 10.

72 Wendt 2006.

73 Adler and Pouliot 2011.

74 Ashley, Richard K. and R.B.J. Walker. 1990. Introduction: Speaking the Language of Exile. *International Studies Quarterly* 34 (3): 259–68.

75 Campbell, David. 1998. *Writing Security: United States Foreign Policy and the Politics of Identity.* Minneapolis: University of Minnesota Press; Doty, Roxanne Lynn. 1993. Foreign Policy as Social Construction: A Post-Positivist Analysis of US Counterinsurgency Policy in the Philippines. *International Studies Quarterly* 37 (3): 297–320.

76 Abbott 2001: 24.

77 Adler 1997; Checkel 1998; Hopf 1998; Finnemore and Sikkink 2001.

78 Abbott 2001: 21.

79 Onuf 2018a.

80 Onuf 2017: *xvii.*

81 Onuf 2018a.

82 See especially Guzzini, Stefano. 2000. A Reconstruction of Constructivism in International Relations. *European Journal of International Relations* 6 (2): 147–82; McCourt, David M. 2016. Practice Theory and Relationalism as the New Constructivism. *International Studies Quarterly* 60 (3): 475–85.

83 Allan, Bentley. 2018. *Scientific Cosmology and International Orders.* Cambridge: Cambridge University Press.

84 Hom, Andrew. 2020. *International Relations and the Problem of Time.* Oxford: Oxford University Press.

85 Ralph, Jason. 2018. What Should Be Done? Pragmatist Constructivist Ethics and the Responsibility to Protect. *International Organization* 72 (1): 173–203.

86 Barkin, J. Samuel and Laura Sjoberg. 2018. *International Relations' Last Synthesis: Decoupling Constructivist and Critical Approaches.* Ann Arbor: University of Michigan Press.

87 See especially Steele, Brent J. 2013. *Alternative Accountabilities in Global Politics: The Scars of Violence.* New York: Routledge; Auchter, Jessica. 2014. *The Politics of Haunting and Memory in International Relations.* New York: Routledge; Solomon, Ty. 2015. *The Politics of Subjectivity in American Foreign Policy Discourses.* Ann Arbor: University of Michigan Press.

88 Durkheim, Emile. 1995 [1912]. *The Elementary Forms of the Religious Life.* New York: Free Press, 424.

89 Du Bois, W.E.B. 1994 [1903]. *The Souls of Black Folk.* New York: Dover.

90 See Owens, Patricia. 2015. Method or Madness? Sociolatry in International Thought. *Review of International Studies* 41, 4: 655–74; Owens, Patricia. 2016. *Economy of Force: Counterinsurgency and the Historical Rise of the Social.* Cambridge: Cambridge University Press.

91 Lake, David. 2011. Why 'Isms' Are Evil: Theory, Epistemology, and Academic Sects as an Impediment to Understanding and Progress. *International Studies Quarterly* 55 (2): 465–80.

92 Jackson, Patrick Thaddeus and Daniel H. Nexon. 2019 Reclaiming the Social: Relationalism in Anglophone International Studies. *Cambridge Review of International Affairs* 32 (5): 582–600.

93 Jackson and Nexon 2009: 907–8.

94 Jackson and Nexon 2009: 907–8.

95 See Espeland, Wendy Nelson and Mitchell L. Stevens. 1998. Commensuration as a Social Process. *Annual Review of Sociology* 24: 313–43.

96 Abbott 2001: 11.

97 Adler 1997: 320.

98 Tilly, Charles. 2002. *Stories, Identities, and Political Change.* Lanham: Rowman and Littlefield, 76.

99 Owens 2015, 2016.

100 Owens 2015: 655.

101 Owens 2015: 655–6.

102 Owens 2015: 658.

103 Owens 2015: 658.

104 Owens 2015: 658.

105 Owens 2015: 658.

106 Owens 2015: 658.

107 Another powerful example of the same is Robert Vitalis' *White World Order, Black Power Politics: The Birth of American International Relations.* Ithaca: Cornell University Press, 2015.

108 See Rohde, Joy. 2013. *Armed with Expertise: The Militarization of American Social Science Research During the Cold War.* Ithaca: Cornell University Press; Price, David H. 2011. *Weaponizing Anthropology.* Petrolia, CA: Counterpunch.

109 Respectively, Vincent Pouliot 2011; Adler-Nissen, Rebecca, ed. 2012. *Bourdieu in International Relations.* London: Routledge; Bueger and Gadinger 2018.

110 Abbott, Andrew. 2016. *Processual Sociology.* Chicago: University of Chicago Press.

111 For example, Pratt, Simon Frankel. 2016. Pragmatism as Ontology, Not (Just) Epistemology: Exploring the Full Horizon of Pragmatism as an Approach to IR Theory. *International Studies Review* 18 (3): 508–27.

112 See Epstein, Charlotte. 2013a. Constructivism or the Eternal Return of Universals in International Relations: Why Returning to Language is Vital for Prolonging the Owl's Flight. *European Journal of International Relations* 19 (3): 499–519; Raymond, Mark. 2019. *Social Practices of Rule-Making in World Politics.* New York: Oxford University Press.

113 Especially in the work of early constructivist Friedrich Kratochwil and Nicholas Onuf. See Kratochwil 1989; Onuf 2012 [1989].

114 See Goldstein, Judith and Robert O. Keohane, eds. 1993. *Ideas and Foreign Policy: Beliefs, Institutions, and Political Change.* Ithaca: Cornell University Press.

115 For example, Rajkovic, Nikolas M. 2011. *The Politics of International Law and Compliance.* London: Routledge; Aalberts, Tanja E. 2012. *Constructing Sovereignty Between Politics and Law.* Abingdon: Routledge; Kratochwil, Friedrich V. 2014. *The Status of Law in World Society: Meditations on the Role and Rule of Law.* Cambridge: Cambridge University Press.

116 See, respectively, Latour, Bruno. 2007. Reassembling the Social: An Introduction to Actor-Network Theory. Oxford: Oxford University Press; Reus-Smit, Christian. 2018. *On Cultural Diversity: International Theory in a World of Difference.* Cambridge: Cambridge University Press.

117 See, for example, Neumann, Iver B. 2012. *At Home With The Diplomats: Inside a European Foreign Ministry.* Ithaca: Cornell University Press; Stampnitzky, Lisa. 2013. *Disciplining Terror: How Experts Invented 'Terrorism'.* Cambridge: Cambridge University Press;

Goetze, Catherine. 2017. *The Distinction of Peace: A Social Analysis of Peacebuilding*. Ann Arbor: University of Michigan Press.

[118] To aid the discussion, I draw on Patrick Thaddeus Jackson's useful distinction between 'methodology' and 'methods'. See Jackson, Patrick Thaddeus. 2016. *The Conduct of Inquiry in International Relations: Philosophy of Science and Its Implications for the Study of World Politics*, 2nd Edition. New York: Routledge.

[119] Early constructivist John Gerard Ruggie hints at this position in Ruggie 1998. The case has been made explicitly by Justin Rosenberg. Rosenberg 1994.

[120] Lechner, Silviya and Mervyn Frost. 2018. *Practice Theory and International Relations*. Cambridge: Cambridge University Press; Weber, Martin. 2020. The Normative Grammar of Relational Analysis: Recognition Theory's Contribution to Understanding Short-Comings in IR's Relational Turn, *International Studies Quarterly*. Online First.

[121] An important source here is Price, Richard, ed. 2008. *Moral Limit and Possibility in World Politics*. Cambridge: Cambridge University Press.

Chapter 1

[1] Alexander Wendt was on one occasion reportedly called 'dangerous' at an International Studies Association panel, for suggesting that national interests were shaped, in part, by the culture of the international system. Constructivists, old and new, would do well to remember that the fear of cultural relativism is real for many self-avowed scientists. Personal anecdote relayed to the author.

[2] Baldwin, David. 1993. *Neorealism and Neoliberalism: The Contemporary Debate*. New York: Columbia University Press.

[3] Grieco, Joseph M. 1988. Anarchy and the Limits of Cooperation: A Realist Critique of the Newest Liberal Institutionalism. *International Organization* 42 (3): 485–507.

[4] Kratochwil and Ruggie 1986.

[5] Kratochwil, Friedrich V. 1989. *Rules, Norms, and Decisions: On the Conditions of Legal and Practical Reasoning in International Relations and Domestic Affairs*. Cambridge: Cambridge University Press.

[6] Onuf, Nicholas Greenwood. 2012 [1989]. *World of Our Making: Rules and Rule in Social Theory and International Relations*. Columbia: University of South Carolina Press.

[7] Wendt, Alexander. 1987. The Agent-Structure Problem in International Relations Theory. *International Organization* 41 (3): 335–70; Wendt, Alexander. 1992. Anarchy is What States Make of It: The Social Construction on Power Politics. *International Organization* 46 (2): 391–425.

[8] See Jepperson, Ronald, Alexander Wendt and Peter Katzenstein. 1996. Norms, Identity, and Culture in National Security. In Peter Katzenstein, ed. *The Culture of National Security: Norms and Identity in World Politics*. New York: Columbia University Press, pp 35–75.

[9] Klotz, Audie. 1995. *Norms in International Relations: The Struggle against Apartheid*. Ithaca: Cornell University Press; Carpenter, R. Charli. 2003. 'Women and Children First.' Gender, Norms, and Humanitarian Evacuation in the Balkans 1991–95. *International Organization* 57 (4): 661–94; see also Tannenwald, Nina. 1999. The Nuclear Taboo: The United States and the Normative Basis of Nuclear Non-Use. *International Organization* 53 (3): 433–68.

[10] Bukovansky, Mlada. 1997. American Identity and Neutral Rights from Independence to the War of 1812. *International Organization* 51 (2): 209–43.

[11] Keck, Margaret and Kathryn Sikkink. 1998. *Activists Beyond Borders: Advocacy Networks in International Politics*. Ithaca: Cornell University Press.

[12] Katzenstein, Peter, ed. 1996b. *Cultural Norms in National Security: Police and Military in Postwar Japan*. Ithaca: Cornell University Press.

[13] I am far from exempt from the pull of this dynamic – see McCourt, David M. 2012b. What's at Stake in the Historical Turn? Theory, Practice, and Phronēsis in International Relations. *Millennium: Journal of International Studies* 41 (1): 23–42; McCourt, David M. 2012c. The 'Problem of Generations' Revisited: Karl Mannheim and the Sociology of Knowledge in International Relations. In Jon Acuff and Brent Steele, ed. *Theory and Practice of the 'Generation' in International Relations and Politics*. New York: Routledge, pp 47–70; McCourt, David M. 2014. *Britain and World Power since 1945: Constructing a Nation's Role in International Politics*. Ann Arbor: University of Michigan Press.

[14] The practice turn wave has yet to crest. See Bicchi, Federica and Niklas Bremberg. 2016. European Diplomatic Practices: Contemporary Challenges and Innovative Approaches. *European Security* 25 (4): 391–406; Bueger, Christian. 2021. *International Organizations in Practice: The United Nations, Peacebuilding, and Praxiography*. London: Routledge.

[15] See McCourt, David M. and Brent J. Steele. 2017. World of Our Making and Second Generation Constructivism. In Harry Gould, ed. *The Art of World-Making: Nicholas Greenwood Onuf and His Critics*. New York: Routledge, pp 1–16.

[16] I am channelling my inner Arthur Stinchcombe here. See his virtuoso defence of the old institutionalism. Stinchcombe, Arthur L. 1997. On the Virtues of the Old Institutionalism. *Annual Review of Sociology* 23: 1–18.

[17] Michael Williams expertly showed, for example, the inseparability of 'security' from culture. See Williams, Michael C. 2007a. *Culture and Security: Symbolic Power and the Politics of International Security*. New York: Routledge.

[18] Katzenstein, Peter, ed. 1996a. *The Culture of National Security: Norms and Identity in World Politics*. New York: Columbia University Press.

[19] Lapid, Yosef and Friedrich Kratocwhil. 1996. *The Return of Culture and Identity in IR Theory*. Boulder: Lynne Reinner.

[20] Geertz, Clifford. 1973. *The Interpretation of Cultures*. New York: Basic Books, 5.

[21] Reus-Smit, Christian. 2018. *On Cultural Diversity: International Theory in a World of Difference*. Cambridge: Cambridge University Press.

[22] Katzenstein 1996a: 6.

[23] Wendt 1992.

[24] Waltz, Kenneth. 1979. *Theory of International Politics*. Reading: Addison-Wesley.

[25] Wendt 1992.

[26] Adler, Emanuel and Michael Barnett. 1998. *Security Communities*. Cambridge: Cambridge University Press.

[27] Ruggie, John Gerard. 1998. What Makes the World Hang Together? Neo-Utilitarianism and the Social Constructivist Challenge? *International Organization* 52 (4): 855–85.

[28] For example, Klotz 1995.

[29] Tannenwald, Nina. 2008. *The Nuclear Taboo: The United States and the Non-Use of Nuclear Weapons since 1945*. Cambridge: Cambridge University Press.

[30] Tannenwald 2008: 45–8.

[31] Dueck, Colin. 2006. *Reluctant Crusaders: Power, Culture, and Change in American Grand Strategy*. Princeton: Princeton University Press.

[32] Katzenstein, Peter, ed. 1996b. *Cultural Norms in National Security: Police and Military in Postwar Japan*. Ithaca: Cornell University Press; Oros, Andrew. 2008. *Normalizing Japan: Politics, Identity, and the Evolution of Security Practice*. Stanford: Stanford University Press.

[33] Eden, Lynn. 2004. *Whole World on Fire: Organizations, Knowledge, and Nuclear Weapons Devastation*. Ithaca: Cornell University Press.

[34] See also Foley, Frank. 2013. *Countering Terrorism: Institutions, Norms, and the Shadow of the Past*. Cambridge: Cambridge University Press.

[35] Hopf, Ted. 2010. The Logic of Habit in International Relations. *European Journal of International Relations* 16 (4): 539–61.

[36] Porter, Patrick. 2018. Why America's Grand Strategy Has Not Changed: Power, Habit, and the US Foreign Policy Establishment. *International Security* 42 (4): 9–46.

[37] See Keohane, Robert O. 1988. International Institutions: Two Approaches. *International Studies Quarterly* 32 (4): 379–96; Zürn, Michael and Jeffrey T. Checkel. 2005. Getting Socialized to Build Bridges: Constructivism and Rationalism, Europe and the Nation-State. *International Organization* 59 (4): 1045–79.

[38] Compare Johnston, Alastair Iain. 1995. Thinking about Strategic Culture. *International Security* 19 (4): 32–64; Meyer, Christoph O. 2007. *The Quest for a European Strategic Culture: Changing Norms on Security and Defense in the European Union*. Basingstoke: Palgrave.

[39] See Fearon, James. 1999. What Is Identity (As We Now Use the Use the Word)? Unpublished Manuscript, Stanford University; Berenskoetter, Felix. 2018. Identity in International Relations. *Oxford Research Encyclopedias*. Oxford: Oxford University Press. Available at https://oxfordre.com/view/10.1093/acrefore/9780190846626.001.0001/acrefore-9780190846626-e-218

[40] Ringmar, Eric. 1996. *Identity, Interest and Action: A Cultural Explanation of Sweden's Intervention in the Thirty Years' War*. Cambridge: Cambridge University Press.

[41] Wendt 1992: 398.

[42] Finnemore, Martha. 1996a. *National Interests in International Society*. Ithaca: Cornell University Press, 1.

[43] Ringmar 1996: 95.

[44] Kratochwil 2006.

[45] Krebs, Ronald R. 2015. *Narrative and the Making of US National Security*. Cambridge: Cambridge University Press.

[46] For example, Little, Richard and Steve Smith, eds. 1988. *Belief Systems in International Relations*. Oxford: Blackwell; Goldstein, Judith and Robert O. Keohane, eds. 1993. *Ideas and Foreign Policy: Beliefs, Institutions, and Political Change*. Ithaca: Cornell University Press.

[47] Steele, Brent J. 2008. *Ontological Security in International Relations: Self-Identity and the IR State*. New York: Routledge.

[48] Hayes, Jarrod. 2013. *Constructing National Security: US Relations with China and India*. Cambridge: Cambridge University Press.

[49] For example, Ross, Andrew A.G. 2014. *Mixed Emotions: Beyond Fear and Hatred in International Conflict*. Chicago: Chicago University Press.

[50] Hymans, Jacques E.C. 2006. *The Psychology of Nuclear Proliferation: Identity, Emotions, and Foreign Policy*. Cambridge: Cambridge University Press.

[51] Hymans 2006.

[52] See, among others, Renshon, Jonathan. 2017. *Fighting for Status: Hierarchy and Conflict in World Politics*. Princeton: Princeton University Press; Murray, Michelle. 2018. *The Struggle for Recognition in International Relations: Status, Revisionism, and Rising Powers*. New York: Oxford University Press.

[53] For an important exception, see Hopf, Ted. 2002. *Social Construction of International Politics: Identities and Foreign Policies, Moscow 1955 and 1999*. Ithaca: Cornell University Press.

[54] Jackson Patrick Thaddeus and Daniel H. Nexon. 1999. Relations before States: Substance, Process and the Study of World Politics. *European Journal of International Relations* 5 (3): 291–332.

[55] Mattern, Janice Bially. 2005. *Ordering International Politics: Identity, Crisis, and Representational Force*. New York: Routledge.

[56] Mattern 2005: 52.

57 Neumann, Iver B. 1998. *Uses of the Other: 'the East' in European Identity Formation.* Minneapolis: University of Minnesota Press; Zarakol, Ayşe. 2010. *After Defeat: How the East Learned to Live with the West.* Cambridge: Cambridge University Press.
58 McCourt, David M. 2011a. Role-Playing and Identity Affirmation in International Politics: Britain's Reinvasion of the Falklands, 1982. *Review of International Studies* 37 (4): 1599–621; McCourt, David M. 2012a. The Roles States Play: A Meadian Interactionist Approach. *Journal of International Relations and Development* 15 (3): 370–92; McCourt 2014.
59 See Clark, Ian. 2011. *Hegemony in International Society.* Oxford: Oxford University Press.
60 Neumann, Iver B. and Ole Jacob Sending. 2010. *Governing the Global Polity: Practice, Mentality, and Rationality.* Ann Arbor: University of Michigan Press.
61 Campbell 1998.
62 Campbell 1998: 61.
63 Ashley, Richard K. 1987. Foreign Policy as Political Performance. *International Studies Notes* 13: 51.
64 Reus-Smit, Christian. 1999. *The Moral Purpose of the State: Culture, Social Identity, and Institutional Rationality in International Relations.* Princeton: Princeton University Press.
65 Ruggie, John Gerard. 1993. *Multilateralism Matters: The Theory and Praxis of an Institutional Form.* New York: Columbia University Press.
66 McCourt, David M. and Andrew Glencross 2018. Great Expectations: The EU's Social Role as Great Power Manager. *New Perspectives* 27 (1): 17–42; Raymond, Mark. 2019. *Social Practices of Rule-Making in World Politics.* New York: Oxford University Press.
67 Reus-Smit 1999: 13.
68 Reus-Smit 1999: 6.
69 Katzenstein 1996b: 22.
70 See, among others, Havercroft, Jonathan. 2011. *Captives of Sovereignty.* Cambridge: Cambridge University Press.
71 Hopf, Ted. 1998. The Promise of Constructivism in International Relations Theory, *International Security* 23 (1): 171–200.
72 Ruggie 1998: 880–2.
73 Zehfuss 2002: 10–23.
74 Katzenstein, Peter J., Robert O. Keohane and Stephen D. Krasner. 1998. International Organization and the Study of World Politics. *International Organization* 52 (4): 645–85.
75 Adler 1997.
76 Ruggie 1998: 857–62; Dessler, David. 1999. Constructivism within a Positivist Social Science. *Review of International Studies* 25 (1): 123–37.
77 Jackson, Patrick Thaddeus. 2011. *The Conduct of Inquiry in International Relations: Philosophy of Science and Its Implications for the Study of World Politics,* 1st Edition. New York: Routledge.
78 Checkel, Jeffrey T. 1998. The Constructivist Turn in International Relations Theory. *International Security* 50 (2): 324–48.
79 Bearce and Bondanella 2007.
80 Dietelhoff 2009.
81 Towns 2012.
82 Notably Hayes 2013; Hopf, Ted. 2002. *Social Construction of International Politics: Identities and Foreign Policies, Moscow, 1955 and 1999.* Ithaca: Cornell University Press; Steele, Brent J. 2008. *Ontological Security in International Relations: Self-Identity and the IR State.* New York: Routledge; Subotic, Jelena. 2009. *Hijacked Justice: Dealing with the Past in the Balkans.* Ithaca: Cornell University Press; Hopf, Ted. 2010. *Reconstructing the Cold War: The Early Years, 1945-58.* Oxford: Oxford University Press; Zarakol, Ayşe. 2010. *After Defeat: How the East Learned to Live With the West* Cambridge: Cambridge University Press.

[83] See, to barely scratch the surface, respectively, Navari, Cornelia. 2011. The Concept of Practice in the English School. *European Journal of International Relations* 17 (4): 611–30; Rosenberg, Justin. 1994. The International Imagination: IR Theory and 'Classic Social Analysis'. *Millennium: Journal of International Studies* 23 (1): 85–108; Tickner, J. Ann. 1988. Hans Morgenthau's Principles of Political Realism: A Feminist Reformulation. *Millennium: Journal of International Studies* 17 (3): 429–40; Linklater, Andrew. 1990. *Beyond Realism and Marxism: Critical Theory and International Relations.* London: Macmillan.

[84] Adbelal, Blyth and Parsons 2011: 2.

[85] Sikkink, Kathryn. 1991. *Ideas and Institutions: Developmentalism in Brazil and Argentina.* Ithaca: Cornell University Press; Goldstein and Keohane 1993.

[86] Adler 1997: 332; Checkel 1998: 325.

[87] Finnemore and Sikkink 2001: abstract.

[88] See also Checkel 1998: 325.

[89] Milliken, Jennifer. 1999. The Study of Discourse in International Relations: A Critique of Research Methods. *European Journal of International Relations* 5 (2): 225–54.

[90] Onuf 2012 [1989].

[91] Buzan, Barry, Ole Waever and Jaap De Wilde. 1997. *Security: A New Framework for Analysis.* Boulder: Lynne Reinner; Hayes 2013.

[92] Onuf 2012 [1989]: 36.

[93] Wendt 1987.

[94] Keck and Sikkink 1999.

[95] Jackson, Patrick Thaddeus. 2007. *Civilizing the Enemy: German Reconstruction and the Invention of the West.* Ann Arbor: University of Michigan Press.

[96] See Sikkink, Kathryn. 2011. *The Justice Cascade: How Human Rights Prosecutions are Changing World Politics.* New York: W.W. Norton. This ignores later works that successfully explore the structure–agency co-constitution. See Gheciu, Alexandra. 2005. Security Institutions as Agents of Socialization? NATO and the 'New Europe.' *International Organization* 59 (4): 973–1012.

[97] Wendt 1998.

[98] Kurki, Milja. 2008. *Causation in International Relations.* Cambridge: Cambridge University Press.

[99] Emirbayer 1997: 307.

[100] Klotz 1995.

[101] Wendt, Alexander. 1999. *Social Theory of International Politics.* Cambridge: Cambridge University Press.

[102] Jackson 2007: *viii.*

[103] Jackson 2007: 43, emphasis in original.

[104] Jackson 2007: 64.

[105] Jackson 2007: 64. See also Ish-Shalom, Piki. 2021. *Concepts at Work: On the Linguistic Infrastructure of World Politics.* Ann Arbor: University of Michigan Press.

[106] Jackson 2007: 77.

[107] See, for example, Rousseau, David L. 2006. *Identifying Threats and Threatening Identities: The Social Construction of Realism and Liberalism.* Stanford: Stanford University Press.

[108] See Hafner-Burton, Emilie M., Miles Kahler, and Alexander H. Montgomery. 2009. Network Analysis for International Relations. *International Organization* 63 (3): 559–92.

[109] Although see Goddard, Stacie E. 2012. Brokering Peace: Networks, Legitimacy, and the Northern Ireland Peace Process. *International Studies Quarterly* 56 (3): 501–15.

[110] Acharya, Amitav. 2004. How Ideas Spread: Whose Norms Matter? Norm Localization and Institutional Change in Asian Regionalism. *International Organization* 58 (2): 239–75.

111 Epstein, Charlotte. 2010. Who Speaks? Discourse, the Subject, and the Study of Identity in International Relations. *European Journal of International Relations* 17 (2): 327–50.
112 Abbott, Andrew. 2001. *Chaos of Disciplines*. Chicago: University of Chicago Press.
113 Abbott 2001: 17.
114 Abbott 2001: 17.

Chapter 2

1   Abbott, Andrew. 2001. *Chaos of Disciplines*. Chicago: University of Chicago Press.
2   Adler, Emanuel and Vincent Pouliot. 2011. *International Practices*. Cambridge: Cambridge University Press; Jackson, Patrick Thaddeus, and Daniel H. Nexon. 2019. Reclaiming the Social: Relationalism in Anglophone International Studies. *Cambridge Review of International Affairs* 32 (5): 583–600.
3   Schatzki, Theodore, Karin Knorr-Cetina and Eike von Savigny. 2001. *The Practice Turn in Contemporary Theory*. New York: Routledge; Bueger and Gadinger 2018; Kustermans 2016.
4   Schatzki et al 2001: 3.
5   Pouliot 2010: 17–22.
6   For insightful applications, see Hopf, Ted. 2013. Common-sense Constructivism and Hegemony in World Politics. *International Organization* 67 (2): 317–54; Autoserre, Séverine. 2014. *Peaceland: Conflict Resolution and the Everyday Politics of International Intervention*. Cambridge: Cambridge University Press; Howard, Lise Morjé. 2015. US Foreign Policy Habits in Ethnic Conflict. *International Studies Quarterly* 59 (4): 721–34.
7   Mattern, Janice Bially. 2005. *Ordering International Politics: Identity, Crisis, and Representational Force*. New York: Routledge; Mattern, Janice Bially. 2011. A Practice Theory of Emotion for International Relations. In Emanuel Adler and Vincent Pouliot, eds. *International Practices*. Cambridge: Cambridge University Press, 63-86; Ross, Andrew A.G. 2014. *Mixed Emotions: Beyond Fear and Hatred in International Conflict*. Chicago: Chicago University Press; Holmes, Marcus. 2015. Believing This and Alieving That: Theorizing Affect and Intuitions in International Politics. *International Studies Quarterly* 59 (4): 706–20.
8   Sharp, Paul. 2009. *Diplomatic Theory of International Politics*. Cambridge: Cambridge University Press.
9   Neumann, Iver B. 2012. *At Home With The Diplomats: Inside a European Foreign Ministry*. Ithaca: Cornell University Press.
10 Mische, Ann. 2011. Relational Sociology, Culture, and Agency. In John Scott and Peter J. Carrington, eds. *The SAGE Handbook of Social Network Analysis*. London: SAGE, pp 80–97; Crossley, Nick. 2012. *Towards Relational Sociology*. London: Routledge; for example, Tilly 2005.
11 Jackson Patrick Thaddeus and Daniel H. Nexon. 1999. Relations before States: Substance, Process and the Study of World Politics. *European Journal of International Relations* 5 (3): 291–332.
12 Emirbayer 1997: 281.
13 Emirbayer 1997: 284.
14 Emirbayer 1997: 307.
15 Elias, Norbert. 2000 [1937]. *The Civilizing Process*. Oxford: Basil Blackwell, 471.
16 Sending, Ole Jacob, Vincent Pouliot and Iver B. Neumann, eds. 2015. *Diplomacy and the Making of World Politics*. Cambridge: Cambridge University Press.
17 Onuf, Nicholas Greenwood. 2012 [1989]. *World of Our Making: Rules and Rule in Social Theory and International Relations*. Columbia: University of South Carolina Press.

[18] See Adler and Pouliot 2011 for a defence of a paradigm-independent practice turn, and Jackson, Patrick Thaddeus and Daniel H. Nexon. 2019 Reclaiming the Social: Relationalism in Anglophone International Studies. *Cambridge Review of International Affairs* 32 (5): 582–600 for the same regarding the relational turn.

[19] For a stimulating set of papers, see the special symposium of *International Studies Quarterly* 'Seizing Constructivist Ground?', 18 June 2017.

[20] See Sending, Pouliot and Neumann 2015: 6–16.

[21] Adler-Nissen, Rebecca, ed. 2012. *Bourdieu in International Relations*. London: Routledge; Bueger, Christian and Frank Gadinger. 2015. The Play of International Practice. *International Studies Quarterly* 59 (3): 449.

[22] See Krasner, Stephen D. 1982. Structural Causes and Regime Consequences: Regimes and Intervening Variables. *International Organization* 36 (2): 185–205.

[23] Adler, Emanuel. 1997. Seizing the Middle Ground: Constructivism in World Politics. *European Journal of International Relations* 3 (3): 319–63.

[24] Adler and Pouliot 2011: 5.

[25] Jackson and Nexon 2009.

[26] Jackson and Nexon 2009: 907–08.

[27] Onuf 2012 [1989]: 13–16.

[28] See Kratochwil and Ruggie 1986: 772.

[29] Katzenstein, Peter J., Robert O. Keohane and Stephen D. Krasner. 1998. International Organization and the Study of World Politics. *International Organization* 52 (4): 645–85.

[30] Martin, John Levi. 2003. What Is Field Theory? *American Journal of Sociology* 109 (1), 1.

[31] Fligstein, Neil and Doug McAdam. 2012. *A Theory of Fields*. Oxford: Oxford University Press.

[32] Adler-Nissen 2012; Leander, Anna. 2011. The Promises, Problems, and Pitfalls of a Bourdieu-inspired Staging of International Relations. *International Political Sociology* 5: 294–313; Villumsen-Berling, Trine. 2015. *The International Political Sociology of Security*. London: Routledge.

[33] Pouliot, Vincent. 2010. *International Security in Practice: The Politics of NATO-Russia Diplomacy*. Cambridge: Cambridge University Press, 33–4.

[34] For an insightful analysis of struggles over cultural capital in great power relations, see Musgrave, Paul and Daniel H. Nexon. 2018. Defending Hierarchy from the Moon to the Indian Ocean. *International Organization* 72 (3): 591–626.

[35] Martin 2003: 314, emphasis added.

[36] Pouliot 2010: 14–27.

[37] Pouliot 2010: 15.

[38] Bourdieu, Pierre, and Loïc J.D. Wacquant. 1992. *An Invitation to Reflexive Sociology*. Chicago: University of Chicago Press; see, for example, Stampnitzky, Lisa. 2013. *Disciplining Terror: How Experts Invented 'Terrorism'*. Cambridge: Cambridge University Press.

[39] Hafner-Burton, Kahler and Montgomery 2009; Goddard 2012; MacDonald, Paul K. 2014. *Networks of Domination: The Social Foundations of Peripheral Conquest in International Politics*. New York: Oxford University Press; Avant, Deborah and Oliver Westerwinter. 2016. *The New Power Politics: Networks and Transnational Security Governance*. New York: Oxford University Press; Avant, Deborah. 2016. Pragmatic Networks and Transnational Governance of Private Military and Security Services. *International Studies Quarterly* 60 (2): 330–42.

[40] Mische 2011: 84–9.

[41] Marin, Alexandra and Barry Wellman. 2011. Social Network Analysis: An Introduction. In John Scott and Peter J. Carrington, eds. *The SAGE Handbook of Social Network Analysis*. London: SAGE, 11.

42 Nexon, Daniel H. 2009. *The Struggle for Power in Early Modern Europe: Religious Conflict, Dynastic Empires, and International Change*. Princeton, NJ: Princeton University Press.

43 Carpenter 2011.

44 Carpenter 2011: 72.

45 See Bueger 2013: 338.

46 Barry, Andrew. 2013. The Translation Zone: Between Actor-Network Theory and International Relations. *Millennium: Journal of International Studies* 41 (3): 413–29; Best, Jacqueline, and William Walters. 2013. Forum on Actor-Network Theory and International Relationality: Lost (and Found) in Translation. *International Political Sociology* 7 (3): 332–49; Bueger and Gadinger 2015.

47 Callon, Michael. 1986. Some Elements of a Sociology of Translation. In John Law, ed. *Power, Action and Belief*. London: Routledge and Kegan Paul, pp 196–233; Latour, Bruno, and Steve Woolgar. 1988. *Laboratory Life: The Construction of Scientific Facts*. Princeton: Princeton University Press; Latour, Bruno. 2005. *Reassembling the Social: An Introduction to Actor-Network Theory*. Oxford: Oxford University Press.

48 Latour 2005: 1–17.

49 Porter, Tony. 2013. Tracing Associations in Global Finance. *International Political Sociology* 7 (3): 334.

50 Leander 2011; Porter 2013.

51 See Milliken 1999.

52 Onuf 2012 [1989]: 40.

53 See, for example, Branch, Jordan. 2014. *The Cartographic State: Maps, Territory, and the Origins of Sovereignty*. Cambridge: Cambridge University Press; Barder, Alexander. 2015. *Empire Within: International Hierarchy and Its Imperial Laboratories of Governance*. New York: Routledge; Branch, Jordan. 2016. Geographic Information Systems (GIS) in International Relations. *International Organization* 70 (4): 845–69; Branch, Jordan. 2018. Technology and Constructivism: Interrogating the Ideational-Material Divide. In Mariano Bertucci, Jarrod Hayes, and Patrick James, eds. *Constructivism Reconsidered: Past, Present, and Future*. Ann Arbor: University of Michigan Press, pp 103–15.

54 Pouliot 2010: 11.

55 Latour 2005: 43.

56 Jackson, Patrick Thaddeus. 2007. *Civilizing the Enemy: German Reconstruction and the Invention of the West*. Ann Arbor: University of Michigan Press.

57 Jackson 2007: 67.

58 Jackson 2007: 43, emphasis in original.

59 Jackson 2007: 64.

60 Jackson 2007; Pouliot, Vincent. 2008. The Logic of Practicality: A Theory of Practice of Security Communities. *International Organization* 62 (2): 257–88; Neumann, Iver B. and Ole Jacob Sending. 2010. *Governing the Global Polity: Practice, Mentality, and Rationality*. Ann Arbor: University of Michigan Press; Zarakol, Ayşe. 2010. *After Defeat: How the East Learned to Live with the West*. Cambridge: Cambridge University Press; Hopf 2012.

61 Hopf, Ted. 1998. The Promise of Constructivism in International Relations Theory. *International Security* 23 (1): 171–200.

62 Jackson 2007. See also Goddard, Stacie E. and Ronald R. Krebs. 2015. Rhetoric, Legitimation, and Grand Strategy. *Security Studies* 24 (1): 5–36.

63 Jackson 2007: 178–9.

64 Neumann and Sending 2010: 93.

65 Neumann and Sending 2010: 70–109.

66 Hopf 2012.

67 Hopf 2012: 248.

68 Morgan, Patrick M. 2011. The Practice of Deterrence. In Emanuel Adler and Vincent Pouliot, eds. *International Practices*. Cambridge: Cambridge University Press, pp 139–73.
69 Morgan 2011: 144, emphasis in original.
70 See Oatley, Thomas. 2011. The Reductionist Gamble: Open Economy Politics in the Global Economy. *International Organization* 65 (2): 311–41.
71 Ruggie, John Gerard. 1998. What Makes the World Hang Together? Neo-Utilitarianism and the Social Constructivist Challenge? *International Organization* 52 (4): 855–85.
72 Katzenstein, Peter J. 2009. Mid-Atlantic: Sitting on the Knife's Sharp Edge. *Review of International Political Economy* 16 (1): 125.
73 Adamson, Fiona B. 2016. Spaces of Global Security: Beyond Methodological Nationalism. *Journal of Global Security Studies* 1 (1): 9–35.
74 Abbott 2001: 88.

Chapter 3

1   Kratochwil, Friedrich V. 1989. *Rules, Norms, and Decisions: On the Conditions of Legal and Practical Reasoning in International Relations and Domestic Affairs*. Cambridge: Cambridge University Press; Onuf, Nicholas Greenwood. 2012 [1989]. *World of Our Making: Rules and Rule in Social Theory and International Relations*. Columbia: University of South Carolina Press.
2   See especially Epstein, Charlotte. 2013a. Constructivism or the Eternal Return of Universals in International Relations: Why Returning to Language is Vital for Prolonging the Owl's Flight. *European Journal of International Relations* 19 (3): 499–519, which I engage in depth throughout the chapter. Also Guzzini, Stefano. 2000. A Reconstruction of Constructivism in International Relations. *European Journal of International Relations* 6 (2): 147–82.
3   See also Neumann, Iver B. 2002. Returning Practice to the Linguistic Turn: The Case of Diplomacy. *Millennium: Journal of International Studies* 31 (3): 625–51.
4   An important exception here is the work of Harry Gould, see Gould, Harry. 2010. *The Legacy of Punishment in International Law*. New York: Palgrave Macmillan.
5   See Kratochwil 2006. For alternative views of progress in the field, and analyses of competing visions, see Elman, Miriam Fendius and Colin Elman. 2003. *Progress in International Relations Theory*. Cambridge, Mass.: MIT Press; Chernoff, Fred. 2014. *Explanation and Progress in Security Studies: Bridging Theoretical Divides in International Relations*. Stanford: Stanford University Press.
6   Epstein 2013a: 502.
7   Epstein 2013a.
8   All the way down through the modern subject, Epstein powerfully argues. Epstein, Charlotte. 2013b. Theorizing Agency in Hobbes's Wake: The Rational Actor, the Self, or the Speaking Subject. *International Organization* 67 (2): 287–316.
9   See Barder, Alexander D. and Daniel J. Levine. 2012. 'The World Is Too Much With Us': Reification and the Depolitising of *Via Media* Constructivist IR. *Millennium: Journal of International Studies* 40 (3): 585–604.
10 Kratochwil and Ruggie 1986.
11 Kratochwil, Friedrich V. 1989. *Rules, Norms, and Decisions: On the Conditions of Legal and Practical Reasoning in International Relations and Domestic Affairs*. Cambridge: Cambridge University Press.
12 Kratochwil, Friedrich V. 2018. Praxis: On Acting and Knowing. Cambridge: Cambridge University Press.
13 Kratochwil 1989: 6.

[14] Fierke, Karin M. 1998. *Changing Games, Changing Strategies: Critical Investigations in Security.* Manchester: Manchester University Press; Duffy, Gavan and Brian Frederking. 2009. Changing the Rules: A Speech Act Analysis of the End of the Cold War. *International Studies Quarterly* 52 (2): 325–47.

[15] Buzan, Barry, Ole Waever and Jaap De Wilde. 1997. *Security: A New Framework for Analysis.* Boulder: Lynne Reinner.

[16] Kratochwil 2018: 7

[17] Kratochwil 2018: 7.

[18] Jepperson, Ronald, Alexander Wendt and Peter Katzenstein. 1996. Norms, Identity, and Culture in National Security. In Peter Katzenstein, ed. *The Culture of National Security: Norms and Identity in World Politics.* New York: Columbia University Press, pp 35–75.

[19] Checkel, Jeffrey T. 1998. The Constructivist Turn in International Relations Theory. *International Security* 50 (2): 324–48.

[20] Epstein, Charlotte. 2013a. Constructivism or the Eternal Return of Universals in International Relations: Why Returning to Language is Vital for Prolonging the Owl's Flight. *European Journal of International Relations* 19 (3): 502.

[21] Epstein 2013a: 501, emphasis in original.

[22] Epstein 2013a: 501.

[23] Epstein 2013a: 502, emphasis in original.

[24] Epstein 2013a: 512.

[25] Epstein 2013a: 501. See also Robert O. Keohane's call for just such a centre in Keohane, Robert O. 1988. International Institutions: Two Approaches. *International Studies Quarterly* 32 (4): 379–96.

[26] Jackson, Patrick Thaddeus. 2007. *Civilizing the Enemy: German Reconstruction and the Invention of the West.* Ann Arbor: University of Michigan Press.

[27] Oren, Ido. 2003. *Our Enemies and US: America's Rivalries and the Making of Political Science.* Ithaca: Cornell University Press.

[28] Epstein, Charlotte. 2021. *Birth of the State: The Place of the Body in Crafting Modern Politics.* Oxford: Oxford University Press.

[29] See, among many others in IR and beyond, Bartelson, Jens. 1995. *A Genealogy of Sovereignty.* Cambridge: Cambridge University Press; Spruyt, Hendrik. 1996. The Sovereign State and Its Competitors. Princeton: Princeton University Press; Krasner, Stephen D. 1999. *Sovereignty: Organized Hypocrisy.* Princeton: Princeton University Press; Bartelson, Jens. 2001. *The Critique of the State.* Cambridge: Cambridge University Press; Osiander, Andreas. 2001. Sovereignty, International Relations, and the Westphalian Myth. *International Organization* 55 (2): 251–87; Philpott, Daniel. 2001. *Revolutions in Sovereignty: How Ideas Shaped Modern International Relations.* Princeton: Princeton University Press; Teschke, Benno. 2003. *The Myth of 1648: Class, Geopolitics and the Making of Modern International Relations.* London: Verso; Bartelson, Jens. 2014. *Sovereignty as Symbolic Form.* London: Routledge.

[30] Hirschman, Daniel and Isaac Ariail Reed. 2014. Foundation Stories and Causality in Sociology. *Sociological Theory* 32 (4): 259–82.

[31] Epstein 2021: 24.

[32] Allan, Bentley B. 2019. *Scientific Cosmology and International Orders.* Cambridge: Cambridge University Press.

[33] Epstein 2021: 25, emphasis in original.

[34] Epstein 2021: 265, emphasis in original.

[35] Epstein 2021: 74. See also Flathman, Richard. 1993. *Thomas Hobbes: Skepticism, Individuality and Chastened Politics.* London: Sage. Epstein thus makes good on a continued

engagement with Hobbes suggested by Michael Williams. See Epstein 2013b and Kratochwil 2018: 32–7.

36 Epstein 2021: 131.
37 Epstein 2021: 127.
38 Epstein 2021: 31–2.
39 Epstein 2021: 172–4.
40 Epstein 2021: 276.
41 Onuf, Nicholas Greenwood. 2018b. Preface: The Dinosaur Speaks! In Mariano Bertucci, Jarrod Hayes, and Patrick James, eds. *Constructivism Reconsidered: Past, Present, and Future*. Ann Arbor: University of Michigan Press, pp xiii–xix, cited in Raymond, Mark. 2019. *Social Practices of Rule-Making in World Politics*. New York: Oxford University Press, emphasis in original.
42 Onuf 2018b: 4, cited in Raymond 2019: 9.
43 See Shotter, John. 1996. 'Now I Can Go On': Wittgenstein and Our Embodied Embeddedness in the 'Hurly Burly' of Life. *Human Studies* 19: 385–407.
44 March, James G. and Johan P. Olsen. 1998. The Institutional Dynamics of International Political Orders. *International Organization* 52 (4): 943–69.
45 March and Olsen 1998.
46 Lechner, Silviya and Mervyn Frost. 2018. *Practice Theory and International Relations*. Cambridge: Cambridge University Press.
47 Lechner and Frost 2018: 3.
48 Lechner and Frost 2018: 1.
49 Lechner and Frost 2018: 11.
50 Lechner and Frost 2018: 11.
51 Lechner and Frost 2018: 44.
52 Lechner and Frost 2018: 42.
53 Lechner and Frost 2018: 45.
54 Lechner and Frost 2018: 45, emphasis added.
55 See especially Latour 2005.
56 Lechner and Frost 2018: 48.
57 Lechner and Frost 2018: 72.
58 Respectively, Bourdieu 2019, 2020, 2006 [1992].
59 Bourdieu, Pierre. 1990. *In Other Words: Essays Towards a Reflexive Sociology*. Stanford: Stanford University Press, emphasis in original.
60 Lechner and Frost 2018: 212.
61 Raymond 2019.
62 Raymond 2020.
63 Raymond 2020: 2.
64 Raymond 2020: 2.
65 Raymond 2020: 8.
66 Raymond 2019: 44–87.
67 Zala, Benjamin. 2017. Great Power Management and Ambiguous Order in Nineteenth-Century International Society. *Review of International Studies* 43 (2): 367–88; McCourt and Glencross 2018.
68 Reus-Smit, Christian. 1997. The Constitutional Structure of International Society. *International Organization* 51 (4): 555–89.
69 Waltz, Kenneth. 1979. *Theory of International Politics*. Reading: Addison-Wesley.
70 Goddard, Stacie E., and Daniel H. Nexon. 2005. Paradigm Lost? Reassessing Theory of International Politics. *European Journal of International Relations* 11 (1): 9–61.

[71] Ruggie, John Gerard. 1993. *Multilateralism Matters: The Theory and Praxis of an Institutional Form*. New York: Columbia University Press.

[72] Raymond 2021: 12.

[73] Kratochwil 1989: 181–211.

[74] Aalberts, Tanja E. 2012. *Constructing Sovereignty Between Politics and Law*. Abingdon: Routledge.

[75] Aalberts 2012: 161.

[76] Aalberts 2012: 158.

[77] Rajkovic, Nikolas M. 2010. 'Global Law' and Governmentality: Reconceptualizing the 'Rule of Law' as Rule 'Through' Law. *European Journal of International Relations* 18 (1): 29–52.

[78] Rajkovic 2010: 38.

[79] Rajkovic 2010: 23.

[80] Epstein 2021: 132.

[81] Neumann 2002: 630.

[82] Onuf 2012 [1989]: 40.

[83] Onuf 2012 [1989]: 40.

[84] Onuf 2012 [1989]: 51.

[85] Onuf 2012 [1989]: 51.

[86] See Hollis and Smith 1991.

[87] Onuf 2012 [1989]: 51.

[88] Onuf 2012 [1989]: 52.

[89] Onuf 2012 [1989]: 52.

[90] Pouliot 2008.

[91] Onuf 2012 [1989]: 49–50.

[92] Onuf 2012 [1989]: 50.

[93] Mills, C. Wright. 1956. *The Power Elite*. New York: Oxford University Press.

[94] See Ruggie, John Gerard. 1998. What Makes the World Hang Together? Neo-Utilitarianism and the Social Constructivist Challenge? *International Organization* 52 (4): 855–85.

[95] Onuf 2012 [1989]: 51, emphasis added.

[96] See, for example, Finnemore and Sikkink 2001, abstract.

[97] Onuf 2012 [1989]: 36.

[98] Onuf 2012 [1989]: 56–7.

[99] Kratochwil 2018: 44

[100] Linklater, Andrew. 2011. *The Problem of Harm in World Politics: Theoretical Investigations*. Cambridge: Cambridge University Press; Linklater 2016.

[101] Agamben, Giorgio. 1995. *Homo Sacer: Sovereign Power and Bare Life*. Stanford: Stanford University Press; Foucault, Michel. 2010. *The Birth of Biopolitics: Lectures at the Collège de France, 1978–1979*. New York: Picador.

Chapter 4

[1] Foucault, Michel. 1989 [1961]. *Discipline and Punish: The Birth of the Prison*. New York: Vintage; Foucault 1989 [1963]; Foucault 1995 [1975]. See also Meyer, John W. and Brian Rowan. 1977. Institutionalized Organizations: Formal Structure as Myth and Ceremony. *American Journal of Sociology* 83 (2): 340–63; Gorski, Philip S. 2003. *The Disciplinary Revolution: Calvinism and the Rise of the State in Early Modern Europe*. Chicago: Chicago University Press.

[2] Guzzini, Stefano. 2000. A Reconstruction of Constructivism in International Relations. *European Journal of International Relations* 6 (2): 147–82.

3   See, respectively, Latour, Bruno. 2005. Reassembling the Social: An Introduction to Actor-Network Theory. Oxford: Oxford University Press; Reus-Smit, Christian. 2018. *On Cultural Diversity: International Theory in a World of Difference*. Cambridge: Cambridge University Press.

4   Amoureux 2016; Amoureux, Jack L. and Brent J. Steele, eds. 2016. *Reflexivity and International Relations: Positionality, Critique, and Practice*. London: Routledge.

5   Löwenheim, Oded. 2010. The 'I' in IR: An Autoethnographic Account. *Review of International Studies* 36 (4): 1023–45.

6   For a good discussion, see Eagleton-Pierce, Matthew. 2011. Advancing a Reflexive International Relations. *Millennium: Journal of International Studies* 39 (3): 805–23.

7   See Jackson, Patrick Thaddeus. 2007. *Civilizing the Enemy: German Reconstruction and the Invention of the West*. Ann Arbor: University of Michigan Press.

8   Wunderlich, Carmen. 2019. *Rogue States as Norm Entrepreneurs: Black Sheep or Sheep in Wolves' Clothing?* New York: Springer.

9   Sunstein, Cass R. 1996. Social Norms and Social Roles. *Columbia Law Review* 96 (4): 903–68.

10 Finnemore 1996b; Florini, Ann. 1996. The Evolution of International Norms. *International Studies Quarterly* 40 (3): 363–89; Finnemore and Sikkink 1998; Keck and Sikkink 1998, 1999; Ingebritsen, Christine. 2002. Norm Entrepreneurs: Scandinavia's Role in World Politics. *Cooperation and Conflict* 37 (1): 11–23.

11 See, among many others, Nadelmann, Ethan A. 1990. Global Prohibition Regimes: The Evolution of Norms in International Society. International Organization 44: 479–526; Slaughter, Anne-Marie. 2005. *A New World Order*. Princeton: Princeton University Press; Sikkink, Kathryn. 2011. *The Justice Cascade: How Human Rights Prosecutions are Changing World Politics*. New York: W.W. Norton; Krook, Mona Lena and Jacqui True. 2012. Rethinking the Life Cycles of International Norms. *European Journal of International Relations* 18 (1): 103–27; Davies, Sara E. and Jacque True. 2017. Norm Entrepreneurship in Foreign Policy: William Hague and the Prevention of Sexual Violence in Conflict. *Foreign Policy Analysis* 13: 701–21.

12 Legro, Jeffrey. 1997. Which Norms Matter? *International Organization* 51 (1): 31–63; Acharya, Amitav. 2004. How Ideas Spread: Whose Norms Matter? Norm Localization and Institutional Change in Asian Regionalism. *International Organization* 58 (2): 239–75.

13 Goddard, Stacie E. 2009. Brokering Change: Networks and Entrepreneurs in International Politics. *International Theory* 1 (2): 249–81.

14 Adler, Emanuel and Vincent Pouliot. 2011. *International Practices*. Cambridge: Cambridge University Press.

15 Adler and Pouliot 2011: 24.

16 Adler and Pouliot 2011: 29–30.

17 Adler and Pouliot 2011: 18–19.

18 Bueger, Christian. 2011. Communities of Practice in World Politics – Theory or Technology? Paper presented at the 52nd Annual Conference of the International Studies Association, Montreal CA, March, 2.

19 Adler and Pouliot 2011.

20 Goetze, Catherine. 2017. *The Distinction of Peace: A Social Analysis of Peacebuilding*. Ann Arbor: University of Michigan Press.

21 Bourdieu, Pierre. 1984. *Distinction: A Social Critique of the Judgment of Taste*. Cambridge, Mass.: Harvard University Press.

22 Goetze 2017: 1.

23 Goetze 2017: 1.

24 Goetze 2017: 3.

25 Goetze 2017: 3.
26 Goetze 2017: 46.
27 Krause, Monika. 2014. *The Good Project: Humanitarian Relief NGOs and the Fragmentation of Reason*. Chicago: University of Chicago Press.
28 Goetze 2017: 195.
29 Goetze 2017: 195.
30 Goetze 2017: 102.
31 Stampnitzky, Lisa. 2013. *Disciplining Terror: How Experts Invented 'Terrorism'*. Cambridge: Cambridge University Press.
32 Stampnitzky 2013: 3.
33 Stampnitzky 2013: 6.
34 Shirk, Mark. 2019. The Universal Eye: Anarchist 'Propaganda of the Deed' and the Development of the Modern Surveillance State. *International Studies Quarterly* 63 (2): 334–45.
35 Shirk 2019.
36 Gallie, W.E.B. 1956. Essentially Contested Concepts. *Proceedings of the Aristotelian Society* 56: 167–98.
37 See Bourdieu, Pierre. 2015. *On the State*. Cambridge: Polity; Morgan, Kimberly J. and Ann Shola Orloff. 2017. *The Many Hands of the State*. New York: Cambridge University Press.
38 Stampnitzky 2013: 11.
39 Sharp, Paul. 2009. *Diplomatic Theory of International Politics*. Cambridge: Cambridge University Press; Banerjee, Kiran, and Joseph MacKay. 2020. Communities of Practice, Impression Management, and Great Power Status: Military Observers in the Russo-Japanese War. *Review of International Studies*. OnlineFirst, 1–20. See also Constantinou, Costas M., Pauline Kerr and Paul Sharp, eds. 2016. *The SAGE Handbook of Diplomacy*. London: SAGE.
40 Neumann, Iver B. 2002. Returning Practice to the Linguistic Turn: The Case of Diplomacy. *Millennium: Journal of International Studies* 31 (3): 627–51.
41 Neumann 2012: 58.
42 Durkheim, Emile. 1982 [1895]. *The Rules of Sociological Method*. New York: Free Press.
43 Neumann, Iver B. 2012. *At Home With The Diplomats: Inside a European Foreign Ministry*. Ithaca: Cornell University Press.
44 Neumann 2012: 61.
45 Neumann 2012: 63.
46 Neumann 2012: 76.
47 Neumann 2012: 66–8.
48 Sending, Ole Jacob, Vincent Pouliot and Iver B. Neumann, eds. 2015. *Diplomacy and the Making of World Politics*. Cambridge: Cambridge University Press. See also Banks, David E. 2019. Fields of Practice: Symbolic Binding and the Qing Defense of Sinocentric Diplomacy. *International Studies Quarterly* 63 (3): 546–57.
49 Seabrooke, Leonard. 2015. Diplomacy as Economic Consultancy. In Ole Jakob Sending, Vincent Pouliot, and I.B. Neumann, eds. *Diplomacy: The Making of World Politics*. Cambridge: Cambridge University Press, p 204. See also Seabrooke, Leonard and Eleni Tsingou. 2014. Distinctions, Affiliations, and Professional Knowledge in Financial Reform Expert Groups. *Journal of European Public Policy* 21 (3): 389–407.
50 Bueger, Christian. 2017. Territory, Authority, Expertise: Global Governance and the Counter-Piracy Assemblage. *European Journal of International Relations* 24 (3): 614–37.
51 Löwenheim, Oded. 2006. *Parasites and Predators: Persistent Agents of Transnational Harm and Great Power Authority*. Ann Arbor: University of Michigan Press.
52 Bueger 2017: 618.

[53] Jackson Patrick Thaddeus and Daniel H. Nexon. 1999. Relations before States: Substance, Process and the Study of World Politics. *European Journal of International Relations* 5 (3): 291–332; Guillaume, Xavier. 2007. Unveiling the 'International': Process, Identity and Alterity. *Millennium: Journal of International Studies* 35 (3): 741–58.

[54] Adler and Pouliot 2011; Bueger, Christian and Frank Gadinger. 2014. *International Practice Theory*. Houndmills: Palgrave.

[55] Best, Jacqueline, and William Walters. 2013. Forum on Actor-Network Theory and International Relationality: Lost (and Found) in Translation. *International Political Sociology* 7 (3): 332–49.

[56] Bueger 2017: 619.

[57] Bueger 2017: 619.

[58] Pouliot, Vincent. 2016. *International Pecking Orders: The Politics and Practice of Multilateral Diplomacy*. Cambridge: Cambridge University Press; Zarakol, Ayşe. 2018. Sovereign Equality as Misrecognition. *Review of International Studies* 44 (5): 848–62.

[59] Bueger 2017: 615.

[60] Compare https://obamawhitehouse.archives.gov/sites/default/files/docs/2015_national_security_strategy_2.pdf pp ii–iii, https://trumpwhitehouse.archives.gov/wp-content/uploads/2017/12/NSS-Final-12-18-2017-0905.pdf, pp 2, 45.

[61] 'Biden, as President, Will Shift US Toolkit on China', *Wall Street Journal* 9 November 2020, www.wsj.com/articles/biden-as-president-will-shift-u-s-toolkit-on-china-11604917800?mod=article_inline

[62] Hayes, Jarrod. 2013. *Constructing National Security: US Relations with China and India*. Cambridge: Cambridge University Press.

[63] Weldes, Jutta. 1999. *Constructing National Interests: The United States and the Cuban Missile Crisis*. Minneapolis: University of Minnesota Press.

[64] Mearsheimer, John. 2001. *The Tragedy of Great Power Politics*. New York: W.W. Norton; Mearsheimer, John. 2006. China's Unpeaceful Rise. *Current History* 105 (690): 160–2.

[65] 'Hong Kong elections: UK and allies condemn moves to "undermine democracy"', *BBC News* 9 August 2020, www.bbc.com/news/world-asia-china-53716538

[66] Goffman, Erving. 1986. *Frame Analysis*. Boston: Northeastern University Press.

[67] Frames function similarly to 'narratives', 'paradigms', and – a more recent concept – 'memes'. See Beeson, Mark and Fujian Li. 2015. What Consensus? Geopolitics and Policy Paradigms in China and the United States. *International Affairs* 91 (1): 93–109; Breuer, Adam and Alastair Iain Johnston. 2019. Memes, Narratives, and the Emergent US-China Security Dilemma. *Cambridge Review of International Affairs* 32 (4): 429–55.

[68] Interviews with China experts, including former policy-makers, academics, think tankers, and for-profit consultants working in the China space. One hundred and seven experts were institutionally located in America, 14 in Australia, and 12 in the UK, although many had experience in more than one field. Interviews were conducted between late 2016 and early 2021. Interviews totaled over 100 hours. Interviewees ranged in age and experience, and were identified using the snowball sampling method.

[69] UK interview D.

[70] UK interview E. As one prominent UK columnist noted, 'For Americans … it very quickly comes round to the question "what does America do? Should we try to thwart them, co-opt them? … In Britain, we don't think that way".' UK interview D.

[71] UK interview E, p 1.

[72] UK interview E, p 8.

[73] *The United States's Strategic Approach to the People's Republic of China*, https://trumpwhitehouse.archives.gov/wp-content/uploads/2020/05/U.S.-Strategic-Approach-to-The-Peoples-Republic-of-China-Report-5.24v1.pdf, p 1.

74 *United States Strategic Approach*, p 1.

75 George, Roger and Harvey Rishikoff, eds. 2017. *The National Security Enterprise.* Washington: Georgetown University Press.

76 US interview A.

77 Drezner, Daniel. 2017. *The Ideas Industry.* New York: Oxford University Press.

78 Compared to the large DC think tanks, 'most British operations are shoestring operations'. UK interview G.

79 Academic literature on political appointees system is surprisingly sparse. Medvetz, Thomas. 2013. *Think Tanks in America.* Chicago: University of Chicago Press; www.therevolvingdoorproject.org

80 Which goes beyond the influence of business elites, see de Graaf, Naná and Bastiaan Van Apeldoorn. 2018. US-China Relations and the Liberal World Order: Contending Elites, Colliding Visions? *International Affairs* 94 (1): 113–31.

81 'American presidents have a long history of walking back tough talk on China', *Washington Post* 6 December 2016, www.washingtonpost.com/news/wonk/wp/2016/12/06/american-presidents-have-a-long-history-of-walking-back-tough-talk-on-china/

82 UK interview F.

83 UK interview G.

84 UK interview G.

85 UK interview B.

86 UK interview B.

87 'AirSea Battle' 18 May 2010, https://csbaonline.org/research/publications/airsea-battle-concept

88 See www.ned.org/wp-content/uploads/2017/12/Sharp-Power-Rising-Authoritarian-Influence-Full-Report.pdf

89 www.cecc.gov/publications/annual-reports; www.uscc.gov/annual-reports

90 See Boon, Hoo Tiang and Hannah Elyse Sworn. 2020. Strategic Ambiguity and the Trumpian Approach to China-Taiwan Relations. *International Affairs* 96 (6): 1487–508.

91 https://presentdangerchina.org/about

92 Gingrich, Newt. 2019. *Trump Vs. China.* New York: Center St; 'China is "Going to Push Biden Around" and US "Must Push Back",' *Fox News* 7 December 2020. www.foxnews.com/world/gordon-chang-china-push-biden-around-dangerous

93 https://2017-2021.state.gov/communist-china-and-the-free-worlds-future-2/index.html

94 'GOP memo urges anti-China assault over Coronavirus', *Politico* 24 April 2020, www.politico.com/news/2020/04/24/gop-memo-anti-china-coronavirus-207244

95 US interview C.

96 Bader, Jeffrey. 2012. *Obama and China's Rise.* Washington DC: Brookings.

97 'How Mnuchin Keeps a Steady Grip'; Henry Paulson, *Dealing with China* (New York: Twelve, 2016); 'How to Fix Our Relationship with China', *Wall St. Journal* 14 December 2020, www.wsj.com/articles/henry-paulson-how-to-fix-our-relationship-with-china-11607943600?mod=hp_featst_pos4

98 'China is Not the Enemy', *Washington Post* 3 July 2019, www.washingtonpost.com/opinions/making-china-a-us-enemy-is-counterproductive/2019/07/02/647d49d0-9bfa-11e9-b27f-ed2942f73d70_story.html

99 'Stay the Course on China', *Journal of Political Risk* 18 July 2019, www.jpolrisk.com/stay-the-course-on-china-an-open-letter-to-president-trump/; 'Why the United States doesn't need to return to a gentler China policy', *Washington Post*, www.washingtonpost.com/opinions/2019/07/09/why-united-states-doesnt-need-return-gentler-china-policy/

[100] 'As Trump attacks Biden on China, he's playing a weak hand', *Los Angeles Times* 27 July 2020, www.latimes.com/politics/story/2020-07-27/attacks-on-joe-bidens-missteps-in-china-blunted-by-trumps-own-failures-there

[101] Kurt Campbell and Ely Ratner, 'The China Reckoning: How Beijing Defied American Expectations', *Foreign Affairs* 97 (2) March/April 2018: 60–70.

[102] 'China is Not the Enemy'.

[103] www.ncsc.gov.uk/information/5g-and-us-sanctions-round-up; blogs.lse.ac.uk/politicsandpolicy/the-citys-pivot-to-china-in-a-post-brexit-world-a-uniquely-vulnerable-policy/

[104] For example, George Magnus' balanced analysis, https://georgemagnus.com/britains-huawei-controversy-has-wider-important-significance

[105] henryjacksonsociety.org/statement-of-principles/

[106] Iain Duncan Smith, 'With hopeless naivety, big business and universities have failed to understand that China is out to destroy our way of life', *The Mail on Sunday* 12 December 2020, www.dailymail.co.uk/debate/article-9046935/IAIN-DUNCAN-SMITH-Big-business-failed-understand-China-destroy-way-life.html

[107] See, for example, www.dailymail.co.uk/news/article-8375447/The-Wolverines-VS-China-Australian-MPs-upset-Beijing.html

[108] https://chinaresearchgroup.org/about

[109] 'Not Cold War, But a Values War; Not Decoupling, But Some Divergence', 2 November 2020, https://chinaresearchgroup.org/research/values-war

[110] https://blogs.lse.ac.uk/politicsandpolicy/labour-china-policy/

[111] https://blogs.lse.ac.uk/politicsandpolicy/labour-china-policy/

Chapter 5

[1] See Jackson, Patrick Thaddeus. 2011. *The Conduct of Inquiry in International Relations: Philosophy of Science and Its Implications for the Study of World Politics*, 1st Edition. New York: Routledge.

[2] Becker, Howard. 1953. Becoming a Marihuana User. *American Journal of Sociology* 59 (3): 235–42.

[3] Jackson 2011: 201–07.

[4] Abbott: 2001: 69.

[5] Mills, C. Wright. 2000 [1959]. *The Sociological Imagination*. Oxford: Oxford University Press.

[6] Rosenberg, Justin. 1994. The International Imagination: IR Theory and 'Classic Social Analysis'. *Millennium: Journal of International Studies* 23 (1): 85–108.

[7] Ruggie, John Gerard. 1998. What Makes the World Hang Together? Neo-Utilitarianism and the Social Constructivist Challenge? *International Organization* 52 (4): 855–85.

[8] Respectively, Onuf, Nicholas Greenwood. 2012 [1989]. *World of Our Making: Rules and Rule in Social Theory and International Relations*. Columbia: University of South Carolina Press; Wendt, Alexander. 1992. Anarchy is What States Make of It: The Social Construction on Power Politics. *International Organization* 46 (2): 391–425; Pouliot, Vincent. 2011. *International Security in Practice: The Politics of NATO-Russia Diplomacy*. Cambridge: Cambridge University Press; Nexon, Daniel H. 2009. *The Struggle for Power in Early Modern Europe: Religious Conflict, Dynastic Empires, and International Change*. Princeton, NJ: Princeton University Press.

[9] Kratochwil 2006.

[10] Mills 2000 [1959]: 121.

[11] For a good overview, see Bevir, Mark and Rod Rhodes. 2015. *Routledge Handbook of Interpretive Political Science*. London: Routledge.

[12] Mills 2000 [1959]: 121.

[13] Mills 2000 [1959]: 224.

[14] McCourt, David M. 2014. *Britain and World Power since 1945: Constructing a Nation's Role in International Politics*. Ann Arbor: University of Michigan Press.

[15] McCourt, David M. 2011b. Rethinking Britain's Role in the World for a New Decade: The Limits of Discursive Therapy and the Promise of Field Theory. *British Journal of Politics and International Relations* 13 (2): 145–64.

[16] For further technical instruction, the reader should see Greenacre, Michael J. and Blasius, Jörg, eds. 1994. Correspondence Analysis in the Social Sciences: Recent Developments and Applications. San Diego: Academic Press; Le Roux, Brigitte and Henry Rouanet. 2004. *Geometric Data Analysis: From Correspondence Analysis to Structured Data Analysis*. Dordrecht: Kluwer Academic Publishers; Grenfell, Michael and Frédéric Lebaron, eds. 2014. *Bourdieu and Data Analysis: Methodological Principles and Practice*. Bern: Peter Lang.

[17] Pouliot, Vincent. 2016. *International Pecking Orders: The Politics and Practice of Multilateral Diplomacy*. Cambridge: Cambridge University Press.

[18] On the historical development of MCA, see Van Meter, Karl M., Marie-Ange Schlitz, Philipp Cibois and Lise Mounier. 1994. Correspondence Analysis: A History and French Sociological Perspective. In Michael J. Greenacre and Jörg Blasius, eds. *Correspondence Analysis in the Social Sciences: Recent Developments and Applications*. San Diego, Calif.: Academic Press, pp 128–38.

[19] Le Roux and Rouanet 2004: 6.

[20] Abbott 1992.

[21] Le Roux and Rouanet 2004: 6.

[22] Laurison, Daniel. 2014. Positions and Position-Takings Among Political Producers: The Field of American Political Consultants. In Michael Grenfell and Frédéric Lebaron, eds. *Bourdieu and Data Analysis: Methodological Principles and Practice*. Bern: Peter Lang, pp 253–72.

[23] Laurison 2014: 260.

[24] Laurison 2014: 260.

[25] Laurison 2014: 260.

[26] Aldenderfer, Mark S. and Roger K. Blashfield. 1984. *Cluster Analysis*. London: Sage.

[27] Bourdieu, Pierre. 1984. *Distinction: A Social Critique of the Judgment of Taste*. Cambridge, Mass.: Harvard University Press; see Robson, Karen and Chris Sanders. 2009. *Quantifying Theory: Pierre Bourdieu*. Dordrecht: Springer.

[28] Fligstein, Neil and Doug McAdam. 2012. *A Theory of Fields*. Oxford: Oxford University Press.

[29] Abbott, Andrew. 2005. Linked Ecologies: States and Universities as Environments for Professions. *Sociological Theory* 23 (3): 246–74.

[30] Allison, Graham and Philip Zelikow. 1999 *The Essence of Decision: Explaining the Cuban Missile Crisis*, 2nd edition. New York, N.Y.: Pearson.

[31] See, for example, Kratochwil 2006.

[32] See Subotic, Jelena. (2017) Constructivism as Professional Practice in the US Academy. *PS: Political Science and Politics* 50 (1): 75–8.

Chapter 6

[1] Lechner, Silviya and Mervyn Frost. 2018. *Practice Theory and International Relations*. Cambridge: Cambridge University Press; Weber, Martin. 2020. The Normative Grammar of Relational Analysis: Recognition Theory's Contribution to Understanding Short-Comings in IR's Relational Turn, *International Studies Quarterly*. Online First.

[2] Barkin, J. Samuel and Laura Sjoberg. 2018. *International Relations' Last Synthesis? Decoupling Constructivist and Critical Approaches*. Ann Arbor: University of Michigan Press.

[3] Price, Richard, ed. 2008. *Moral Limit and Possibility in World Politics*. Cambridge: Cambridge University Press.

[4] Sikkink, Kathryn. 2008. The Role of Consequences, Comparison and Counterfactuals in Constructivist Ethical Thought. In Richard Price, ed. *Moral Limit and Possibility in World Politics*. Cambridge: Cambridge University Press, 83.

[5] Oren, Ido. 2003. *Our Enemies and US: America's Rivalries and the Making of Political Science*. Ithaca: Cornell University Press.

[6] See Price, Richard, and Christian Reus-Smit. 1998. Dangerous Liaisons? Critical International Theory and Constructivism. *European Journal of International Relations* 4 (3): 259–94, who reject the notion of such 'dangerous liaisons'.

[7] Wendt 1999: 141. As one early constructivist has quipped to the author, 'I know what rump steak is, but what even is rump materialism?'

[8] Dessler, David. 1999. Constructivism within a Positivist Social Science. *Review of International Studies* 25 (1): 123–37.

[9] Price 2008: 192.

[10] Price 2008: 192.

[11] Price 2008: 192.

[12] Crawford, Neta. 2002. *Argument and Change in World Politics: Ethics, Decolonization, and Humanitarian Intervention*. Cambridge: Cambridge University Press.

[13] Erskine, Toni. 2012. Whose Progress, Which Morals? Constructivism, Normative IR Theory and the Limits and Possibilities of Studying Ethics in World Politics. *International Theory* 4 (3): 466.

[14] Snyder, Jack, and Leslie Vinjamuri. 2012. Principled Pragmatism and the Logic of Consequences. *International Theory* 4 (3): 435.

[15] Snyder and Vinjamuri 2012: 435.

[16] Rengger, Nicholas. 2012. Progress With a Price? *International Theory* 4 (3): 473.

[17] Rengger 2012: 475.

[18] Haacke, Jürgen. 2005. 'The Frankfurt School and International Relations: On the Centrality of Recognition.' *Review of International Studies* 31: 181–94; Fabry, Mikulas. 2010. *Recognizing States: International Society and the Recognition of New States Since 1776*. Oxford: Oxford University Press; Lindemann, Thomas. 2010. *Causes of War: The Struggle for Recognition*. Colchester: ECPR Press; Wolf, Richard. 2011. Respect and Disrespect in International Politics: The Significance of Status Recognition. *International Theory* 3 (1): 105–42; Murray, Michelle. 2018. *The Struggle for Recognition in International Relations: Status, Revisionism, and Rising Powers*. New York: Oxford University Press.

[19] Fabry 2010; Reus-Smit, Christian. 2013. *Individual Rights and the Making of the International System*. Cambridge: Cambridge University Press.

[20] Bartelson, Jens. 2013. Three Concepts of Recognition. *International Theory* 5 (1): 107–29.

[21] Bartelson 2013: 126.

[22] Matthieu, Xavier. 2020. Sovereign Myths in International Relations: Sovereign Equality and the Reproduction of Eurocentric Blindness. *Journal of International Political Theory* 16 (3): 339–60. See also Vucetic, Srdjan. 2011. *The Anglosphere: A Geneaology of a Racialized Identity in International Relations*. Stanford: Stanford University Press.

[23] Ralph, Jason. 2018. What Should Be Done? Pragmatic Constructivist Ethics and the Responsibility to Protect. *International Organization* 72 (1): 175–203.

[24] Ralph 2018: 176.

[25] Erskine 2012: 465.

[26] Ralph 2018:174.

[27] Ralph 2018: 174.

[28] Ralph 2018: 198.

29 Cochran, Molly. 1999. *Normative Theory in International Relations: A Pragmatic Approach.* Cambridge: Cambridge University Press; Cochran, Molly. 2002. Deweyan Pragmatism and Post-Positivist Social Science in IR. *Millennium: Journal of International Studies* 31 (3): 525–48; Owen, David. 2002. Re-orienting International Relations: On Pragmatism, Pluralism and Practical Reasoning. *Millennium* 31 (3): 653–73; Widmaier, Wesley. 2004. Theory as Factor and Theorist as Actor. *International Studies Review* 6 (3): 427–45; Friedrichs, Jörg, and Friedrich Kratochwil. 2009. On Acting and Knowing: How Pragmatism Can Advance International Relations Research and Methodology. *International Organization* 63 (4):701–31; Hellmann, Gunther. 2009. Beliefs as Rules of Action: Pragmatism as Theory of Thought and Action. *International Studies Review* 11: 638–63; Abraham, Kavi Joseph, and Yehonatan Abraham. 2015. A Pragmatist Vocation for International Relations: The (Global) Public and Its Problems. *European Journal of International Relations* 23 (1): 26–48; Dancy, Geoff. 2016. Human Rights Pragmatism: Belief, Inquiry and Action. *European Journal of International Relations* 22 (3): 512–35.

30 Ralph 2018: 188.

31 Hoffmann, Matthew J. 2009. Is Constructivist Ethics an Oxymoron? *International Studies Review* 11 (2): 231–52.

32 Ralph 2018: 181.

33 Ralph 2018: 181.

34 Ralph 2018: 181–2.

35 Ralph 2018: 174.

36 Sikkink, Kathryn. 1991. *Ideas and Institutions: Developmentalism in Brazil and Argentina.* Ithaca: Cornell University Press; Checkel 1997a, 1997b.

37 Weber, Martin 2014. Between 'Isses' and 'Oughts:' IR Constructivism, Critical Theory, and the Challenge of Political Philosophy. *European Journal of International Relations* 20 (2): 533.

38 Weber 2012: 533.

39 Weber 2020: 533

40 Price and Reus-Smit 1999.

41 Price 2008: 208–09.

42 Keohane, Robert O. 1988. International Institutions: Two Approaches. *International Studies Quarterly* 32 (4): 379–96.

43 Barkin and Sjoberg 2018: 4, emphasis in original.

44 Scauso, Marcos S. 2018. Researching Within the Instability of Meaning: Decolonial Voices and Practices. In Brent J. Steele, Harry Gould, and Oliver Kessler, eds. *Tactical Constructivism: Expressing Method in International Relations.* New York: Routledge, pp 157–69.

45 Neumann, Iver B. 1995. *Russia and the Idea of Europe: A Study in Identity and International Relations.* Minneapolis: University of Minnesota Press; Zarakol, Ayşe. 2010. *After Defeat: How the East Learned to Live with the West.* Cambridge: Cambridge University Press.

46 Shilliam, Robbie. 2014. "Open the Gates Mek We Repratriate": Caribbean Slavery, Constructivism, and Hermeneutic Tensions. *International Theory* 6 (2): 352.

47 Shilliam 2014: 352.

48 Shilliam 2014: 351.

49 Holmwood, John. 2010. "The Challenge of Global Social Inquiry." Social Science Research Online 14(4) http://www.socresonline.org.uk/14/4/13.html

50 Shilliam 2018.

51 Shilliam 2018: 360.

52 Shilliam 2018: 364.

53 Shilliam 2018: 365.

54 Shilliam 2018: 365.
55 Locher, Birgit, and Elisabeth Prügl. 2001. Feminism and Constructivism: Worlds Apart or Sharing a Middle Ground? *International Studies Quarterly* 45 (1): 112.
56 Locher and Prügl 2001: 112.
57 Locher and Prügl 2001: 112–13.
58 Locher and Prügl 2001: 113.
59 Locher and Prügl 2001: 113.
60 Towns, Ann E. 2010. *Women and States: Norms and Hierarchies in International Society.* Cambridge: Cambridge University Press; Towns, Ann E. and Bahar Rumelili. 2007. Taking the Pressure: Unpacking the Relations Between Norms, Social Hierarchies, and Social Pressures on States. *European Journal of International Relations* 23 (4): 756–70.
61 Sjoberg, Laura. 2012. Gender, Structure, and War: What Waltz Couldn't See. *International Theory* 4 (1): 1–38; Sjoberg, Laura. 2017. The Invisible Structures of Anarchy: Gender, Orders, and Global Politics. *Journal of International Political Theory* 13 (3): 325–40.
62 Standfield, Catriona. 2020. Gendering the Practice Turn in Diplomacy. *European Journal of International Relations* 26 (S1): 140–65.
63 Standfield 2020: 141.
64 Standfield 2020: 143–6.
65 Standfield 2020: 147.
66 Rösch, Felix. Forthcoming. Affect, Practice, and Change: Dancing World Politics at the Congress of Vienna. *Cooperation and Conflict.*
67 Rösch 2020: 9.
68 Rösch 2020: 9.
69 Rösch 2020: 9.
70 Rösch 2020: 10.
71 Rösch 2020: 11.
72 Rösch 2020: 11.
73 Rösch 2020: 12.
74 Craig, Maxine. 2013. *Sorry I Don't Dance: Why Men Refuse to Move.* New York: Oxford University Press.
75 Towns, Ann. 2020. 'Diplomacy is a Feminine Art': Feminised Figurations of the Diplomat. *Review of International Studies* 46 (5): 547.

Chapter 7

1 Wolin, Sheldon. 1969. Political Theory as a Vocation. *American Political Science Review* 63 (4): 1062–82.
2 Toulmin, Stephen. 2001. *Return to Reason.* Cambridge: Harvard University Press.
3 Gunnell, John. 1998. *The Orders of Discourse.* Lanham: Rowman and Littlefield.
4 Teschke, Benno. 2003. *The Myth of 1648: Class, Geopolitics and the Making of Modern International Relations.* London: Verso.
5 Smith, Thomas. 1999. *History and International Relations.* London: Routledge; Isacoff, Jonathan. 2002. On the Historical Imagination of International Relations. *Millennium: Journal of International Studies* 31 (3): 603–26; Puchala, Donald. 2003. *Theory and History in International Relations.* London: Routledge.
6 Haber, Stephen, David Kennedy and Stephen Krasner. 1997. Brothers Under the Skin: Diplomatic History and International Relations. *International Security* 22 (1): 34–43; Kennedy-Pipe, Caroline. 2000. International History and International Relations Theory. *International Affairs* 76 (4): 741–54.

[7] Vaughan-Williams, Nick. 2005. International Relations and the 'Problem of History'. *Millennium: Journal of International Studies* 34 (1): 115–36.

[8] Buzan, Barry and Richard Little. 2000. *International Systems in World History.* Oxford: Oxford University Press; Keene, Edward. 2008. The English School and British Historians. *Millennium: Journal of International Studies* 37 (2): 381–93.

[9] Roberts, Geoffrey. 2006. History, theory and the Narrative Turn in IR. *Review of International Studies* 32 (4): 703–14; Suganami, Hidemi. 2008. Narrative Explanation and International Relations. *Millennium: Journal of International Studies* 37 (2): 327–56.

[10] Hutchings, Kimberley. 2008. *Time and World Politics.* Manchester: Manchester University Press.

[11] Bell, Duncan. 2001. International Relations: The Dawn of a Historiographical Turn? *British Journal of Politics and International Relations* 3 (1): 115–26.

[12] Lawson, George. 2006. The Promise of Historical Sociology in International Relations. *International Studies Review* 8 (3): 397–423.

[13] Bell 2001: 115.

[14] Curtis, Simon and Marjo Koivisto. 2010. Towards a Second 'Second Debate'? *International Relations* 24 (4): 433–55; May, Ernest R., Richard Rosecrance and Zara Steiner, eds. 2010. *History and Neorealism.* Cambridge: Cambridge University Press; Yetiv, Steve. 2011. History, International Relations, and Integrated Approaches. *International Studies Perspectives* 12 (2): 94–118; Glencross, Andrew. 2015. From 'Doing History' to Thinking Historically: Historical Consciousness Across Historical and International Relations. *International Relations* 29 (4): 413–33; MacKay, Joseph and Christopher David LaRoche. 2017. The Conduct of History in International Relations: Rethinking Philosophy of History in IR. *International Theory* 9 (2): 203–36.

[15] Curtis and Koivisto 2010.

[16] I follow Patrick Jackson's use of 'neo-positivism' rather than 'positivism' to make clear the distinction between neo-positivism as a methodology of social science as used today and the various positivisms that have emerged in the philosophy of science. See Jackson 2011. The most fully elaborated discussion of neo-positivism in the social sciences remains King, Gary, Robert Keohane and Sidney Verba. 1994. *Designing Social Inquiry.* Princeton.

[17] Gadamer, Hans Georg. 1975. *Truth and Method.* London: Continuum.

[18] Despite two decades of challenge, a 2011 survey of IR in the US concluded that there is 'a remarkable and growing consensus that positivist epistemology should guide IR research'. Maliniak, Daniel, Amy Oakes, Susan Peterson, and Michael J. Tierney. 2011. International Relations in the US Academy. *International Studies Quarterly* 55 (2): 437–64.

[19] Cited in Smith 1999: 7.

[20] Buzan and Little 2000.

[21] *International Security* 22, (1) (Summer 1997), later published as Elman, Colin, and Miriam Fendius Elman, eds. 2001. *Bridges and Boundaries: Historians, Political Scientists, and the Study of International Relations.* Cambridge: MIT Press.

[22] Lebow, Richard Ned and Thomas Risse-Kappen. 1995. *International Relations Theory and the End of the Cold War.* New York: Columbia University Press.

[23] Kratochwil, Friedrich. 1993. The Embarrassment of Changes. *Review of International Studies* 19 (1): 63–80.

[24] Gunnell, John G. 1993. *The Descent of Political Theory.* Chicago: The University of Chicago Press.

[25] Jackson 2011.

[26] Jackson 2011: 41–71.

[27] Kratochwil 2006: 16. See also Friedrich Nietzsche, 'On the Use and Abuse of History for Life'. Available at: https://la.utexas.edu/users/hcleaver/330T/350kPEENietzscheAbuseTableAll.pdf

[28] Cox, Robert. 1981. Social Forces, States and World Order: Beyond International Relations Theory. *Millennium: Journal of International Studies* 10 (2): 126–55.

[29] Kratochwil 2006; Ferguson, Yale F. and Richard W. Mansbach. 2004. *Remapping Global Politics*. Cambridge: Cambridge University Press.

[30] Collingwood, R.G. 1946. *The Idea of History*. Oxford: Clarendon Press.

[31] Oakeshott, Michael. 1933. *Experience and Its Modes*. Cambridge: Cambridge University Press.

[32] Lustick, Ian. 1996. History, Historiography, and Political Science. *American Political Science Review* 90 (3): 605–18.

[33] See the debate over Andrew Moravcsik's *The Choice for Europe* (New York: Routledge, 1999) in the special issue of *Journal of Cold War Studies* 2 (3) (2000).

[34] Osiander, Andreas. 2007. *Before the State*. Oxford: Oxford University Press.

[35] This is an important theme in Hoffman, Stanley. 1959. International Relations: The Long Road to Theory. *World Politics* 11 (3): 346–77.

[36] Oren, Ido. 2003. *Our Enemies and US: America's Rivalries and the Making of Political Science*. Ithaca: Cornell University Press.

[37] Oren, Ido. 1995. The Subjectivity of the 'Democratic' Peace. *International Security* 20: 147–84.

[38] Bernstein, Richard. 1983. *Beyond Objectivism and Relativism: Science, Hermeneutics, and Praxis*. Oxford: Basil Blackwell.

[39] Political science has long been firmly within the Cartesian anxiety's thrall, clearly visible in its perennial identity crisis regarding its scientific status. See Gunnell, John. 2011. *Political Theory and Social Science*. Houndmills: Palgrave Macmillan.

[40] See Widmaier, Wesley. 2004. Theory as Factor and Theorist as Actor. *International Studies Review* 6 (3): 427–45. The classic work on objectivism within History is Novick, Peter. 1988. *That Noble Dream*. Cambridge: Cambridge University Press.

[41] See Brown, Chris. 1994. Turtles All the Way Down. *Millennium: Journal of International Studies* 23 (2): 213–36; Monteiro, Nuno P. and Kevin Ruby. 2009. IR and the False Promise of Philosophical Foundations. *International Theory* 1 (1): 15–48.

[42] The best treatment is Jackson, Patrick Thaddeus. 2011. *The Conduct of Inquiry in International Relations: Philosophy of Science and Its Implications for the Study of World Politics*, 1st Edition. New York: Routledge.

[43] Bernstein 1983.

[44] Bernstein 1983: 1–49.

[45] See Knorr-Cetina, Karin. 1999. *Epistemic Cultures*. Cambridge: Harvard University Press.

[46] Kuhn, Thomas. 1970. *The Structure of Scientific Revolutions*. Chicago: Chicago University Press.

[47] See Weber, Max. 1949. *The Methodology of the Social Sciences*. New York: Free Press; Bourdieu, Pierre. 2004. *Science of Science and Reflexivity*. Cambridge: Polity Press.

[48] Feyerabend, Paul. 1987. *Farewell to Reason*. London: Verso.

[49] Rorty, Richard. 1980. *Philosophy and the Mirror of Nature*. Princeton: Princeton University Press.

[50] See Kuhn, Thomas. 1974. *Objectivity, Value Judgment, and Theory Choice, in The Essential Tension*. Chicago: The University of Chicago Press, pp 356–69.

[51] Mieland, Jack and Michael Krausz. 1982. Introduction in Mieland and Krausz, eds. *Relativism: Cognitive and Moral*. Notre Dame: University of Notre Dame Press.

[52] Bernstein 1983: 11.

[53] Bernstein 1983: 9.
[54] Bernstein 1983.
[55] Mieland, Jack, and Michael Krausz. 1982. Introduction. In Jack Mieland and Krausz, eds. *Relativism: Cognitive and Moral.* Notre Dame: University of Notre Dame Press, 1–2.
[56] Mieland and Krausz 1989: 4.
[57] Hopf, Ted. 2002. *Social Construction of International Politics: Identities and Foreign Policies, Moscow, 1955 and 1999.* Ithaca: Cornell University Press.
[58] Bernstein, Richard. 1976. *The Restructuring of Social and Political Theory.* Oxford: Blackwell.
[59] Bernstein 1976: 53.
[60] Bernstein 1976: *xxii.*
[61] See Neufeld, Mark. 1995. *The Restructuring of International Relations Theory.* Cambridge: Cambridge University Press.
[62] See Ferguson, Yale F. and Richard Mansbach. 1988. *The Elusive Quest.* Columbia: South Carolina Press. Some would say too closely, see Oren, Ido. 2003. *Our Enemies and US: America's Rivalries and the Making of Political Science.* Ithaca: Cornell University Press.
[63] Keohane, Robert O. 1984. *After Hegemony.* Princeton: Princeton University Press.
[64] Guilhot, Nicolas, ed. 2011. *The Invention of International Relations Theory.* New York: Columbia University Press.
[65] See Lepgold, Joseph and Miroslav Nincic. 1999. *Beyond the Ivory Tower.* New York: Columbia University Press.
[66] In particular Gadamer 1975: 310–21.
[67] Gadamer 1975; Arendt, Hannah. 1958. *The Human Condition.* Chicago: Chicago University Press.
[68] Aristotle. 1953. *The Ethics.* London: Penguin.
[69] Aristotle 1953: 207.
[70] Aristotle 1953: 207, emphasis added.
[71] Aristotle 1953.
[72] See in particular the work of Williams, Michael C. 2005. *The Realist Tradition and the Limits of International Relations.* Cambridge: Cambridge University Press; Williams, Michael C., ed. 2007b. *Realism Reconsidered.* Oxford: Oxford University Press.
[73] Lebow, Richard Ned. 2003. *The Tragic Vision of Politics.* Cambridge: Cambridge University Press.
[74] X (George Kennan). 1947. The Sources of Soviet Conduct. *Foreign Affairs* 25 (4): 566–82.
[75] Macchiavelli, Niccolo. 1988. *The Prince.* Cambridge: Cambridge University Press.
[76] Macchiavelli 1988; Kratochwil, Friedrich V. 1989. *Rules, Norms, and Decisions: On the Conditions of Legal and Practical Reasoning in International Relations and Domestic Affairs.* Cambridge: Cambridge University Press.
[77] Kratochwil 2006.
[78] Bull, Hedley. 1966. International Theory: The Case for a Classical Approach. *World Politics* 18 (3): 361–77; Shapcott, Richard. 2004. IR as Practical Philosophy. *British Journal of Politics and International Relations* 6: 271–91.
[79] Flyvbjerg, Bent. 2001. *Making Social Science Matter.* Cambridge: Cambridge University Press.
[80] Kupchan, Charles. 2010. *How Enemies Become Friends.* Princeton: Princeton University Press.
[81] Wohlforth, William. 2009. Unipolarity, Status Competition, and Great Power War. *World Politics* 61 (1): 28–57.
[82] Kupchan, 2010: 73–111, 351–64.
[83] Kupchan, 2010: 414.
[84] Wohlforth 2009: 30.

85 Wohlforth 2009: 40.
86 Wohlforth 2009: 57.
87 Gadamer 1975: 315–21.
88 Gadamer 1975: 318.
89 Bernstein 1983: 157.
90 Toulmin 2001: 78.
91 See Gunnell 1998.
92 Bernstein 1983: 160–1.
93 Bernstein 1983:141.
94 Bernstein 1983:161.
95 Gunnell 1998: 17–46.
96 It is important to note here a more recent 'turn': the reflexive turn. See Hamati-Attaya, Inanna. 2011. The 'Problem of Values' and International Relations Scholarship. *International Studies Review* 13: 259–87.
97 See Parmar, Inderjeet. 2004. *Think Tanks and Power in Foreign Policy*. Basingstoke: Palgrave; Stone, Diane and Andrew Denham. 2004. Think Tank Traditions. Manchester: Manchester University Press.
98 Gunnell 1998: 91.
99 Gunnell 1998: 215.
100 See Nussbaum, Martha. 1994. *The Therapy of Desire*. Princeton: Princeton University Press.

Conclusion

1   Wendt, Alexander. 1995. Constructing International Politics. *International Security* 20 (1): 80, emphasis added.
2   Wendt 1995: 74.
3   Wendt, Alexander. 1992. Anarchy is What States Make of It: The Social Construction on Power Politics. *International Organization* 46 (2): 391–425.
4   Wendt 1995: 77.
5   Onuf, Nicholas Greenwood. 2012 [1989]. *World of Our Making: Rules and Rule in Social Theory and International Relations*. Columbia: University of South Carolina Press.
6   Onuf 2012 [1989]: 49–50.
7   Kratochwil, Friedrich V. 1989. *Rules, Norms, and Decisions: On the Conditions of Legal and Practical Reasoning in International Relations and Domestic Affairs*. Cambridge: Cambridge University Press.
8   Ruggie, John Gerard. 1998. What Makes the World Hang Together? Neo-Utilitarianism and the Social Constructivist Challenge? *International Organization* 52 (4): 855–85.
9   Onuf 2012 [1989]: 33.
10 Lapid, Yosef. 1996. Culture's Ship: Returns and Departures in IR Theory. In Yosef Lapid and Friedrich V. Kratochwil, eds. *The Return of Culture and Identity in IR Theory*. Boulder: Lynn Reiner, 6, 8.
11 Kratochwil and Ruggie 1986.
12 Kratochwil and Ruggie 1986: 772.
13 Katzenstein, Peter J., Robert O. Keohane and Stephen D. Krasner. 1998. International Organization and the Study of World Politics. *International Organization* 52 (4): 645–85.
14 Milner 1998.
15 See Maliniak, Daniel, Amy Oakes, Susan Peterson, and Michael J. Tierney. 2011. International Relations in the US Academy. *International Studies Quarterly* 55 (2): 437–64.
16 Maliniak et al 2011: 14.
17 Maliniak et al 2011: 25.

[18] Jackson and Nexon 2009; Jackson, Patrick Thaddeus. 2011. *The Conduct of Inquiry in International Relations: Philosophy of Science and Its Implications for the Study of World Politics*, 1st Edition. New York: Routledge.

[19] Jackson 2011: 41–71.

[20] Waever, Ole. 1998. The Sociology of a Not So International Discipline. *International Organization* 52 (4): 687–727.

[21] Katzenstein, Keohane and Krasner 1998: 646.

[22] Maliniak et al 2011: 9.

[23] Oatley 2011.

[24] Kratochwil 1989: 261.

[25] Keohane, Robert O. 2009. The Old IPE and the New. *Review of International Political Economy* 16 (1): 34–46.

[26] Checkel, Jeffrey T. 1998. The Constructivist Turn in International Relations Theory. *International Security* 50 (2): 324–48.

[27] Tilly 2002: 71.

[28] Ruggie 1998: 867.

[29] Fearon, James. 1995. Rationalist Explanations for War. *International Organization* 49 (3): 379–414; Wagner, R. Harrison. 2007. *War and the State: The Theory of International Politics*. Ann Arbor: University of Michigan Press; Glaser, Charles. 2010. *Rational Theory of International Politics: The Logic of Competition and Cooperation*. Princeton: Princeton University Press.

[30] *International Organization* 55 (4): 2001.

[31] Ruggie 1998: 880.

[32] Abbott, Andrew. 2001. *Chaos of Disciplines*. Chicago: University of Chicago Press.

[33] Katzenstein 2009: 125.

[34] Keohane 2009: 38.

[35] Kratochwil, Friedrich V. 2011. Making Sense of International Practices. In Emanuel Adler and Vincent Pouliot, eds. *International Practices*. Cambridge: Cambridge University Press, pp 36–60.

[36] Jewett, Andrew. 2012. *Science, Democracy, and the American University: From the Civil War to the Cold War*. Cambridge: Cambridge University Press.

[37] Jewett 2012: 240.

[38] Jewett 2012: 243.

[39] Jewett 2012: 336.

[40] Reisch, George A. 2005. *How the Cold War Transformed Philosophy of Science: To the Icy Slopes of Logic*. Cambridge: Cambridge University Press.

[41] Amadae, S.M. 2003. *Rationalizing Capitalist Democracy: The Cold War Origins of Rational Choice Liberalism*. Chicago: University of Chicago Press.

[42] Isaac, Joel. 2012. *Working Knowledge: Making the Human Sciences from Parsons to Kuhn*. Harvard: Harvard University Press.

[43] Jewett 2012: 317.

[44] Snow, C.P. 2012 [1959]. *The Two Cultures*. Cambridge: Cambridge University Press.

[45] Snow 2012 [1959]: 334.

[46] Kuhn, Thomas. 1962. *The Structure of Social Revolutions*. Chicago: University of Chicago Press.

[47] Knorr-Cetina, Karin. 1999. *Epistemic Cultures*. Cambridge: Harvard University Press.

[48] Fuller, Steve. 2000. *Thomas Kuhn: A Philosophical History for Our Times*. Chicago: Chicago University Press.

[49] Abbott 2001: 88.

[50] Abbott 2001: 69.

[51] Jackson 2011.

References

Aalberts, Tanja E. 2012. *Constructing Sovereignty Between Politics and Law*. Abingdon: Routledge.

Abbott, Andrew. 1992. What Do Cases Do? Some Notes on Activity in Sociological Analysis. In *What Is A Case? Exploring the Foundations of Social Inquiry*. Cambridge: Cambridge University Press, pp 53–82.

Abbott, Andrew. 2001. *Chaos of Disciplines*. Chicago: University of Chicago Press.

Abbott, Andrew. 2005. Linked Ecologies: States and Universities as Environments for Professions. *Sociological Theory* 23 (3): 246–74.

Abbott, Andrew. 2016. *Processual Sociology*. Chicago: University of Chicago Press.

Abdelal, Rawi, Mark Blyth, and Craig Parsons, eds. 2011. *Constructing the International Economy*. Ithaca: Cornell University Press.

Abraham, Kavi Joseph and Yehonatan Abraham. 2015. A Pragmatist Vocation for International Relations: The (Global) Public and Its Problems. *European Journal of International Relations* 23 (1): 26–48.

Acharya, Amitav. 2004. How Ideas Spread: Whose Norms Matter? Norm Localization and Institutional Change in Asian Regionalism. *International Organization* 58 (2): 239–75.

Acharya, Amitav. 2014. Global International Relations (IR) and Regional Worlds: A New Agenda for International Relations. *International Studies Quarterly* 58 (4): 647–59.

Adamson, Fiona B. 2016. Spaces of Global Security: Beyond Methodological Nationalism. *Journal of Global Security Studies* 1 (1): 9–35.

Adler, Emanuel. 1997. Seizing the Middle Ground: Constructivism in World Politics. *European Journal of International Relations* 3 (3): 319–63.

Adler, Emanuel and Michael Barnett. 1998. *Security Communities*. Cambridge: Cambridge University Press.

Adler, Emanuel and Vincent Pouliot. 2011. *International Practices*. Cambridge: Cambridge University Press.

Adler-Nissen, Rebecca, ed. 2012. *Bourdieu in International Relations*. London: Routledge.

Agamben, Giorgio. 1995. *Homo Sacer: Sovereign Power and Bare Life.* Stanford: Stanford University Press.

Aldenderfer, Mark S. and Roger K. Blashfield. 1984. *Cluster Analysis.* London: Sage.

Allan, Bentley B. 2018. *Scientific Cosmology and International Orders.* Cambridge: Cambridge University Press.

Allison, Graham and Philip Zelikow. 1999 *The Essence of Decision: Explaining the Cuban Missile Crisis*, 2nd edition. New York: Pearson.

Amadae, S.M. 2003. *Rationalizing Capitalist Democracy: The Cold War Origins of Rational Choice Liberalism.* Chicago: University of Chicago Press.

Amoureux, Jack L. 2016. *A Practice of Ethics for Global Politics: Ethical Reflexivity.* London: Routledge.

Amoureux, Jack L. and Brent J. Steele, ed. 2016. *Reflexivity and International Relations: Positionality, Critique, and Practice.* London: Routledge.

Arendt, Hannah. 1958. *The Human Condition.* Chicago: Chicago University Press.

Aristotle. 1953. *The Ethics.* London: Penguin.

Ashley, Richard K. 1987. Foreign Policy as Political Performance. *International Studies Notes* 13: 51.

Ashley, Richard K. and R.B.J. Walker. 1990. Introduction: Speaking the Language of Exile. *International Studies Quarterly* 34 (3): 259–68.

Auchter, Jessica. 2014. *The Politics of Haunting and Memory in International Relations.* New York: Routledge.

Autoserre, Séverine. 2014. *Peaceland: Conflict Resolution and the Everyday Politics of International Intervention.* Cambridge: Cambridge University Press.

Avant, Deborah. 2016. Pragmatic Networks and Transnational Governance of Private Military and Security Services. *International Studies Quarterly* 60 (2): 330–42.

Avant, Deborah and Oliver Westerwinter. 2016. *The New Power Politics: Networks and Transnational Security Governance.* New York: Oxford University Press.

Bader, Jeffrey. 2012. *Obama and China's Rise.* Washington DC: Brookings.

Baldwin, David. 1993. *Neorealism and Neoliberalism: The Contemporary Debate.* New York: Columbia University Press.

Banerjee, Kiran and Joseph MacKay. 2020. Communities of Practice, Impression Management, and Great Power Status: Military Observers in the Russo-Japanese War. *Review of International Studies.* OnlineFirst, 1–20.

Banks, David E. 2019. Fields of Practice: Symbolic Binding and the Qing Defense of Sinocentric Diplomacy. *International Studies Quarterly* 63 (3): 546–57.

Barder, Alexander. 2015. *Empire Within: International Hierarchy and Its Imperial Laboratories of Governance.* New York: Routledge.

Barder, Alexander D. and Daniel J. Levine. 2012. 'The World Is Too Much With Us': Reification and the Depolitising of *Via Media* Constructivist IR. *Millennium: Journal of International Studies* 40 (3): 585–604.

Barkin, J. Samuel and Laura Sjoberg. 2018. *International Relations' Last Synthesis: Decoupling Constructivist and Critical Approaches.* Ann Arbor: University of Michigan Press.

Barry, Andrew. 2013. The Translation Zone: Between Actor-Network Theory and International Relations. *Millennium: Journal of International Studies* 41 (3): 413–29.

Bartelson, Jens. 1995. *A Genealogy of Sovereignty.* Cambridge: Cambridge University Press.

Bartelson, Jens. 2001. *The Critique of the State.* Cambridge: Cambridge University Press.

Bartelson, Jens. 2013. Three Concepts of Recognition. *International Theory* 5 (1): 107–29.

Bartelson, Jens. 2014. *Sovereignty as Symbolic Form.* London: Routledge.

Bearce, David H. and Stacey Bondanella. 2007. Intergovernmental Organizations, Socialization, and Member-State Interest Convergence. *International Organization* 61 (4): 703–33.

Becker, Howard. 1953. Becoming a Marihuana User. *American Journal of Sociology* 59 (3): 235–42.

Beeson, Mark and Fujian Li. 2015. What Consensus? Geopolitics and Policy Paradigms in China and the United States. *International Affairs* 91 (1): 93–109.

Bell, Duncan. 2001. International Relations: The Dawn of a Historiographical Turn? *British Journal of Politics and International Relations* 3 (1): 115–26.

Berenskoetter, Felix. 2018. Identity in International Relations. *Oxford Research Encylopedias.* Oxford: Oxford University Press. Available at https://oxfordre.com/view/10.1093/acrefore/9780190846626.001.0001/acrefore-9780190846626-e-218

Bernstein, Richard. 1976. *The Restructuring of Social and Political Theory.* Oxford: Blackwell.

Bernstein, Richard. 1983. *Beyond Objectivism and Relativism: Science, Hermeneutics, and Praxis.* Oxford: Basil Blackwell.

Bertucci, Mariano, Jarrod Hayes, and Patrick James, eds. 2018. *Constructivism Reconsidered: Past, Present, and Future.* Ann Arbor: University of Michigan Press.

Best, Jacqueline and William Walters. 2013. Forum on Actor-Network Theory and International Relationality: Lost (and Found) in Translation. *International Political Sociology* 7 (3): 332–49.

Bevir, Mark and Rod Rhodes. 2015. *Routledge Handbook of Interpretive Political Science.* London: Routledge.

Bicchi, Federica and Niklas Bremberg. 2016. European Diplomatic Practices: Contemporary Challenges and Innovative Approaches. *European Security* 25 (4): 391–406.

Boon, Hoo Tiang and Hannah Elyse Sworn. 2020. Strategic Ambiguity and the Trumpian Approach to China-Taiwan Relations. *International Affairs* 96 (6): 1487–508.

Bourdieu, Pierre. 1984. *Distinction: A Social Critique of the Judgment of Taste.* Cambridge: Harvard University Press.

Bourdieu, Pierre. 1990. *In Other Words: Essays Towards a Reflexive Sociology.* Stanford: Stanford University Press.

Bourdieu, Pierre. 2004. *Science of Science and Reflexivity.* Cambridge: Polity Press.

Bourdieu, Pierre. 2006 [1992]. *The Rules of Art: Genesis and Structure of the Literary Field.* Stanford: Stanford University Press.

Bourdieu, Pierre. 2015. *On the State.* Cambridge: Polity.

Bourdieu, Pierre. 2019. *Classification Struggles.* Cambridge: Polity.

Bourdieu, Pierre. 2020. *Habitus and Field.* Cambridge: Polity.

Bourdieu, Pierre and Loïc J.D. Wacquant. 1992. *An Invitation to Reflexive Sociology.* Chicago: University of Chicago Press.

Branch, Jordan. 2014. *The Cartographic State: Maps, Territory, and the Origins of Sovereignty.* Cambridge: Cambridge University Press.

Branch, Jordan. 2016. Geographic Information Systems (GIS) in International Relations. *International Organization* 70 (4): 845–69.

Branch, Jordan. 2018. Technology and Constructivism: Interrogating the Ideational-Material Divide. In Mariano Bertucci, Jarrod Hayes, and Patrick James, eds. *Constructivism Reconsidered: Past, Present, and Future.* Ann Arbor: University of Michigan Press, pp 103–15.

Breuer, Adam and Alastair Iain Johnston. 2019. Memes, Narratives, and the Emergent US-China Security Dilemma. *Cambridge Review of International Affairs* 32 (4): 429–55.

Brown, Chris. 1994. Turtles All the Way Down: Anti-Foundationalism, Critical Theory, and International Relations. *Millennium: Journal of International Studies* 23 (2): 213–36.

Bueger, Christian. 2011. Communities of Practice in World Politics – Theory or Technology? Paper presented at the 52nd Annual Conference of the International Studies Association, Montreal CA, March, 2.

Bueger, Christian. 2017. Territory, Authority, Expertise: Global Governance and the Counter-Piracy Assemblage. *European Journal of International Relations* 24 (3): 614–37.

Bueger, Christian. 2021. *International Organizations in Practice: The United Nations, Peacebuilding, and Praxiography.* London: Routledge.

Bueger, Christian and Frank Gadinger. 2014. *International Practice Theory.* Houndmills: Palgrave.

Bueger, Christian and Frank Gadinger. 2015. The Play of International Practice. *International Studies Quarterly* 59 (3): 449–60.

Bueger, Christian and Frank Gadinger. 2018. *International Practice Theory: New Perspectives*, 2nd edition. Basingstoke: Palgrave.

Bukovansky, Mlada. 1997. American Identity and Neutral Rights from Independence to the War of 1812. *International Organization* 51 (2): 209–43.

Bukovansky, Mlada. 1999. *Legitimacy and Power Politics: The American and French Revolutions in International Political Culture*. Ithaca: Cornell University Press.

Bull, Hedley. 1966. International Theory: The Case for a Classical Approach. *World Politics* 18 (3): 361–77.

Bush, Sarah Sunn. 2011. International Politics and the Spread of Quotas for Women in Legislatures. *International Organization* 65 (1): 103–37.

Buzan, Barry and Richard Little. 2000. *International Systems in World History.* Oxford: Oxford University Press.

Buzan, Barry, Ole Waever and Jaap De Wilde. 1997. *Security: A New Framework for Analysis.* Boulder: Lynne Reinner.

Callon, Michael. 1986. Some Elements of a Sociology of Translation. In John Law, ed. *Power, Action and Belief.* London: Routledge and Kegan Paul, pp 196–233.

Campbell, David. 1998. *Writing Security: United States Foreign Policy and the Politics of Identity.* Minneapolis: University of Minnesota Press.

Campbell, Kurt and Ely Ratner. 2018. The China Reckoning: How Beijing Defied American Expectations. *Foreign Affairs* 97 (2): 60–70.

Carpenter, R. Charli. 2003. 'Women and Children First.' Gender, Norms, and Humanitarian Evacuation in the Balkans 1991-95. *International Organization* 57 (4): 661–94.

Checkel, Jeffrey T. 1997a. International Norms and Domestic Politics: Bridging the Rationalist-Constructivist Divide. *European Journal of International Relations* 3 (4): 473–95.

Checkel, Jeffrey T. 1997b. *Ideas and International Political Change.* New Haven: Yale University Press.

Checkel, Jeffrey T. 1998. The Constructivist Turn in International Relations Theory. *International Security* 50 (2): 324–48.

Chernoff, Fred. 2014. *Explanation and Progress in Security Studies: Bridging Theoretical Divides in International Relations.* Stanford: Stanford University Press.

Clark, Ian. 2011. *Hegemony in International Society*. Oxford: Oxford University Press.

Cochran, Molly. 1999. *Normative Theory in International Relations: A Pragmatic Approach.* Cambridge: Cambridge University Press.

Cochran, Molly. 2002. Deweyan Pragmatism and Post-Positivist Social Science in IR. *Millennium: Journal of International Studies* 31 (3): 525–48.

Collingwood, R.G. 1946. *The Idea of History.* Oxford: Clarendon Press.

Constantinou, Costas M., Pauline Kerr and Paul Sharp, eds. 2016. *The SAGE Handbook of Diplomacy*. London: SAGE.

Cox, Robert. 1981. Social Forces, States and World Order: Beyond International Relations Theory. *Millennium: Journal of International Studies* 10 (2): 126–55.

Craig, Maxine. 2013. *Sorry I Don't Dance: Why Men Refuse to Move*. New York: Oxford University Press.

Crawford, Neta C. 1994. A Security Regime Among Democracies: Cooperation Among Iroquois Nations. *International Organization* 48 (3): 345–85.

Crawford, Neta. 2002. *Argument and Change in World Politics: Ethics, Decolonization, and Humanitarian Intervention*. Cambridge: Cambridge University Press.

Crossley, Nick. 2012. *Towards Relational Sociology*. London: Routledge.

Curtis, Simon and Marjo Koivisto. 2010. Towards a Second 'Second Debate'? *International Relations* 24 (4): 433–55.

Dancy, Geoff. 2016. Human Rights Pragmatism: Belief, Inquiry and Action. *European Journal of International Relations* 22 (3): 512–35.

Davies, Sara E. and Jacque True. 2017. Norm Entrepreneurship in Foreign Policy: William Hague and the Prevention of Sexual Violence in Conflict. *Foreign Policy Analysis* 13: 701–21.

de Graaf, Naná and Bastiaan Van Apeldoorn. 2018. US–China Relations and the Liberal World Order: Contending Elites, Colliding Visions? *International Affairs* 94 (1): 113–31.

Dessler, David. 1999. Constructivism within a Positivist Social Science. *Review of International Studies* 25 (1): 123–37.

Dietelhoff, Nicole. 2009. The Discursive Process of Legalization: Charting Islands of Persuasion in the ICC Case. *International Organization* 63 (1): 33–65.

Doty, Roxanne Lynn. 1993. Foreign Policy as Social Construction: A Post-Positivist Analysis of US Counterinsurgency Policy in the Philippines. *International Studies Quarterly* 37 (3): 297–320.

Drezner, Daniel. 2017. *The Ideas Industry*. New York: Oxford University Press.

Du Bois, W.E.B. 1994 [1903]. *The Souls of Black Folk*. New York: Dover.

Dueck, Colin. 2006. *Reluctant Crusaders: Power, Culture, and Change in American Grand Strategy*. Princeton: Princeton University Press.

Duffy, Gavan and Brian Frederking. 2009. Changing the Rules: A Speech Act Analysis of the End of the Cold War. *International Studies Quarterly* 52 (2): 325–47.

Durkheim, Emile. 1982 [1895]. *The Rules of Sociological Method*. New York: Free Press.

Durkheim, Emile. 1995 [1912]. *The Elementary Forms of the Religious Life*. New York: Free Press.

Eagleton-Pierce, Matthew. 2011. Advancing a Reflexive International Relations. *Millennium: Journal of International Studies* 39 (3): 805–23.

Eden, Lynn. 2004. *Whole World on Fire: Organizations, Knowledge, and Nuclear Weapons Devastation.* Ithaca: Cornell University Press.

Elias, Norbert. 2000 [1937]. *The Civilizing Process.* Oxford: Basil Blackwell

Elman, Colin and Mirium Fendius Elman. 2001. *Bridges and Boundaries: Historians, Political Scientists, and the Study of International Relations.* Cambridge: MIT Press.

Elman, Miriam Fendius and Colin Elman. 2003. *Progress in International Relations Theory.* Cambridge: MIT Press.

Emirbayer, Mustafa. 1997. Manifesto for a Relational Sociology. *American Journal of Sociology* 103 (2): 281–317.

Enloe, Cynthia. 1989. *Bananas, Beaches, and Bases: Making Feminist Sense of International Politics.* Berkeley: University of California Press.

Epstein, Charlotte. 2010. Who Speaks? Discourse, the Subject, and the Study of Identity in International Relations. *European Journal of International Relations* 17 (2): 327–50.

Epstein, Charlotte. 2013a. Constructivism or the Eternal Return of Universals in International Relations: Why Returning to Language is Vital for Prolonging the Owl's Flight. *European Journal of International Relations* 19 (3): 499–519.

Epstein, Charlotte. 2013b. Theorizing Agency in Hobbes's Wake: The Rational Actor, the Self, or the Speaking Subject. *International Organization* 67 (2): 287–316.

Epstein, Charlotte. 2021. *Birth of the State: The Place of the Body in Crafting Modern Politics.* Oxford: Oxford University Press.

Erskine, Toni. 2012. Whose Progress, Which Morals? Constructivism, Normative IR Theory and the Limits and Possibilities of Studying Ethics in World Politics. *International Theory* 4 (3): 449–68.

Espeland, Wendy Nelson and Mitchell L. Stevens. 1998. Commensuration as a Social Process. *Annual Review of Sociology* 24: 313–43.

Fabry, Mikulas. 2010. *Recognizing States: International Society and the Recognition of New States Since 1776.* Oxford: Oxford University Press.

Fearon, James. 1995. Rationalist Explanations for War. *International Organization* 49 (3): 379–414.

Fearon, James. 1999. *What Is Identity (As We Now Use the Use the Word)?* Unpublished Manuscript, Stanford University.

Fearon, James and Alexander Wendt. 2002. Rationalism Vs. Constructivism: A Skeptical View. In Walter Carlsnaes, Thomas Risse, and Beth Simmons, eds. *The SAGE Handbook of International Relations.* London: SAGE, pp 52–72.

Ferguson, Yale F. and Richard Mansbach. 1988. *The Elusive Quest.* Columbia: South Carolina Press.

Ferguson, Yale F. and Richard W. Mansbach. 2004. *Remapping Global Politics.* Cambridge: Cambridge University Press.

Feyerabend, Paul. 1987. *Farewell to Reason.* London: Verso.

Fierke, Karin M. 1998. *Changing Games, Changing Strategies: Critical Investigations in Security.* Manchester: Manchester University Press.

Finnemore, Martha. 1996a. *National Interests in International Society.* Ithaca: Cornell University Press.

Finnemore, Martha. 1996b. Norms, Culture, and World Politic: Insights from Sociology's Institutionalism. *International Organization* 53 (4): 699 – 72.

Finnemore, Martha and Kathryn Sikkink. 2001. Taking Stock: The Constructivist Research Program in International Relations and Comparative Politics. *Annual Review of Political Science.* 4: 391–416.

Flathman, Richard. 1993. *Thomas Hobbes: Skepticism, Individuality and Chastened Politics.* London: Sage.

Fligstein, Neil and Doug McAdam. 2012. *A Theory of Fields.* Oxford: Oxford University Press.

Florini, Ann. 1996. The Evolution of International Norms. *International Studies Quarterly* 40 (3): 363–89.

Flyvbjerg, Bent. 2001. *Making Social Science Matter.* Cambridge: Cambridge University Press.

Foley, Frank. 2013. *Countering Terrorism: Institutions, Norms, and the Shadow of the Past.* Cambridge: Cambridge University Press.

Foucault, Michel. 1989 [1961]. *Discipline and Punish: The Birth of the Prison.* New York: Vintage.

Foucault, Michel. 1989 [1963]. *Madness and Civilization.* London: Routledge.

Foucault, Michel. 1995 [1975]. *The Birth of the Clinic.* London: Routledge.

Foucault, Michel. 2010. *The Birth of Biopolitics: Lectures at the Collège de France, 1978–1979.* New York: Picador.

Friedrichs, Jörg. 2004. *European Approaches to International Relations Theory: A House With Many Mansions.* London: Routledge.

Friedrichs, Jörg and Friedrich V. Kratochwil. 2009. On Acting and Knowing: How Pragmatism Can Advance International Relations Research and Methodology. *International Organization* 63 (4): 701–31.

Fuller, Steve. 2000. *Thomas Kuhn: A Philosophical History for Our Times.* Chicago: Chicago University Press.

Gadamer, Hans Georg. 1975. *Truth and Method.* London: Continuum.

Gallie, W.E.B. 1956. Essentially Contested Concepts. *Proceedings of the Aristotelian Society* 56: 167–98.

Geertz, Clifford. 1973. *The Interpretation of Cultures.* New York: Basic Books

George, Roger and Harvey Rishikoff, eds. 2017. *The National Security Enterprise.* Washington: Georgetown University Press.

Gheciu, Alexandra. 2005. Security Institutions as Agents of Socialization? NATO and the 'New Europe'. *International Organization* 59 (4): 973–1012.

Gingrich, Newt. 2019. *Trump Vs. China*. New York: Center St.

Glaser, Charles. 2010. *Rational Theory of International Politics: The Logic of Competition and Cooperation*. Princeton: Princeton University Press.

Glencross, Andrew. 2015. From 'Doing History' to Thinking Historically: Historical Consciousness Across Historical and International Relations. *International Relations* 29 (4): 413–33.

Goddard, Stacie E. 2009. Brokering Change: Networks and Entrepreneurs in International Politics. *International Theory* 1 (2): 249–81.

Goddard, Stacie E. 2012. Brokering Peace: Networks, Legitimacy, and the Northern Ireland Peace Process. *International Studies Quarterly* 56 (3): 501–15.

Goddard, Stacie E. and Ronald R. Krebs. 2015. Rhetoric, Legitimation, and Grand Strategy. *Security Studies* 24 (1): 5–36.

Goetze, Catherine. 2017. *The Distinction of Peace: A Social Analysis of Peacebuilding*. Ann Arbor: University of Michigan Press.

Goffman, Erving. 1986. *Frame Analysis*. Boston: Northeastern University Press.

Goldstein, Judith and Robert O. Keohane, eds. 1993. *Ideas and Foreign Policy: Beliefs, Institutions, and Political Change*. Ithaca: Cornell University Press.

Gorski, Philip S. 2003. *The Disciplinary Revolution: Calvinism and the Rise of the State in Early Modern Europe*. Chicago: Chicago University Press.

Gould, Harry. 2010. *The Legacy of Punishment in International Law*. New York: Palgrave Macmillan.

Greenacre, Michael J. and Jörg Blasius, eds. 1994. *Correspondence Analysis in the Social Sciences: Recent Developments and Applications*. San Diego: Academic Press.

Grenfell, Michael and Frédéric Lebaron, eds. 2014. *Bourdieu and Data Analysis: Methodological Principles and Practice*. Bern: Peter Lang.

Grieco, Joseph M. 1988. Anarchy and the Limits of Cooperation: A Realist Critique of the Newest Liberal Institutionalism. *International Organization* 42 (3): 485–507.

Guilhot, Nicolas, ed. 2011. *The Invention of International Relations Theory*. New York: Columbia University Press.

Guillaume, Xavier. 2007. Unveiling the 'International': Process, Identity and Alterity. *Millennium: Journal of International Studies* 35 (3): 741–58.

Gunnell, John G. 1993. *The Descent of Political Theory*. Chicago: The University of Chicago Press.

Gunnell, John. 1998. *The Orders of Discourse*. Lanham: Rowman and Littlefield.

Gunnell, John. 2011. *Political Theory and Social Science*. Houndmills: Palgrave Macmillan.

Guzzini, Stefano. 2000. A Reconstruction of Constructivism in International Relations. *European Journal of International Relations* 6 (2): 147–82.

Guzzini, Stefano and Anna Leander, eds. 2006. *Constructivism and International Relations.* New York: Routledge.

Haacke, Jürgen. 2005. The Frankfurt School and International Relations: On the Centrality of Recognition. *Review of International Studies* 31: 181–94.

Haber, Stephen, David Kennedy and Stephen Krasner. 1997. Brothers Under the Skin: Diplomatic History and International Relations. *International Security* 22 (1): 34–43.

Hafner-Burton, Emilie M., Miles Kahler, and Alexander H. Montgomery. 2009. Network Analysis for International Relations. *International Organization* 63 (3): 559–92.

Hall, Rodney Bruce. 1999. *National Collective Identity: Social Constructs and Internationlal Systems.* New York: Columbia University Press.

Hamati-Attaya, Inanna. 2011. The 'Problem of Values' and International Relations Scholarship. *International Studies Review* 13: 259–87.

Havercroft, Jonathan. 2011. *Captives of Sovereignty.* Cambridge: Cambridge University Press.

Hayes, Jarrod. 2013. *Constructing National Security: US Relations with China and India.* Cambridge: Cambridge University Press.

Hayes, Jarrod. 2017. Reclaiming Constructivism: Identity and the Practice of the Study of International Relations. *PS: Political Science and Politics* 50 (1): 89–92.

Hirschman, Daniel and Isaac Ariail Reed. 2014. Foundation Stories and Causality in Sociology. *Sociological Theory* 32 (4): 259–82.

Hoffman, Stanley. 1959. International Relations: The Long Road to Theory. *World Politics* 11 (3): 346–77.

Hoffmann, Matthew J. 2009. Is Constructivist Ethics an Oxymoron? *International Studies Review* 11 (2): 231–52.

Hollis, Martin and Steve Smith. 1991. *Explaining and Understanding International Relations.* Oxford: Clarendon Press.

Holmes, Marcus. 2015. Believing This and Alieving That: Theorizing Affect and Intuitions in International Politics. *International Studies Quarterly* 59 (4): 706–20.

Hom, Andrew. 2020. *International Relations and the Problem of Time.* Oxford: Oxford University Press.

Hopf, Ted. 1998. The Promise of Constructivism in International Relations Theory. *International Security* 23 (1): 171–200.

Hopf, Ted. 2002. *Social Construction of International Politics: Identities and Foreign Policies, Moscow, 1955 and 1999.* Ithaca: Cornell University Press.

Hopf, Ted. 2010. The Logic of Habit in International Relations. *European Journal of International Relations* 16 (4): 539–61.

Hopf, Ted. 2013. Common-sense Constructivism and Hegemony in World Politics. *International Organization* 67 (2): 317–54.

Howard, Lise Morjé. 2015. US Foreign Policy Habits in Ethnic Conflict. *International Studies Quarterly* 59 (4): 721–34.

Hutchings, Kimberley. 2008. *Time and World Politics*. Manchester: Manchester University Press.

Hyde, Susan D. 2015. Experiments in International Relations: Laboratory, Survey, and Field. *Annual Review of Political Science* 18: 403–24.

Hymans, Jacques E.C. 2006. *The Psychology of Nuclear Proliferation: Identity, Emotions, and Foreign Policy*. Cambridge: Cambridge University Press.

Hynek, Nik and Andrea Teti. 2010. Saving Identity from Postmodernism? The Normalization of Constructivism in International Relations. *Contemporary Political Theory* 9 (1): 171–99.

Ingebritsen, Christine. 2002. Norm Entrepreneurs: Scandinavia's Role in World Politics. *Cooperation and Conflict* 37 (1): 11–23.

Isaac, Joel. 2012. *Working Knowledge: Making the Human Sciences from Parsons to Kuhn*. Harvard: Harvard University Press.

Isacoff, Jonathan. 2002. On the Historical Imagination of International Relations. *Millennium: Journal of International Studies* 31 (3): 603–26.

Ish-Shalom, Piki. 2021. *Concepts at Work: On the Linguistic Infrastructure of World Politics*. Ann Arbor: University of Michigan Press.

Jackson, Patrick Thaddeus. 2007. *Civilizing the Enemy: German Reconstruction and the Invention of the West*. Ann Arbor: University of Michigan Press.

Jackson, Patrick Thaddeus. 2011. *The Conduct of Inquiry in International Relations: Philosophy of Science and Its Implications for the Study of World Politics*, 1st Edition. New York: Routledge.

Jackson, Patrick Thaddeus. 2016. *The Conduct of Inquiry in International Relations: Philosophy of Science and Its Implications for the Study of World Politics*, 2nd Edition. New York: Routledge.

Jackson Patrick Thaddeus and Daniel H. Nexon. 1999. Relations before States: Substance, Process and the Study of World Politics. *European Journal of International Relations* 5 (3): 291–332.

Jackson, Patrick Thaddeus and Daniel H. Nexon. 2009. Paradigmatic Faults in International-Relations Theory. *International Studies Quarterly* 53 (4): 907–30.

Jackson, Patrick Thaddeus and Daniel H. Nexon. 2019. Reclaiming the Social: Relationalism in Anglophone International Studies. *Cambridge Review of International Affairs* 32 (5): 582–600.

Jepperson, Ronald, Alexander Wendt and Peter Katzenstein. 1996. Norms, Identity, and Culture in National Security. In Peter Katzenstein, ed. *The Culture of National Security: Norms and Identity in World Politics*. New York: Columbia University Press, pp 33–75.

Jewett, Andrew. 2012. *Science, Democracy, and the American University: From the Civil War to the Cold War*. Cambridge: Cambridge University Press.

Johnson, James. 2002. How Conceptual Problems Migrate: Rational Choice, Interpretation, and the Hazards of Pluralism. *Annual Review of Political Science.* 5: 223–48.

Johnston, Alastair Iain. 1995. Thinking about Strategic Culture. *International Security* 19 (4): 32–64.

Katzenstein, Peter, ed. 1996a. *The Culture of National Security: Norms and Identity in World Politics.* New York: Columbia University Press.

Katzenstein, Peter, ed. 1996b. *Cultural Norms in National Security: Police and Military in Postwar Japan.* Ithaca: Cornell University Press.

Katzenstein, Peter J. 2009. Mid-Atlantic: Sitting on the Knife's Sharp Edge. *Review of International Political Economy* 16, 1: 122–35.

Katzenstein, Peter J., Robert O. Keohane and Stephen D. Krasner. 1998. International Organization and the Study of World Politics. *International Organization* 52 (4): 645–85.

Keck, Margaret and Kathryn Sikkink. 1998. *Activists Beyond Borders: Advocacy Networks in International Politics.* Ithaca: Cornell University Press.

Keene, Edward. 2008. The English School and British Historians. *Millennium: Journal of International Studies* 37 (2): 381–93.

Kennedy-Pipe, Caroline. 2000. International History and International Relations Theory. *International Affairs* 76 (4): 741–54.

Keohane, Robert O. 1984. *After Hegemony.* Princeton: Princeton University Press.

Keohane, Robert O. 1988. International Institutions: Two Approaches. *International Studies Quarterly* 32 (4): 379–96.

Keohane, Robert O. 2009. The Old IPE and the New. *Review of International Political Economy* 16 (1): 34–46.

King, Gary, Robert Keohane and Sidney Verba. 1994. *Designing Social Inquiry.* Princeton: Princeton University Press.

Klotz, Audie. 1995. *Norms in International Relations: The Struggle against Apartheid.* Ithaca: Cornell University Press.

Klotz, Audie, and Cecilia Lynch. 2007. *Strategies for Research in Constructivist International Relations.* New York: Routledge.

Knorr-Cetina, Karin. 1999. *Epistemic Cultures.* Cambridge: Harvard University Press.

Krasner, Stephen D. 1982. Structural Causes and Regime Consequences: Regimes and Intervening Variables. *International Organization* 36 (2): 185–205.

Krasner, Stephen D. 1999. *Sovereignty: Organized Hypocrisy.* Princeton: Princeton University Press.

Kratochwil, Friedrich V. 1989. *Rules, Norms, and Decisions: On the Conditions of Legal and Practical Reasoning in International Relations and Domestic Affairs.* Cambridge: Cambridge University Press.

Kratochwil, Friedrich V. 1993. The Embarrassment of Changes. *Review of International Studies* 19 (1): 63–80.

Kratochwil, Friedrich V. 2006. History, Action, and Identity: Revisiting the 'Second' Great Debate and Assessing its Importance for Social Theory. *European Journal of International Relations* 12 (1): 5–29.

Kratochwil, Friedrich V. 2011. Making Sense of International Practices. In Emanuel Adler and Vincent Pouliot, eds. *International Practices*. Cambridge: Cambridge University Press, pp 36–60.

Kratochwil, Friedrich V. 2014. *The Status of Law in World Society: Meditations on the Role and Rule of Law*. Cambridge: Cambridge University Press.

Kratochwil, Friedrich V. 2018. Praxis: On Acting and Knowing. Cambridge: Cambridge University Press.

Kratochwil, Friedrich V. and John Gerard Ruggie. 1986. International Organization: A State of the Art on an Art of the State. *International Organization* 40 (4): 753–75.

Krause, Monika. 2014. *The Good Project: Humanitarian Relief NGOs and the Fragmentation of Reason*. Chicago: University of Chicago Press.

Krebs, Ronald R. 2015. *Narrative and the Making of US National Security*. Cambridge: Cambridge University Press.

Krook, Mona Lena and Jacqui True. 2012. Rethinking the Life Cycles of International Norms. *European Journal of International Relations* 18 (1): 103–27.

Kubálková, Vendulka, Paul Kowert, and Nicholas Onuf, eds. 1998. *International Relations in a Constructed World*. Armonk: M.E. Sharpe.

Kuhn, Thomas. 1962. *The Structure of Social Revolutions*. Chicago: University of Chicago Press.

Kuhn, Thomas. 1970. *The Structure of Scientific Revolutions*. Chicago: Chicago University Press.

Kuhn, Thomas. 1974. *Objectivity, Value Judgment, and Theory Choice, in The Essential Tension*. Chicago: The University of Chicago Press, pp 356–69.

Kupchan, Charles. 2010. *How Enemies Become Friends*. Princeton: Princeton University Press.

Kurki, Milja. 2008. *Causation in International Relations*. Cambridge: Cambridge University Press.

Kustermans, Jorg. 2016. Parsing the Practice Turn. Practice, Practical Knowledge, Practices. *Millennium: Journal of International Studies* 44 (2): 175–96.

Lake, David. 2011. Why 'Isms' Are Evil: Theory, Epistemology, and Academic Sects as an Impediment to Understanding and Progress. *International Studies Quarterly* 55 (2): 465–80.

Lapid , Yosef. 1996. Culture's Ship: Returns and Departures in IR Theory. In Yosef Lapid and Friedrich V. Kratochwil, eds. *The Return of Culture and Identity in IR Theory*. Boulder: Lynn Reiner, pp 3–20.

Lapid, Yosef and Friedrich Kratocwhil. 1996. *The Return of Culture and Identity in IR Theory.* Boulder: Lynne Reinner.

Latour, Bruno. 2005. Reassembling the Social: An Introduction to Actor-Network Theory. Oxford: Oxford University Press.

Latour, Bruno and Steve Woolgar. 1988. *Laboratory Life: The Construction of Scientific Facts.* Princeton: Princeton University Press.

Laurison, Daniel. 2014. Positions and Position-Takings Among Political Producers: The Field of American Political Consultants. In Michael Grenfell and Frédéric Lebaron, eds. *Bourdieu and Data Analysis: Methodological Principles and Practice.* Bern: Peter Lang, pp 253–72.

Lawson, George. 2006. The Promise of Historical Sociology in International Relations. *International Studies Review* 8 (3): 397–423.

Leander, Anna. 2011. The Promises, Problems, and Pitfalls of a Bourdieu-inspired Staging of International Relations. *International Political Sociology* 5: 294–313.

Lebow, Richard Ned. 2003. *The Tragic Vision of Politics.* Cambridge: Cambridge University Press.

Lebow, Richard Ned and Thomas Risse-Kappen. 1995. *International Relations Theory and the End of the Cold War.* New York: Columbia University Press.

Lechner, Silviya and Mervyn Frost. 2018. *Practice Theory and International Relations.* Cambridge: Cambridge University Press.

Legro, Jeffrey. 1997. Which Norms Matter? *International Organization* 51 (1): 31–63.

Lepgold, Joseph and Miroslav Nincic. 1999. *Beyond the Ivory Tower.* New York: Columbia University Press.

Le Roux, Brigitte and Henry Rouanet. 2004. *Geometric Data Analysis: From Correspondence Analysis to Structured Data Analysis.* Dordrecht: Kluwer Academic Publishers.

Lindemann, Thomas. 2010. *Causes of War: The Struggle for Recognition.* Colchester: ECPR Press.

Linklater, Andrew. 1990. *Beyond Realism and Marxism: Critical Theory and International Relations.* London: Macmillan.

Linklater, Andrew. 2011. *The Problem of Harm in World Politics: Theoretical Investigations.* Cambridge: Cambridge University Press.

Linklater, Andrew. 2016. *Violence and Civilization in the Western States-System.* Cambridge: Cambridge University Press.

Little, Richard and Steve Smith, eds. 1988. *Belief Systems in International Relations.* Oxford: Blackwell.

Locher, Birgit and Elisabeth Prügl. 2001. Feminism and Constructivism: Worlds Apart or Sharing a Middle Ground? *International Studies Quarterly* 45 (1): 111–29.

Löwenheim, Oded. 2006. *Parasites and Predators: Persistent Agents of Transnational Harm and Great Power Authority*. Ann Arbor: University of Michigan Press.

Löwenheim, Oded. 2010. The 'I' in IR: An Autoethnographic Account. *Review of International Studies* 36 (4): 1023–45.

Lustick, Ian. 1996. History, Historiography, and Political Science. *American Political Science Review* 90 (3): 605–18.

Macchiavelli, Niccolo. 1988. *The Prince*. Cambridge: Cambridge University Press.

MacDonald, Paul K. 2014. *Networks of Domination: The Social Foundations of Peripheral Conquest in International Politics*. New York: Oxford University Press.

MacKay, Joseph and Christopher David LaRoche. 2017. The Conduct of History in International Relations: Rethinking Philosophy of History in IR. *International Theory* 9 (2): 203–36.

Maliniak, Daniel, Amy Oakes, Susan Peterson, and Michael J. Tierney. 2011. International Relations in the US Academy. *International Studies Quarterly* 55 (2): 437–64.

March, James G. and Johan P. Olsen. 1998. The Institutional Dynamics of International Political Orders. *International Organization* 52 (4): 943–69.

Marin, Alexandra and Barry Wellman. 2011. Social Network Analysis: An Introduction. In John Scott and Peter J. Carrington, eds. *The SAGE Handbook of Social Network Analysis*. London: SAGE, pp 11–25.

Martin, John Levi. 2003. What Is Field Theory? *American Journal of Sociology* 109 (1): 1–49.

Mattern, Janice Bially. 2005. *Ordering International Politics: Identity, Crisis, and Representational Force*. New York: Routledge.

Mattern, Janice Bially. 2011. A Practice Theory of Emotion for International Relations. In Emanuel Adler and Vincent Pouliot, eds. *International Practices*. Cambridge: Cambridge University Press, pp 63–86.

Matthieu, Xavier. 2020. Sovereign Myths in International Relations: Sovereign Equality and the Reproduction of Eurocentric Blindness. *Journal of International Political Theory* 16 (3): 339–60.

May, Ernest R., Richard Rosecrance and Zara Steiner, eds. 2010. *History and Neorealism*. Cambridge: Cambridge University Press.

McCourt, David M. 2011a. Role-Playing and Identity Affirmation in International Politics: Britain's Reinvasion of the Falklands, 1982. *Review of International Studies* 37 (4): 1599–621.

McCourt, David M. 2011b. Rethinking Britain's Role in the World for a New Decade: The Limits of Discursive Therapy and the Promise of Field Theory. *British Journal of Politics and International Relations* 13 (2): 145 – 64.

McCourt, David M. 2012a. The Roles States Play: A Meadian Interactionist Approach. *Journal of International Relations and Development* 15 (3): 370–92.

McCourt, David M. 2012b. What's at Stake in the Historical Turn? Theory, Practice, and Phronēsis in International Relations. *Millennium: Journal of International Studies* 41 (1): 23–42.

McCourt, David M. 2012c. The 'Problem of Generations' Revisited: Karl Mannheim and the Sociology of Knowledge in International Relations. In Jon Acuff and Brent Steele, ed. *Theory and Practice of the 'Generation' in International Relations and Politics.* New York: Routledge, pp 47–70.

McCourt, David M. 2014. *Britain and World Power since 1945: Constructing a Nation's Role in International Politics.* Ann Arbor: University of Michigan Press.

McCourt, David M. 2016. Practice Theory and Relationalism as the New Constructivism. *International Studies Quarterly* 60 (3): 475–85.

McCourt, David M. and Brent J. Steele. 2017. World of Our Making and Second Generation Constructivism. In Harry Gould, ed. *The Art of World-Making: Nicholas Greenwood Onuf and His Critics.* New York: Routledge, pp 1–16.

McCourt, David M. and Andrew Glencross 2018. Great Expectations: The EU's Social Role as Great Power Manager. *New Perspectives* 27 (1): 17–42.

Mearsheimer, John. 2001. *The Tragedy of Great Power Politics.* New York: W.W. Norton.

Mearsheimer, John. 2006. China's Unpeaceful Rise. *Current History* 105 (690): 160–2.

Medvetz, Thomas. 2013. *Think Tanks in America.* Chicago: University of Chicago Press.

Meyer, Christoph O. 2007. *The Quest for a European Strategic Culture: Changing Norms on Security and Defense in the European Union.* Basingstoke: Palgrave.

Meyer, John W. and Brian Rowan. 1977. Institutionalized Organizations: Formal Structure as Myth and Ceremony. *American Journal of Sociology* 83 (2): 340–63.

Mieland, Jack and Michael Krausz. 1982. Introduction. In Mieland and Krausz, eds. *Relativism: Cognitive and Moral.* Notre Dame: University of Notre Dame Press.

Milliken, Jennifer. 1999. The Study of Discourse in International Relations: A Critique of Research Methods. *European Journal of International Relations* 5 (2): 225–54.

Mills, C. Wright. 1956. *The Power Elite.* New York: Oxford University Press.

Mills, C. Wright. 2000 [1959]. *The Sociological Imagination.* Oxford: Oxford University Press.

Milner, Helen. 1998. Rationalizing Politics: The Emerging Synthesis of International, American, and Comparative Politics. *International Organization* 52 (4): 759–86.

Mische, Ann. 2011. Relational Sociology, Culture, and Agency. In John Scott and Peter J. Carrington, eds. *The SAGE Handbook of Social Network Analysis*. London: SAGE, pp 80–97.

Monteiro, Nuno P. and Kevin Ruby. 2009. IR and the False Promise of Philosophical Foundations. *International Theory* 1 (1): 15–48.

Moravcsik, Andrew. 2000. *The Choice for Europe*. New York: Routledge.

Morgan, Kimberly J. and Ann Shola Orloff. 2017. *The Many Hands of the State*. New York: Cambridge University Press.

Morgan, Patrick M. 2011. The Practice of Deterrence. In Emanuel Adler and Vincent Pouliot, eds. *International Practices*. Cambridge: Cambridge University Press, pp 139–73.

Murray, Michelle. 2018. *The Struggle for Recognition in International Relations: Status, Revisionism, and Rising Powers*. New York: Oxford University Press.

Musgrave, Paul and Daniel H. Nexon. 2018. Defending Hierarchy from the Moon to the Indian Ocean. *International Organization* 72 (3): 591–626.

Nadelmann, Ethan A. 1990. Global Prohibition Regimes: The Evolution of Norms in International Society. *International Organization* 44: 479–526.

Navari, Cornelia. 2011. The Concept of Practice in the English School. *European Journal of International Relations* 17 (4): 611–30.

Neufeld, Mark. 1995. *The Restructuring of International Relations Theory*. Cambridge: Cambridge University Press.

Neumann, Iver B. 1995. *Russia and the Idea of Europe: A Study in Identity and International Relations*. Minneapolis: University of Minnesota Press.

Neumann, Iver B. 1998. *Uses of the Other: 'the East' in European Identity Formation*. Minneapolis: University of Minnesota Press.

Neumann, Iver B. 2002. Returning Practice to the Linguistic Turn: The Case of Diplomacy. *Millennium: Journal of International Studies* 31 (3): 625–51.

Neumann, Iver B. 2012. *At Home With The Diplomats: Inside a European Foreign Ministry*. Ithaca: Cornell University Press.

Neumann, Iver B. and Ole Jacob Sending. 2010. *Governing the Global Polity: Practice, Mentality, and Rationality*. Ann Arbor: University of Michigan Press.

Nexon, Daniel H. 2009. *The Struggle for Power in Early Modern Europe: Religious Conflict, Dynastic Empires, and International Change*. Princeton: Princeton University Press.

Nietzsche, Friedrich. *On the Use and Abuse of History for Life*. Available at: https://la.utexas.edu/users/hcleaver/330T/350kPEENietzscheAbuseTableAll.pdf

Novick, Peter. 1988. *That Noble Dream*. Cambridge: Cambridge University Press.

Nussbaum, Martha. 1994. *The Therapy of Desire*. Princeton: Princeton University Press.

Oakeshott, Michael. 1933. *Experience and Its Modes*. Cambridge: Cambridge University Press.

Oatley, Thomas. 2011. The Reductionist Gamble: Open Economy Politics in the Global Economy. *International Organization* 65 (2): 311–41.

Onuf, Nicholas Greenwood. 2012 [1989]. *World of Our Making: Rules and Rule in Social Theory and International Relations*. Columbia: University of South Carolina Press.

Onuf, Nicholas Greenwood. 2017. The Bigger Story. *PS: Political Science and Politics* 50 (1): 93–6.

Onuf, Nicholas Greenwood. 2018a. *The Mightie Frame: Epochal Change and the Modern World*. New York: Oxford University Press.

Onuf, Nicholas Greenwood. 2018b. Preface: The Dinosaur Speaks! In Mariano Bertucci, Jarrod Hayes, and Patrick James, eds. *Constructivism Reconsidered: Past, Present, and Future*. Ann Arbor: University of Michigan Press, pp xiii–xix.

Oren, Ido. 1995. The Subjectivity of the 'Democratic' Peace. *International Security* 20: 147–84.

Oren, Ido. 2003. *Our Enemies and US: America's Rivalries and the Making of Political Science*. Ithaca: Cornell University Press.

Oros, Andrew. 2008. *Normalizing Japan: Politics, Identity, and the Evolution of Security Practice*. Stanford: Stanford University Press.

Osiander, Andreas. 2007. *Before the State*. Oxford: Oxford University Press.

Osiander, Andreas. 2001. Sovereignty, International Relations, and the Westphalian Myth. *International Organization* 55 (2): 251–87.

Owen, David. 2002. Re-orienting International Relations: On Pragmatism, Pluralism and Practical Reasoning. *Millennium* 31 (3): 653–73.

Owens, Patricia. 2015. Method or Madness? Sociolatry in International Thought. *Review of International Studies* 41, 4: 655–74.

Owens, Patricia. 2016. *Economy of Force: Counterinsurgency and the Historical Rise of the Social*. Cambridge: Cambridge University Press.

Parmar, Inderjeet. 2004. *Think Tanks and Power in Foreign Policy*. Basingstoke: Palgrave.

Philpott, Daniel. 2001. *Revolutions in Sovereignty: How Ideas Shaped Modern International Relations*. Princeton: Princeton University Press.

Porter, Patrick. 2018. Why America's Grand Strategy Has Not Changed: Power, Habit, and the US Foreign Policy Establishment. *International Security* 42 (4): 9–46.

Porter, Tony. 2013. Tracing Associations in Global Finance. *International Political Sociology* 7 (3): 334–8.

Pouliot, Vincent. 2008. The Logic of Practicality: A Theory of Practice of Security Communities. *International Organization* 62 (2): 257–88.

Pouliot, Vincent. 2011. *International Security in Practice: The Politics of NATO-Russia Diplomacy*. Cambridge: Cambridge University Press.

Pouliot, Vincent. 2016. *International Pecking Orders: The Politics and Practice of Multilateral Diplomacy*. Cambridge: Cambridge University Press.

Pratt, Simon Frankel. 2016. Pragmatism as Ontology, Not (Just) Epistemology: Exploring the Full Horizon of Pragmatism as an Approach to IR Theory. *International Studies Review* 18 (3): 508–27.

Price, David H. 2011. *Weaponizing Anthropology*. Petrolia, CA: Counterpunch.

Price, Richard. 1998. Reversing the Gun Sights: Transnational Civil Society Targets Land Mines. *International Organization* 52 (3): 613–44.

Price, Richard, ed. 2008. *Moral Limit and Possibility in World Politics*. Cambridge: Cambridge University Press.

Puchala, Donald. 2003. *Theory and History in International Relations*. London: Routledge.

Rajkovic, Nikolas M. 2010. 'Global Law' and Governmentality: Reconceptualizing the 'Rule of Law' as Rule 'Through' Law. *European Journal of International Relations* 18 (1): 29–52.

Rajkovic, Nikolas M. 2011. *The Politics of International Law and Compliance*. London: Routledge.

Ralph, Jason. 2018. What Should Be Done? Pragmatist Constructivist Ethics and the Responsibility to Protect. *International Organization* 72 (1): 173–203.

Raymond, Mark. 2019. *Social Practices of Rule-Making in World Politics*. New York: Oxford University Press.

Raymond, Mark. 2020. Social Practices for Rule-Making for International Law in the Cyber Domain. *Journal of Global Security Studies* 6 (2): 1–24.

Reisch, George A. 2005. *How the Cold War Transformed Philosophy of Science: To the Icy Slopes of Logic*. Cambridge: Cambridge University Press.

Rengger, Nicholas. 2012. Progress With a Price? *International Theory* 4 (3): 468–77.

Renshon, Jonathan. 2017. *Fighting for Status: Hierarchy and Conflict in World Politics*. Princeton: Princeton University Press.

Reus-Smit, Christian. 1997. The Constitutional Structure of International Society. *International Organization* 51 (4): 555–89.

Reus-Smit, Christian. 1999. *The Moral Purpose of the State: Culture, Social Identity, and Institutional Rationality in International Relations*. Princeton: Princeton University Press.

Reus-Smit, Christian. 2008. Constructivism and the Structure of Ethical Reasoning. In Richard Price, ed. *Moral Limit and Possibility in World Politics*, Cambridge: Cambridge University Press, pp 53–82.

Reus-Smit, Christian. 2013. *Individual Rights and the Making of the International System*. Cambridge: Cambridge University Press.

Reus-Smit, Christian. 2018. *On Cultural Diversity: International Theory in a World of Difference*. Cambridge: Cambridge University Press.

Ringmar, Eric. 1996. *Identity, Interest and Action: A Cultural Explanation of Sweden's Intervention in the Thirty Years' War.* Cambridge: Cambridge University Press.

Risse, Thomas. 2000. 'Let's Argue!' Communicative Action in World Politics. *International Organization* 54 (1): 1–39.

Roberts, Geoffrey. 2006. History, theory and the Narrative Turn in IR. *Review of International Studies* 32 (4): 703–14.

Robson, Karen and Chris Sanders. 2009. *Quantifying Theory: Pierre Bourdieu.* Dordrecht: Springer.

Rohde, Joy. 2013. *Armed with Expertise: The Militarization of American Social Science Research During the Cold War.* Ithaca: Cornell University Press.

Rorty, Richard. 1980. *Philosophy and the Mirror of Nature.* Princeton: Princeton University Press.

Rösch, Felix. Forthcoming. Affect, Practice, and Change: Dancing World Politics at the Congress of Vienna. *Cooperation and Conflict.*

Rosenberg, Justin. 1994. The International Imagination: IR Theory and 'Classic Social Analysis'. *Millennium: Journal of International Studies* 23 (1): 85–108.

Ross, Andrew A. G. 2006. Coming in from the Cold: Constructivism and Emotions. *European Journal of International Relations* 12 (2): 197–222.

Ross, Andrew A.G. 2014. *Mixed Emotions: Beyond Fear and Hatred in International Conflict.* Chicago: Chicago University Press.

Rousseau, David L. 2006. *Identifying Threats and Threatening Identities: The Social Construction of Realism and Liberalism.* Stanford: Stanford University Press.

Ruggie, John Gerard. 1993. *Multilateralism Matters: The Theory and Praxis of an Institutional Form.* New York: Columbia University Press.

Ruggie, John Gerard. 1998. What Makes the World Hang Together? Neo-Utilitarianism and the Social Constructivist Challenge? *International Organization* 52 (4): 855–85.

Scauso, Marcos S. 2018. Researching Within the Instability of Meaning: Decolonial Voices and Practices. In Brent J. Steele, Harry Gould, and Oliver Kessler, eds. *Tactical Constructivism: Expressing Method in International Relations.* New York: Routledge, pp 157–69.

Schatzki, Theodore, Karin Knorr-Cetina and Eike von Savigny. 2001. *The Practice Turn in Contemporary Theory.* New York: Routledge.

Seabrooke, Leonard. 2015. Diplomacy as Economic Consultancy. In Ole Jacob Sending, Vincent Pouliot, and Iver B. Neumann, eds. *Diplomacy and the Making of World Politics.* Cambridge: Cambridge University Press, pp 195–219.

Seabrooke, Leonard and Eleni Tsingou. 2014. Distinctions, Affiliations, and Professional Knowledge in Financial Reform Expert Groups. *Journal of European Public Policy* 21 (3): 389–407.

Sellar, Walter Carruthers and Robert Julian Yeatman. 1930. *1066 and All That*. London: Methuen.

Sending, Ole Jacob, Vincent Pouliot and Iver B. Neumann, eds. 2015. *Diplomacy and the Making of World Politics*. Cambridge: Cambridge University Press.

Shapcott, Richard. 2004. IR as Practical Philosophy. *British Journal of Politics and International Relations* 6: 271–91.

Sharp, Paul. 2009. *Diplomatic Theory of International Politics*. Cambridge: Cambridge University Press.

Shilliam, Robbie. 2014. 'Open the Gates Mek We Repratriate': Caribbean Slavery, Constructivism, and Hermeneutic Tensions. *International Theory* 6 (2): 349–72.

Shirk, Mark. 2019. The Universal Eye: Anarchist 'Propaganda of the Deed' and the Development of the Modern Surveillance State. *International Studies Quarterly* 63 (2): 334–45.

Shotter, John. 1996. 'Now I Can Go On': Wittgenstein and Our Embodied Embeddedness in the 'Hurly Burly' of Life. *Human Studies* 19: 385–407.

Sikkink, Kathryn. 1991. *Ideas and Institutions: Developmentalism in Brazil and Argentina*. Ithaca: Cornell University Press.

Sikkink, Kathryn. 2008. The Role of Consequences, Comparison and Counterfactuals in Constructivist Ethical Thought. In Richard Price, ed. *Moral Limit and Possibility in World Politics*. Cambridge: Cambridge University Press, pp 83–111.

Sikkink, Kathryn. 2011. *The Justice Cascade: How Human Rights Prosecutions are Changing World Politics*. New York: W.W. Norton.

Sil, Rudra and Peter J. Katzenstein. 2010. *Beyond Paradigms: Analytical Eclecticism in the Study of World Politics*. New York: Palgrave.

Sjoberg, Laura. 2012. Gender, Structure, and War: What Waltz Couldn't See. *International Theory* 4 (1): 1–38.

Sjoberg, Laura. 2017. The Invisible Structures of Anarchy: Gender, Orders, and Global Politics. *Journal of International Political Theory* 13 (3): 325–40.

Slaughter, Anne-Marie. 2005. *A New World Order*. Princeton: Princeton University Press.

Smith, Thomas. 1999. *History and International Relations*. London: Routledge.

Snow, C.P. 2012 [1959]. *The Two Cultures*. Cambridge: Cambridge University Press.

Snyder, Jack, and Leslie Vinjamuri. 2012. Principled Pragmatism and the Logic of Consequences 4 (3): 434–48.

Solomon, Ty. 2015. *The Politics of Subjectivity in American Foreign Policy Discourses*. Ann Arbor: University of Michigan Press.

Spruyt, Hendrik. 1996. *The Sovereign State and Its Competitors*. Princeton: Princeton University Press.

Stampnitzky, Lisa. 2013. *Disciplining Terror: How Experts Invented 'Terrorism'*. Cambridge: Cambridge University Press.

Steele, Brent J. 2008. *Ontological Security in International Relations: Self-Identity and the IR State*. New York: Routledge.

Steele, Brent J. 2013. *Alternative Accountabilities in Global Politics: The Scars of Violence*. New York: Routledge.

Steele, Brent J. 2017. Introduction: The Politics of Constructivist International Relations in the US Academy. *PS: Political Science and Politics* 50 (1): 71–3.

Stinchcombe, Arthur L. 1997. On the Virtues of the Old Institutionalism. *Annual Review of Sociology* 23: 1–18.

Stone, Diane and Andrew Denham. 2004. *Think Tank Traditions*. Manchester: Manchester University Press.

Struett, Michael J. 2017. Reading and Writing Constructivist Research in American Political Science. *PS: Political Science and Politics* 50 (1): 79–83.

Subotic, Jelena. 2009. *Hijacked Justice: Dealing with the Past in the Balkans*. Ithaca: Cornell University Press.

Subotić, Jelena. 2017. Constructivism as Professional Practice in the US Academy. *PS: Political Science and Politics* 50 (1): 75–8.

Suganami, Hidemi. 2008. Narrative Explanation and International Relations. *Millennium: Journal of International Studies* 37 (2): 327–56.

Sunstein, Cass R. 1996. Social Norms and Social Roles. *Columbia Law Review* 96 (4): 903–68.

Szent-Iványi, Balázs and Pēteris Timofejevs. 2020. Selective Norm Promotion in International Development Assistance: The Drivers of Naming and Shaming Advocacy Among European Non-Governmental Development Organisations. *International Relations* 35 (1): 23–46.

Tannenwald, Nina. 1999. The Nuclear Taboo: The United States and the Normative Basis of Nuclear Non-Use. *International Organization* 53 (3): 433–68.

Tannenwald, Nina. 2008. *The Nuclear Taboo: The United States and the Non-Use of Nuclear Weapons since 1945*. Cambridge: Cambridge University Press.

Teschke, Benno. 2003. *The Myth of 1648: Class, Geopolitics and the Making of Modern International Relations*. London: Verso.

Tickner, J. Ann. 1988. Hans Morgenthau's Principles of Political Realism: A Feminist Reformulation. *Millennium: Journal of International Studies* 17 (3): 429–40.

Tickner, Arlene B. and Ole Waever, eds. 2009. *International Relations Scholarship Around the World*. Abingdon: Routledge.

Tilly, Charles. 2002. *Stories, Identities, and Political Change*. Lanham: Rowman and Littlefield.

Toulmin, Stephen. 2001. *Return to Reason*. Cambridge: Harvard University Press.

Towns, Ann E. 2010. *Women and States: Norms and Hierarchies in International Society*. Cambridge: Cambridge University Press.

Towns, Ann E. 2012. Norms and Social Hierarchies: Understanding International Policy Diffusion "From Below." *International Organization* 66 (2): 179–209.

Towns, Ann E. 2020. 'Diplomacy is a Feminine Art': Feminised Figurations of the Diplomat. *Review of International Studies* 46 (5): 573–93.

Towns, Ann E. and Bahar Rumelili. 2007. Taking the Pressure: Unpacking the Relations Between Norms, Social Hierarchies, and Social Pressures on States. *European Journal of International Relations* 23 (4): 756–70.

United States' Strategic Approach to China, May 2020. Available at https://trumpwhitehouse.archives.gov/wp-content/uploads/2020/05/U.S.-Strategic-Approach-to-The-Peoples-Republic-of-China-Report-5.24v1.pdf

US NSS 2015. Security Strategy of the United States of America. Available at https://obamawhitehouse.archives.gov/sites/default/files/docs/2015_national_security_strategy_2.pdf

Van Meter, Karl M., Marie-Ange Schlitz, Philipp Cibois, and Lise Mounier. 1994. Correspondence Analysis: A History and French Sociological Perspective. In Michael J. Greenacre and Jörg Blasius, eds. *Correspondence Analysis in the Social Sciences: Recent Developments and Applications*. San Diego, Calif.: Academic Press, pp 128–38.

Vaughan-Williams, Nick. 2005. International Relations and the 'Problem of History'. *Millennium: Journal of International Studies* 34 (1): 115–36.

Villumsen-Berling, Trine. 2015. *The International Political Sociology of Security*. London: Routledge.

Vitalis, Robert. 2015. *White World Order, Black Power Politics: The Birth of American International Relations*. Ithaca: Cornell University Press.

Vucetic, Srdjan. 2011. *The Anglosphere: A Geneaology of a Racialized Identity in International Relations*. Stanford: Stanford University Press.

Waever, Ole. 1998. The Sociology of a Not So International Discipline. *International Organization* 52 (4): 687–727.

Wagner, R. Harrison. 2007. *War and the State: The Theory of International Politics*. Ann Arbor: University of Michigan Press.

Waltz, Kenneth. 1979. *Theory of International Politics*. Reading: Addison-Wesley.

Weber, Martin. 2014. Between 'Isses' and 'Oughts:' IR Constructivism, Critical Theory, and the Challenge of Political Philosophy. *European Journal of International Relations* 20 (2): 516–43.

Weber, Martin. 2020. The Normative Grammar of Relational Analysis: Recognition Theory's Contribution to Understanding Short-Comings in IR's Relational Turn. *International Studies Quarterly*. Online First.

Weber, Max. 1949. *The Methodology of the Social Sciences*. New York: Free Press.

Weldes, Jutta. 1999. *Constructing National Interests: The United States and the Cuban Missile Crisis*. Minneapolis: University of Minnesota Press.

Wendt, Alexander. 1987. The Agent-Structure Problem in International Relations Theory. *International Organization* 41 (3): 335–70.

Wendt, Alexander. 1992. Anarchy is What States Make of It: The Social Construction on Power Politics. *International Organization* 46 (2): 391–425.

Wendt, Alexander. 1995. Constructing International Politics. *International Security* 20 (1): 71–81.

Wendt, Alexander. 1998. On Constitution and Causation in International Relations. *Review of International Studies* 24 (5): 101–17.

Wendt, Alexander. 1999. *Social Theory of International Politics*. Cambridge: Cambridge University Press.

Wendt, Alexander. 2006. Social Theory as Cartesian Science: An Auto-Critique from a Quantum Perspective. In Stefano Guzzini and Anna Leander, eds. *Constructivism and International Relations*. New York: Routledge, pp 181–219.

Wendt, Alexander. 2015. *Quantum Mind and Social Science: Unifying Physical and Social Ontology*. Cambridge: Cambridge University Press.

Widmaier, Wesley. 2004. Theory as Factor and Theorist as Actor. *International Studies Review* 6 (3): 427–45.

Williams, Michael C. 2005. *The Realist Tradition and the Limits of International Relations*. Cambridge: Cambridge University Press.

Williams, Michael C. 2007a. *Culture and Security: Symbolic Power and the Politics of International Security*. New York: Routledge.

Williams, Michael C., ed. 2007b. *Realism Reconsidered*. Oxford: Oxford University Press.

Wohlforth, William. 2009. Unipolarity, Status Competition, and Great Power War. *World Politics* 61 (1): 28–57.

Wolf, Richard. 2011. Respect and Disrespect in International Politics: The Significance of Status Recognition. *International Theory* 3 (1): 105–42.

Wolin, Sheldon. 1969. Political Theory as a Vocation. *American Political Science Review* 63 (4): 1062–82.

Wunderlich, Carmen. 2019. *Rogue States as Norm Entrepreneurs: Black Sheep or Sheep in Wolves' Clothing?* New York: Springer.

X (George Kennan). 1947. The Sources of Soviet Conduct. *Foreign Affairs* 25 (4): 566–82.

Yetiv, Steve. 2011. History, International Relations, and Integrated Approaches. *International Studies Perspectives* 12 (2): 94–118.

Zala, Benjamin. 2017. Great Power Management and Ambiguous Order in Nineteenth-Century International Society. *Review of International Studies* 43 (2): 367–88.

Zarakol, Ayşe. 2010. *After Defeat: How the East Learned to Live with the West*. Cambridge: Cambridge University Press.

Zarakol, Ayşe. 2017. TRIPping Constructivism. *PS: Political Science and Politics* 50 (1): 75–8.

Zarakol, Ayşe. 2018. Sovereign Equality as Misrecognition. *Review of International Studies* 44 (5): 848–62.

Zehfuss, Maja. 2002. *Constructivism in International Relations*. Cambridge: Cambridge University Press.

Zürn, Michael and Jeffrey T. Checkel. 2005. Getting Socialized to Build Bridges: Constructivism and Rationalism, Europe and the Nation-State. *International Organization* 59 (4): 1045–79.

Index